ElderHouse

ElderHouse

PLANNING YOUR BEST HOME EVER

Adelaide Altman

CHELSEA GREEN PUBLISHING COMPANY

White River Junction, Vermont

Designed by Dede Cummings Designs

Printed in Canada.

Printed on recycled, chlorine-free paper.

First printing, October 2002.

05 04 03 02   1 2 3 4 5

Library of Congress Cataloging-in-Publication Data

Elderhouse: planning your best home ever / Adelaide Altman.
    p.   cm.
Includes bibliographical references and index.
ISBN 1-931498-11-3 (alk. paper)
    1. Aged—Dwellings. 2. Architecture, Domestic—Psychological aspects.
3. Architecture—Human factors. 4. Architecture, Domestic—Designs and
plans. I. Title: Elder house.

NA7195.A4 E38 2002   2002031481
720'.84'6—DC21

Chelsea Green Publishing Company
Post Office Box 428
White River Junction, VT 05001
www.chelseagreen.com

With love to
Chip,
Stephanie and Micah,
Robert and Lucy.

In loving memory of
Sadye
and
Michael,
and
Gram

CONTENTS

PART II.

SMALL GEMS ARE BETTER THAN
WHITE ELEPHANTS

PART III.

PLANNING YOUR HOME—YOUR WAY

Preface

ELDERHOUSE is not an old folks' book. Or a rich man's book, or a poor man's book. Or a book for special interest groups.

This is a book for everyone concerned with, and enthralled by, the magnificent gift of longevity. It's for the teens and twenties who are becoming aware of their legacy . . . the thirties and forties, who are elated by its promise . . . the fifties who see it happening as they prepare elder homes for their parents and for themselves . . . and the sixties and onward who suddenly realize that elder means them.

ElderHouse is for you, me, your next-door neighbor, and the family down the street—in the next town, the next state, the next nation—everybody who wants to live their bonus years safely, comfortably, in their own homes.

Welcome.

ACKNOWLEDGMENTS

I T IS TO MY FAMILY, friends, clients, and colleagues that I tender my ineffable thanks. Their voices, past and present, have layered into the help and confidence I needed to complete this book. Among many are:

My husband, Francis, for his love, patience, and support.

Barbara (Barnes) Murdoch, my dear friend and mentor.

Michael Albert, who taught me to love a good tale.

Sharon Nelton, my first editor, lifesaver, and longtime friend.

Sydney Clary, friend, writer, and steadfast cheerleader.

Shelly B. Franks, manager of the disabilities program of the U.S. Securities and Exchange Commission.

Diana Gould, my agent, and Alan Berolzheimer, my editor at Chelsea Green.

INTRODUCTION
Where Will You Live When You Grow Up?

There is no alternative to aging. No one stays young forever, but growing older does not have to be a painful process anymore.

—Dr. Isadore Rosenfeld,
LIVE NOW—AGE LATER

LOOK AT IT THIS WAY: While most of us aspire to longevity, no one really wants to be old. In some parts of the world, old age is disparaged, while in others, it is considered life's crowning glory. In our society, it can be either. The choice is our own.

We are the lucky generations—far ahead of our forebears, on the cutting edge of tomorrows more incredible that humankind ever has dared to predict! We have great new moments to live, new challenges, new joys. We have more time. With a nod to the past and an eye to the future, we can avail ourselves of alternatives now, revel in choices, celebrate the wonderful possibilities of longer, better lives.

It would be tragic to forfeit those years to an accident that might have been avoided, or to chores and responsibilities that deprive you of sweet opportunities life can offer. The mission of this book is to encourage you to be aware of your options, and be prepared—*before the fact*. The need is easy to understand.

People age. Most dwellings do not keep pace. Our once-comfortable homes, designed for earlier years and different needs, have changed overnight, it seems, into obstacle courses and booby traps determined to infuse our lives with havoc and unwanted work. But this need not be that way. Many homes today are built comfortably downsized, designed to live in for a lifetime, replacing "big white elephants" with small gems of *comfort, accessibility, safety,* and *easy-care,* and are at one with their environment, wherever it may be. In most cases, special considerations can be made to prevent accidents, the major cause of injury among elders.

Aging is part of living, and the point of extended life is extended well-being. In addition to medical and technological advancements, great importance is now placed on living in elder-friendly, up-beat environments. Scientists say that successful aging depends more on attention to *safe environments,* as well as self-repair and enriching the brain, than on family genes, now estimated to account for only about 20 to 30 percent of age determination.

"How well we age depends more on how we live than on our genes," says the MacArthur Foundation Consortium on Successful Aging. Being surrounded by safe material comforts goes a long way, the experts say. They further state that an elder-oriented home will both comfort us and discourage apathy because our relationship to our environment heavily determines our mental attitude and behavior. Up-beat homes that emphasize our abilities, not our disabilities, are not only more fun, but tantamount to successful aging.

Accentuating the good news of longer and healthier lives, studies continue to prove that we are less likely to become incapacitated by age than heretofore assumed. According to researchers of Duke University, Stanford University, and the University of Pennsylvania, disability rates are decreasing among the elderly, challenging the theory of steady deterioration. A study by the National Institute of Aging states, "The accelerating decline is dramatic and important news . . . as the older generation grows significantly, offering further evidence that we may be able to influence how we age."

Knowing they will benefit by today's research, the now fifty-something Baby Boomer generation and the Gen-Xers are ecstatic; their elders, equally so. But a big question remains—*Where will we all live?* Most homes occupied by elders are not safe. And alternative so-called senior facilities generally are greeted like news of an outbreak of the bubonic plague. The obvious answer, of course, is to adapt our own homes to present and future needs or to create new, more appropriate homes, sustainable homes that we will not "outgrow."

Although studies have shown that today's elders just want to stay put, close to friends and family in familiar surroundings, we sometimes forget that this may not be possible if our homes no longer are safe or appropriate for our aging selves. For example, they may be too big and too costly to care for, the neighborhood may have deteriorated, or bath-rooms, kitchens, and stairways might be accidents waiting to happen. Sad to say, current statistics show that the majority of the elderly will do nothing about it—until it's too late.

This book was written to help you avoid the home catastrophes that often befall elders, and to encourage your aging offspring to prepare their own homes, present or future, for almost certain longer lives. Its inspiration was born several years ago as a promise to Barbara.

At about sixty-five, Barbara was still catching rainbows, dreaming dreams, and working, always working, for others. At that time, after a long career as a journalist on a large city newspaper, a World War II correspondent, cause-advocate, trusted friend, and mentor to many, she was a volunteer public relations counselor for the Society of Friends and UNICEF. She spoke little about herself. I remember expressing my feelings to my longtime friend and mentor. "I want to be just like you when I grow up," I said.

I did. I truly did. She understood.

About fifteen years later, she did get around to talking about Barbara. She had a problem, she said, and needed my professional help. The problem was the three-story Victorian home she had occupied for forty-six years. It wasn't that she was incapacitated in any way, I must understand, just that she'd been noticing lately that the stairs seemed steeper and harder to navigate, and Seymour, her longtime feline companion who shook paws with you, still wanted his breakfast at six A.M.

"I'm afraid I shouldn't live here much longer," she said, "and I don't know what to do. Should I rent a small apartment? Go to a community for seniors? Move into my granddaughter's guest cottage? What should I take with me? All of this won't fit." Her graceful hands gestured toward the furnishings of the room that held so many memories, and then softly asked, "Where will *you* live when *you* grow up?"

Busy trying to balance life between my kids and my career, I hadn't given any thought to where I wanted to live later on in life. I mumbled something about maybe moving to a warm climate, some day. Then Barbara spoke words I never thought I'd hear from her. "Will you help me? I can't seem to make this decision myself."

Of course I would, I replied.

"And will you also write it all down for others like me?"

"Yes, that too," I said, having no idea at that time that my promise was the first step of a long pilgrimage of my own.

She continued, "Things are not the way they were when I was your age. Old people seemed older then. Nowadays, they're living longer. But faster. Everything's faster. The older I become, the more life seems to be dancing to a different beat around me. There's too much to keep up with."

She was right. Times have changed. New technologies are evolving even as we begin to understand the old, scientific breakthroughs that affect our daily lives, from the food we eat to the air we breathe. The future appears less mysterious, less intangible, and we are better able to plan for it. For example, large numbers of former Baby Boomers are assuming the responsibility for providing safe homes for their elders and planning ahead for their own tomorrows, even as they fervently assert that middle age does not begin until sixty. And seventy is young-old, and the *real* old-old doesn't start until after eighty-five, if then! Words like *pastures* and *rocking chairs* have disappeared from their vocabularies. They are the beginning of "an ageless society." Age is just a number! they say, and rate independence high on priority lists.

Independence is the magic wand of the future—if we do not ignore old age but, rather, embrace it, prepare for it, and then go on living the full good life, in comfort and safety. As my friend Barbara does.

She now enjoys the small first-floor apartment that we designed from the outdated kitchen, butler's pantry, morning room, and verandah of her big, old house. The apartment overlooks the garden she still loves and tends, and is furnished with her favorite books, art, and family treasures. Financed by a home-building loan, the rest of the house has been converted into rental apartments, which provide Barbara with a comfortable income.

With that twinkle in her eye I know so well, and a lilt to her voice, she said one day, "A very attractive older gentleman moved in last week. Perhaps I shall invite him in for cocktails."

This book fulfills my promise to Barbara: to help and encourage people of all ages, everywhere, to plan homes for when they "grow up." This book also is meant to echo the way Barbara lives. "No!" she says, "Aging is not doom and gloom. Aging is continuing to do what I've always done, with a lot more wisdom, and less speed, which is good. It's funny, the older I get, the less I hurry, and the more progress I seem to make! Life keeps getting better and better."

The new millennium has only begun. Today, we are healthier and smarter, more active, longer-lived than ever before in history. Think of the possibilities—on the farm or the fast track, in a cottage or a condo— life past sixty, seventy, eighty, and onward can continue to be, or can become, our finest passage.

Whether we pare down or fix up, stay put or move on to where the grass is greener all year 'round, our basic expectations of our homes do not change, regardless of our age. They must provide safe shelter and comfort for our bodies and sustenance for our souls, and feelings of domestic peace in these times of world turmoil. Our homes are extensions of ourselves, our pleasures and, often, our dreams. It matters little whether they are old or new, mouse holes or mansions. Our homes are where we want to be.

Let *ElderHouse* help you stay there.

Part 1, Obstacle Courses and Booby Traps, expresses the need to be prepared for your elder years, to *act before the fact*. Because elders are just as heterogeneous as any other age group, the options are wide for adapting homes (retrofitting) to personal needs for safety and comfort: navigable stairs, compatible kitchens, safe bathrooms, as examples. Discussions and details are listed within the order of a "walk-through" in an average house, from the front door to the garden to the basement. Also discussed is sustainable living; that is, the use of human systems, such as passive solar design, that work with, not against, nature. References to requirements by the Americans with Disabilities Act (ADA) also are included for those who are physically challenged.

Part 2, Small Gems Are Better than White Elephants, is about adjusting to and furnishing your downsized home. It also discusses the principles and advantages of ecological housing and sustainable design. This section is arranged according to basic interior design elements such as color, lighting, scale, ecology, and the like. Finally, in part 3, Building Your Home—Your Way, I provide pencil-to-paper directions and design aids. Throughout, you will find real life stories to inspire you and small hints to help you.

It is my true warm wish that this book add pleasure and enthusiasm as well as direction to the planning of your elder home. Think of it as the first step toward a safe, independent, upbeat place to live, and as a catalyst to your own creativity, waiting like the genie in the bottle to be uncorked. Joyful anticipation has a way of becoming happy reality. Thoughts are things.

Your elder home can be a gem—small perhaps, but well set, sparkling, and prized. Living well has no dimensions, no price tag. And no age limit.

To your good life—go well!
Adelaide Altman
Boca Raton, Florida, 2002

PART I

OBSTACLE COURSES AND BOOBY TRAPS

Chapter One

OLD ISN'T OLD ANYMORE

Whatever you do, do it now. For life is time, and time is all there is.

—GLORIA STEINEM

AGE IS BECOMING FACELESS.

Our attitude, our activities, our place in the community, even our faces and physiques, all belie what the calendar says. And we are enjoying every minute of it! Age is just a number, we say. It really is!

As we gradually, imperceptibly, evolve from one stage of our lives into the next, most of us do not even realize it until we're there. Youth, middle age, young-old, old, old-old—it has become difficult to know for sure when one stage ends and the next one begins. Maybe that's the reason we're referred to as the "ageless generation." Old isn't old anymore.

But it is—eventually. The trick is to *act before the fact*; prepare our homes and our lives for elderhood. Then go on to enjoy the fulfilling years still ahead!

Science has shown that successful aging depends on good lifetime habits; to a lesser extent, good genes; and, to an increasingly *greater* extent, an environment favorable to your physical and emotional selves. Your own home is of primary importance, and deserves more than a random pile of mental promissory notes: you will fix those steps . . . you will do something about that kitchen . . . you will install a grab bar in the bathtub. Prepare now for future safety, accessibility, and comfort, for yourself and those who matter to you. And do it now.

The problem is that, dear as they may be, most of our homes have not "aged" with us, and remain designed for who we *were*—a society that was conditioned to expect age-related maladies to besiege us—rather than for the healthier, longer-lived folks we are becoming. But an out-grown house does not necessitate moving away. Not at all. It is possible to prepare your home for a lifetime of comfort and convenience, right where you are. Modification of some design aspects of your home will increase its comfort and prevent accidents for elders—and for everyone else. While this has always been the case, it's more important and feasible now that we are living longer than ever before in history.

America's over-sixty population is expected to more than double in the foreseeable future. And an estimated 83 percent of older Americans want to continue to live where they celebrated their sixty-fifth birthday—independently, on their own terms, at home—reports a recent survey by the National Institute on Aging. That probability grows stronger every day. Old is not old anymore!

Miracles await us. Incredible as it seems, the fundamental understanding of how we age has increased at an amazing, perhaps alarming, rate. Science may soon be able to slow, stop, or even reverse the human aging process. It is reasonable to believe that answers to the puzzles of the ages may emerge within the next five, surely within the next twenty years. We know now that life is not programmed to go off at a given time, like some sort of time bomb, that human lifespan probably is 120 to 125 years without benefit of replacement parts or regenerating organs. In fact, in areas of Russia and in island pockets near Japan, this has been reported as a regular occurrence.

Falls are the leading cause of death and injuries to elders, and most falls are suffered at home during everyday activities, states the American Academy of Orthopaedic Surgeons. Falls are not natural occurrences; most are preventable. Often, all it takes to make a home safer are simple measures such as rearranging furniture to open traffic lanes, or increasing the wattage to accommodate dimming vision, or changing door handles. Sometimes, more extensive improvements may be necessary, such as replanning kitchens for accessibility, or correcting the dangers lurking in bathrooms. There are scores of everyday considerations that will help us age safely and independently at home, stay in control of our lives, and benefit those about us. Changing push-button electric switches to rocker switches, for example, will also help anyone with arms full of groceries.

Retrofitting is the term used for making changes and adding conveniences that were not included or available when our older homes originally were built. Another term, *universal design*, usually refers to new construction where special considerations have been made for all family members, "from cradle to old age"; that is, child-proofing and age-proofing built in from the foundation up. While this concept gradually is taking hold—particularly among the Baby Boomers and Gen-Xers, with a deep bow to environmental considerations—most developers still are building the old way, and will continue to do so as long as the public doesn't demand better, or until today's lucrative rush of nursing homes and conglomerate elder facilities ebbs. Or until we get smarter. Meanwhile, there's help ahead.

Retrofitting a home may not seem much fun at first, but accidents and nursing homes are far worse. It is crucial to re-evaluate your homes in the light of present and near-future needs, to remove the accident-causing obstacles and inaccessibility, the "obstacle courses and booby traps," so prevalent in today's homes. To clear the national landscape of such impediments, the Americans with Disabilities Act (ADA), was enacted into law in 1990. It mandates that companies provide spaces for elder citizens and folks with disabilities. The ADA requirements are finely tuned, and all must follow them or face the threat of U.S. Justice Department sanctions. Where applicable, this book has adapted ADA rulings to augment information directed to the physically challenged.

However, much can be accomplished to alter the physical qualities of your home without following to the letter the rigid ADA restrictions, originally created for disabled citizens in the public provenance. Often, too, your renovations need not cost very much money. What follows will help you to understand your options. While you may need to consider many factors, such as aesthetics, cost, gender, cultural appropriateness, and ecological impact, ultimately no one but you can determine what you need in your home, and which tools and amenities are worthy of your time, energy, and money.

But oh! there's too much to do, too much to consider, you might say. Not necessarily. Just remember that all suggestions do not fit all people, and choose accordingly, and keep the inappropriate suggestions on hand for future use, should they ever be needed. One good method of separating real needs from wants, even fantasies (although this may be the time to indulge them), is to set them down on paper. For most people, this is the start of making things happen. And don't be afraid of new things. Here's a fun fact to keep in mind: Noah's ark was built by amateurs, the Titanic by pros.

Prepare a list of your daily activities and pastimes, then compare the items on the list with the places in your living quarters in which you perform them. Are they safe? Easy to access? Easy to use? Pleasing to the eye? Write down the needed improvements. These lists will help you to draw up a plan for modifying your home, or planning a new one, and for prioritizing your needs and finances—that is, determining what you must do first, and how to set a realistic budget and time frame. Later on, the lists also can serve as purchasing guides and controls.

Consider all the things that help your home run efficiently. These are your tools of living—possessions large and small, plain and fancy, serious and just for fun. Human needs are basic: a place to prepare food and to eat; facilities for personal hygiene; somewhere to relax, to nourish body and spirit, and to sleep. As we age, we may choose to own less, but expect it to do more, be higher quality, to promote independence without compromising comfort and aesthetics—and so importantly, to be safe. The conveniences you add today may well be your necessities of tomorrow.

Insight without action is entertainment at best. So this book will show you how to plan your home now for the additional years of life that scientific and technological marvels continue to make possible. To perform a home audit, all you need are a pad of paper and two different colored pens (a third color might be useful to denote future investigation). You can troubleshoot each room on a walk-through on floor plans, or through the actual dwelling itself. A pocket recorder might also be helpful. The information in part 1 will point out what to look for in each area. Your house audit will be a valuable tool for ensuring your future safety, comfort and accessibility, which, together, can equal independence in your elder years. The audit will also give you a brighter outlook on life, and provide a good measure of relief for your loved ones. Awareness counts.

Our homes are so much more than bricks and mortar, or merely places to hang our hats for the rest of our days. They are extensions of ourselves, our safe harbors, scrapbooks of our lives. Few words hold so many connotations or evoke such deep feeling as "home." Much like "love" or "beauty," home cannot be fully defined in words.

Whether we are presently aware of it, or will soon come to realize and revere it, home also means our planet Earth, Mother Earth, if you will, home to us all. In the name of Progress (a euphemism for multinational power lust?), or in the misappropriated name of God, humankind has been killing, plundering, and gluttonously consuming Earth's diminishing, finite bounty, with no thought of tomorrow.

Still, it's not too late.

Good design can extend the life of your home, where you can live for a very long time, even a lifetime. In addition to providing safety, accessibility, and comfort, you can install systems in your home that work in concert with nature, not against it, protecting Earth's bounty, not wantonly destroying it. Sustainable or ecological living has many aspects. As discussed in part 2, a downsized home, for example would be your first major step; the smaller the house, the smaller its ecological impact (referred to as its *footprint*) on the planet in every respect. There are numerous ecologically friendly measures to consider: passive solar designs for heating and cooling systems, for example, conserve energy, and are, in fact, far more economical over time than conventional methods. Passive solar systems also can be incorporated by retrofitting and remodeling already existing homes. The truth is, the more fossil fuel you burn, the more you pollute.

Other sustainable living issues include adequate and appropriately positioned daylighting (doors, windows, and skylights) to provide natural, cheerful, interior lighting while reducing electrical demand—sunlight is one of "the best things in life (that) are free." Another consideration is adequate sealing of your home to keep out the elements, and proper insulation to retain or deflect interior warmth and cooling. You might also want to consider financial and ecological burdens of nonrenewable materials and the energy consumed in manufacturing and transporting them. Water usage, alternate means of construction, the toxic properties of many products inside your home, and other "green" issues conducive to independent, sustainable living are too numerous to cover here. Please refer to the bibliography for additional sources of information.

Feeling good about yourself and your place on Earth is the immeasurable, immutable bonus of sustainable living. All the millions of flora, fins, fur, and feathers of the world will thank you, as will generations of humankind yet to come. If you support Mother Earth, she will continue to support you. It's not too late to live in balance, although for now, it possibly may be only one house at a time. Will it be yours?

Let's now begin to evaluate your home, or home-to-be, in general ways: What obstacle courses and booby traps will you encounter? How will you fix them or replace them? What are the choices? Let's start at the beginning, the approach to your home.

Chapter Two

Approaching Your Home A Safe Hello

The beginning of wisdom is to get you a roof.

—West African proverb

Coming home . . .

These two small words speak volumes, recalling some of life's most satisfying moments, especially as you grow older. The means by which you enter and leave should say a great deal more than "in" and "out," such as "welcome home" and "hurry back."

Entrances establish mood and indicate what to expect inside. That's why the hospitality industry makes a great effort and spends formidable sums of money to lure guests across their thresholds and to send messages of welcome long before the front desk is approached. It is done with light, color, cheerful amenities, plantings, and pleasant faces. These make you want to come in. You can and should enhance your own homecomings, as well. This is your home, your good nurturing friend.

The means of entrance also should be designed for ease of approach, accident avoidance, and security. Check the following suggestions in your present house or your apartment building, or your new home if you're contemplating a move.

DRIVEWAYS

CURBS: Eliminate them, if possible, or introduce gently sloping curb cuts. All changes in level should be easy to negotiate, no more than a quarter-inch from one level to the next.

PLACEMENT: Your driveway should be reasonably close to the door, preferably with an overhang to provide protection from the elements, if there is no garage. A flowering vine on the overhang will create a very attractive approach to your home, but be sure it will not drop flowers, seeds, or fruit that would make the entrance slippery and attract insects and birds.

Welcome home!

Surfacing: Driveways should be even. Avoid decorative surfaces such as pebbles or uneven bricks, and paving stones where moss and tiny plants can fill the cracks; they can be slippery. (Can you picture our forebears with hobble skirts on cobblestones?) Steps should be covered with a rough-surfaced paint or abrasive strips. Spread sand on icy walkways.

Steep inclines: These are risky, especially in northern climates. Radiant heating coils embedded in the surface will melt ice and snow. Expensive, but cheaper than medical bills.

Width: Driveways should allow enough space for easy car entrance and exit, additional width if a wheelchair is to be accommodated. There also must be a 5-by-5-foot minimum maneuvering space. Be sure to measure the wheelchair; they vary in size.

WALKWAYS

Placement: Walkways should be continuous from the driveway to the house, or from a detached garage to the house, and at least 36 inches wide (six inches wider to accommodate most wheelchairs; be sure to measure).

Materials: Good candidates include concrete, grouted brick, wood composite. In cold climates, consider embedded heating coils in the cement. Expensive? Perhaps. But less costly than broken bones. It's best to avoid slate and flagstone; although very attractive, they can be slippery when wet.

Definition: *Important!* Walkways must be easily seen, particularly for the sight-impaired. Consider flower borders, motion-activated lights, and handrails. Garden walkways should be equipped with handrails where the ground rises, falls, or is subject to dampness, and should be well lit.

Special walkway requirements: Please keep in mind that the following measurements do not allow for objects protruding into walkways. These may include wall-mounted objects, such as light fixtures; free-standing, such as decorative fountains or sculpture; suspended, such as lanterns and low-hanging branches; or hinged, such as gateposts or signs.

~ *For the sight impaired:* Walking with a stick: six to ten inches required each side; 32 inches to the front. Walking with a seeing-eye dog: 32 inches to one side; 48 inches front to back.

~ *For the motion impaired:* Using crutches: 36 inches side to side; 48 inches front to back. Using a walker: 32 inches side-to-side; front extension 14 to 17 inches. Using a motorized scooter: 27 inches side-to-side, 42 inches front to back.

~ *Walking with a baby carriage:* 24 inches total width; 60 inches front to back.

DOORS AND ENTRANCES

> **ELDER-AID:**
> Create rough surfaced paint by adding sand to deck paint. Check with a paint store for the best kind to use for particular types of paint. Investigate ready-made versions; some are resilient to soften falls.

Accent lighting (as opposed to overall lighting) creates a warm hello at the entrance to reinforce feelings of familiarity and security. This is particularly effective in apartment houses. An entrance bench, shelf, or garden chair is convenient for resting parcels (or yourself) before entering your house. Space permitting, a potted plant adds cheer.

SIZE: Minimum width of a single door is 32 inches; minimum door height is 6 feet, 8 inches. An intercom and door buzzer should be adjacent to the door. Also helpful is a closed-circuit TV camera connected to a communications center inside.

AUTOMATED DOOR OPENERS: Rarely used for residential entrances, these mechanisms may be necessary when doors are very heavy or landings are small, and for wheelchair- and walker-users. Electro-mechanical openers plug into outlets and operate by sensors or remote controls. Pneumatic systems are expensive, and usually are found only in commercial buildings.

WEIGHT: Doors should not require more than 5 pounds of pressure for ease of handling.

MATERIAL: Solid-core wood or metal are preferred, with a peep-hole and/or a view panel at the appropriate height, or a full-length sidelight. Glass should be non-breakable, wired for safety.

GRAB BAR: Install one outside the doorway, for extra safety in entering, particularly when the doorsill is higher than 1/4 inch.

ADDRESS NUMBERS: High-visibility address numbers are helpful, especially in "cookie cutter" communities where finding your own unit can be a challenge.

DOOR HARDWARE

LEVER HANDLES: Knobs often are difficult to turn, or they slip in your hands, particularly in inclement weather or when fingers have lost some flexibility. Check for lever door handles that will fit over existing knobs.

HANDLE HEIGHT: Door handles should be about 42 inches from the ground for most people, but measure for your own comfortable height.

OPERATION: Knobs and handles should be operable with one hand without tight grasping, pinching, or wrist twisting.

MATERIAL: Choose wood or another textured material, molded to fit the hand comfortably for good grip. Also consider loop handles, push plates, or rubberlike sleeves that stretch over knobs (and faucet handles).

HIGH-TECH HARDWARE: More costly installations are available, such as power doors with push plates, magnetic card readers, remote-control locks, and push-button-controlled magnetic locks, even voice-activated controls. Automatic closers must be adjusted to prevent closing too quickly. These kinds of hardware are expensive, and generally are used for commercial and institutional applications.

> **∽ ELDER-AID:**
> Apply a faux (imitation) wood grain finish to beautify institutional-looking metal doors. Then replace knobs with attractive lever handles.

LATCHES: Latches may need to be taken off doors to remove extra weight and lessen the effort needed to operate them. Investigate lever hardware or lever arms for existing cylindrical latches.

LOCK HARDWARE: Locks may present problems for less dexterous fingers. Push-button locks operate easily but do not provide the security of a dead-bolt mechanism. Try slide bolts instead.

DOORS FOR WHEELCHAIR USERS

DOORWAY WIDTHS: The rule of thumb is that the width should be one and a half times that of an average standing person. It's best to measure the vehicle itself because sizes vary. The space needed between two hinged doors is 48 inches minimum. An average wheelchair measures 32 inches side to side and 48 inches front to back, but they vary.

DOOR OPENING AND CLOSING: Allow adequate floor space in front of the door on both sides, and include a pull-bar for ease in closing the door.

TURNAROUND SPACE: Allow 5 feet diameter clear floor area to complete a 360-degree turn on the handle side of the door.

MAIL SLOT AND PEEPHOLE: Place these at wheelchair-accessible height in the door.

ENTRANCE LIGHTING AND DOORBELLS

For much more on lighting, see chapter 22.

WALKWAY LIGHTING: Entrance lighting should include illumination of the walkway, if you have one.

LIGHT FIXTURES: Use frosted bulbs to prevent glare, and position fixtures on either side of or above the front door.

HOUSE NUMBERS AND KEYHOLES: House or apartment numbers and keyholes should be well lit.

MOTION-ACTIVATED LIGHTING: Consider sensors that turn lights on automatically when someone approaches entrances—all around the house for added security. Also, photocell lighting, controlled by light, automatically goes on at dusk and turns off at dawn.

FLASHING LIGHTS, DOORBELLS: If you have a small hearing loss, install several chimes throughout the house. For those more seriously hearing-impaired, you may wish to install an electrical relay system, which activates flashing lights when the doorbell is rung, and a bedrocker, to wake you if you are sleeping when someone is at the door.

> **ELDER-AID:**
> A key ring with a mini-flashlight on it will help you to find the keyhole.

WIRELESS CHIMES: Install the transmitter at the front door and attach the chimes to the walls of other much-used areas.

THRESHOLDS AND SILLS

HEIGHT: The threshold should be ¼-inch maximum height, 1/2-inch if tapered (or beveled) to ¼-inch, but ideally, flush with the floor. To avoid tripping, be sure all level changes are easily navigated. Sometimes it is possible to install small, securely fastened wedges between levels.

GRAB BARS: Choose contrasting colors for easy visibility. Install to one side of the entrance door.

SILLS: Sills should be removed or never built in at all. They cause tripping.

DOOR MATS: These are potential trippers unless recessed at floor level (expensive!) or secured with nails or double-faced tape (not fool-proof), or have rubber backing or rubber underpads to hold them in place. At best, they are hazardous, and should be avoided.

STEPS: Carefully check their condition, and add railings for safety.

RAMPS AND RAILINGS

Ramps (or another gently sloping entry route with an easy grade) often are the best way to make level changes easy, which is indispensable for walking-aid users. Interestingly, it has been found that even though walkers and wheelchairs may never be necessary, ramps are easier for most people to navigate and result in fewer accidents than steps. It's a good idea to have at least one sloping entryway, which is also handy for grocery and outdoor serving carts. Ramps look good, too, providing landscape interest.

SURFACING: The ramp floor surface should be made of a stable, firm, hard finished, non-slip material such as concrete or wood painted with non-skid deck paint.

WET OR ICY CONDITIONS: Ramps are dangerous in wet, frosty weather. Approach them very carefully. Build ramps on the sunny side of the house, if possible, to expedite melting of ice and snow, and design them so that water does not accumulate on the surfaces.

SLOPE: Exterior ramps should have a 1:12 slope; that is, 1 inch of rise to every 12 inches of length. Minimum width (between handrails) is 36 inches.

RAILINGS: Railings on ramps are extra safety measures. Install them on both sides, extended 12 inches beyond the first and last step, for additional support getting on and off. Allow for finger and knuckle room, about 1½ inches if the ramp is attached to a wall. Avoid rough-textured walls. Railings should be rough-textured for better grip, and light colored for visibility. They should be placed between 34 inches and 38 inches above the ramp surface.

GARAGES

ACCESS: The garage should lead directly into the home to avoid bad weather, ideally with no steps between the garage and the house.

ELECTRONICALLY OPERATED GARAGE DOORS: These are vital to avoid undue physical exertion and accidents. Provide manual controls in case of power outages. If automatic doors are not affordable, manually operated doors should be lightweight and equipped with tension-spring mechanisms for manageability.

LIGHTS: These should go on automatically when the garage door is activated, illuminating the entire garage and garage door area. Safety signals, usually blinking lights, will alert you in case of trouble, such as the car not clearing the door, or someone standing under the doors.

"Dear Star Door"

Even as she tells about it now, Maggie trembles and becomes pale. An automatic garage door saved her much grief, possibly her life.

It was the proverbial dark and stormy night when Maggie, who lived alone, returned home from a club meeting. She activated the automatic garage door, drove in all snug and dry, and then depressed the button to close the door behind her before entering the house. The lights blinked a warning. The door would not close. She depressed the button to raise the door and tried again to close it. Again, the lights blinked their warning.

Maggie walked toward the door to investigate. The garage was well lit. She noticed an unusual shadow cast across the threshold and moved back just as an arm shot out, grabbing for her. A man's voice snarled obscenities. Maggie managed to duck his approach, dashed through the door into the adjacent laundry room and locked it, but purposely did not disengage the burglar alarm. She waited. The alarm went off. The intruder fled.

The police arrived a short time later, and stated that several other people in the neighborhood had had similar experiences. The intruder was later apprehended. Maggie sent the Star Garage Door Company an unsolicited endorsement: "Dear Star Door, may you blink forever and ever. You saved my life. Love, Maggie."

FOYERS AND VESTIBULES

MATS: As discussed under "Thresholds" above, mats should be used only if absolutely necessary. These must be skid-proof and securely fastened.

WALLS: Light, cheerful colors are best, such as warm off-white (pure or bluish white is glary), soft peach, warm beige, or warm yellow. Most folks prefer warm colors for a warm welcome. A change of texture from the rest of the rooms, such as a stippled (bumpy), stucco, or flocked (raised velvety figures) wall covering, will help the sight-impaired to know where the next room begins.

LIGHTING: Use a warm, no-glare overhead light or wall sconces. Avoid fluorescent lighting, said to be harmful to aging eyes. Place a light switch on the same line as or slightly above the doorknob for quick illumination. Or install sensor lights that are activated by movement.

MAILBOXES: Door slots are preferred to out-of-doors mailboxes for both convenience and safety. Place the slot at arm height to avoid stooping.

FOYER BENCH: A small bench near the entrance is useful for putting on boots, resting, or holding packages, if it does not block passage. A bench may also be necessary to double as a transfer bench, to help you slide more easily in and out of wheelchairs.

SHELF OR SMALL CONSOLE: Although handy to hold parcels, purses, or mail, an entrance piece should not interfere with clear passage. Inches in depth often can be saved by wall mounting a shelf made of a slab of wood, stone, or laminate (Formica, Nevamar, or similar), or urethane-treated material. Some scaled-down consoles are available for tight spaces, as shallow as 9 to 12 inches. The top should be about 36 inches from the floor. Take care that any shelf unit does not interfere with the entrance door swing.

CLOSET FOR OUTERWEAR: Your closet should be located near the entrance door and be fitted with reachable shelves or compartments for hats, boots, and other outerwear. If you're physically challenged, consider a pull-down counter-weighted clothes pole, or low-hung, reachable clothes rods (see "Closets" in

An accessible foyer.

chapter 7). The closet should be large enough to store a wheelchair or
other aids. Install a closet light that goes on when the door is opened. Pull-
chain lights can be glary and hot if unshaded, and difficult to reach.

VESTIBULES: Designed to prevent the elements from entering,
vestibules should contain nothing except, perhaps, an umbrella stand in a
corner if it's out of the way of passage. Walls and floors generally are covered with hard surface washable materials, so beware of slipping. It's better to replace the floor with a non-skid, waterproof flooring material
(please refer to "Flooring in General" in chapter 12).

Emergency Access and Rescue Provisions

The following ADA requirements are important to mobility-impaired folks considering an apartment house, condominium, or apartment hotel residency. *They could save your life!*

- WINDOWS: One operable door or window is required in each sleeping room below the fourth floor, and in basements, as follows: Minimum net area: 5.7 square feet; minimum openable height, 24 inches; minimum openable width, 27 inches; maximum sill height, 44 inches.

> **ELDER-AID:**
>
> **Very important.** The Fair Housing Act mandates that tenants cannot be refused the right to make "reasonable" modifications to accommodate their physical needs if they are willing to pay for the changes. However, most landlords also require that tenants pay to have the modifications removed and the property restored to its original condition when they move.

- DOORS: The minimum width for wheelchair users is 36 to 38 inches. Minimum door height is 6 feet, 8 inches, swinging in the direction of exit travel. Both sides of double doors must be operable with a 90-degree opening.
- CORRIDORS: For wheelchair users, the minimum access width is 36 inches, the minimum passing space is 60 inches, and the minimum turn-around space must be 60 inches in diameter. The minimum exit corridor ceiling height is 7 feet. The exit route must be free of obstacles with no angles and sharp turns because straight lines and paths are easier to navigate.
- STAIRS: The minimum headroom is 6 feet, 8 inches above the nosing; the minimum width, 44 inches. Risers should be no higher than 7 inches; treads, a minimum of 4 inches.
- HANDRAILS ON STAIRS: These should be 1¼ inches to 1½ inches (standard pipe sizes) in diameter and, ideally, installed on both sides of a staircase, and fixed so they do not rotate within their fittings. The handrail should extend 12 inches plus one tread beyond the bottom step. The railing height is to be 30 to 34 inches above stairs; spaced away from wall from 1½ inches minimum to 3 inches maximum. Railing color should contrast with the walls behind them for clear definition. Gripping surface should be non-slip and continuous, without obstructions or missing segments. Landings should be as wide as the stairs and approximately as long.
- RAMPS: There should be less than ½-inch change from ground level to ramp level. The minimum width should be equal to that of the walkway, the maximum slope no greater than 1 inch rise

for every 12 inches in the run, and the maximum rise, 30 inches. Minimum depth should be 60 inches, and at least 72 inches at the bottom. The ramp surface must be non-slip.

- RAMP HANDRAIL: If a ramp rises more than 6 inches or is longer than 72 inches, the tops of the handrails are to be 34 to 38 inches above the ramp surface, ends rounded or returned smoothly to the floor, wall, or post. Handrails should be provided on both sides of the ramp segments, and the inside rail on any switchback or dogleg should be continuous. (Please see "Ramps and Railings" above.)
- RAMP LANDINGS: These must be level, with landing width at least equal to that of the ramp, and at least 60 inches long.
- ACCESSIBLE ROUTES: Each room or area must connect with at least one accessible entrance. Routes should be 36 inches wide at a minimum; 42 inches is preferred, and provide a 60-inch diameter, 180-degree turning or passing space and a "T" intersection (where two corridors or walks meet) 36 inches wide by 60 inches deep.
- FIRE ALARMS: Emergency lighting, audible alarms, and flashing lights for the hearing impaired at a frequency of one cycle per second.
- PARKING SPACE (IN LIEU OF GARAGE): Accessible space needs to be at least 96 inches wide with a clearly demarcated level access aisle at least 60 inches wide.

Charles's and Jane's Retrofits

When Charles, a widower, built his tri-level dream home twenty-five years ago, no one ever could have convinced him that it would one day be a hostile environment. He never imagined a car accident would leave him with physical problems that made it impossible for him to navigate the approach to his beautiful mountainside home, or climb the interior steps, or even enter his shower, or work in his kitchen. He tried to use his house, but nothing was ever the same.

Charles investigated other properties, but they were too expensive for him now, and did not have the beautiful view he loved. He evaluated the possibility of retrofitting, that is, remodeling the house to accommodate his physical problems. But what could be done with three levels and the hilly terrain? He could rearrange the rooms, install a chairlift, refit the car. The garage already was on the ground level.

A little-used garden room became a ground-floor bedroom; the powder room, enlarged to a fully accessible bathroom; the two-car garage, a comfortable living room/home office. A new garage was added. His newly divorced daughter and her teen-age son moved in, so Charles did not need to use the kitchen. Even so, the kitchen underwent changes, should he ever need or want to cook for himself again. Charles complains, "Nobody makes my gassy chili anymore. They say it's not good for me. Baloney!"

Yes, the renovations were costly but affordable because Charles did not have a mortgage on his property. "Besides," he said, "no other place would feel like home."

Jane's story is similar: she began to have physical problems her snug two-story house couldn't accommodate. She was forced to move because of the stairs, the old-fashioned tub she could no longer get into, a garage she couldn't use, and grounds she was unable to tend. Jane chose to rent a nearby condominium unit, which was retrofitted to her needs.

Did Jane like condo living? Well, yes and no. "When I got sick last month, my next-door neighbor brought in the best chicken soup I've ever had. It's nice to have people close by."

The negative side was not having a house, a whole house, to herself. Yet the following year she laughed about this and announced she'd never own a house again. "You know, now if the toilet won't work, all I have to do is pick up the phone and tell Maintenance to come fix *their* plumbing."

Chapter Three

NAVIGATING YOUR HOME
Getting from Here to There—
No Problem!

Whether people are fully conscious of this or not, they actually derive countenance and sustenance from the atmosphere of the things they live in or with.

—FRANK LLOYD WRIGHT

Moving from one area to another in their own homes often causes many elders to have accidents—in corridors, on stairways, wherever the floor level changes, for example. Once considered "normal" for aging folks, medical advances and the advent of the Americans with Disabilities Act (ADA) in 1990 have disproved this assumption. Unless you believe in poltergeists, accidents don't "just happen." They are caused, usually by negligence or ignorance, or by overestimating your own agility and strength.

It is very important to have a continuous and unobstructed passage to and from your home, and through your home. Although safe passageways in your own home need not necessarily meet requirements as stringent as those offered by the ADA, some corridors or hallways can mean trouble, being both obstacle courses and booby traps. Here are some suggestions for both house and apartment dwellers to help make wayfinding safe and easy for elders and for people of all ages.

CORRIDOR LIGHTING

Good corridor lighting is crucial. Shadowed or dark areas can hide places to trip and things to bump into. Overhead lighting is considered best because portable lamps and dangling cords can be dangerous. Experts disagree on the most appropriate type. Environmentalists state that compact fluorescent bulbs are cool and most energy-efficient, while gerontologists usually agree that incandescent lighting is less harmful to aging eyes. Keep in mind, though, that ceiling fixtures and recessed lights tend to trap heat; voltage that is too high or the wrong type may overheat and cause fire. So take your choice. What is most important to you, and most suitable for the application?

WATTAGE: Use higher wattage bulbs, if necessary, and distribute the light evenly.

> **ﾟ ELDER-AID:**
> To locate the bathroom door easily, close the door most of the way and turn on a night light inside the room. This will outline the door in light, a good trick to use for unfamiliar places such as hotels or someone else's house.

EFFICIENCY: Fixtures should be kept clean for maximum efficiency. Frosted bulbs, indirect lighting, and globes can be used to cut glare, but also can be less efficient. Check with a lighting consultant, registered electrician, or trained store personnel.

NIGHT LIGHTS: Night lights should be small and unobtrusive, located near door openings, at both ends of corridors, near stairways, and in bathrooms. Photosensitive lights (activated by movement) work well.

LIGHT SWITCHES: Light switches should be easy to find, reach, and operate. Install them at both ends of corridors and at both ends of stairways. For easy recognition, be sure the color of the switch plates contrasts with the walls (light against dark, dark against light). Choose switches that can be seen in the dark (luminous), and install them 42 inches (or whatever is comfortable) from the floor, rather than the usual 48 inches from the floor.

CONSISTENCY: Maintain light consistency between hallways and bedrooms. Drastic change in light levels may impair vision.

ENDS OF CORRIDORS: Cover windows with blinds, film, or curtains that don't get in the way. Walking into glare cuts vision and causes accidents.

CORRIDOR COLOR

BRIGHTNESS AND CONTRAST: Avoid dark or saturated colors, dark blue or bright green, for example. Select any light to medium-light tone such as ivory, pale blue, or light rose. To aid sight-impaired people, paint woodwork a deep color such as dark blue or brown, for better definition of openings. Because corridors are transition zones between one area and the next, they also should merge color brightness between bright and dark areas that may exist in adjacent rooms. Try an intermediate tone in both areas if sharp contrasts in brightness cannot be avoided.

COLOR CODING: When many doors open from a corridor, it helps to paint them different cheerful colors. They can be good guides and quite attractive. This method has been successfully implemented in schools and public buildings.

FIRE EXITS: All fire exits should be clearly marked. Hang signs lower for those in wheelchairs.

CORRIDOR FURNISHINGS, DOORS, AND RAILINGS

FREE-STANDING OBSTACLES: A good rule of thumb for free-standing furnishings in corridors: Don't have any. Free-standing objects can be obstacles and are best avoided, unless the corridors are exceptionally wide. Even then, for

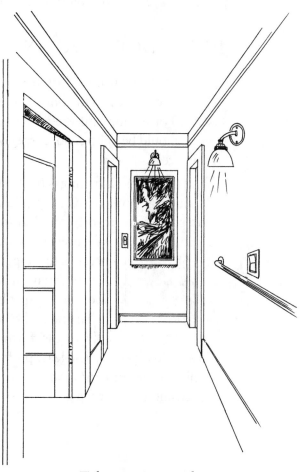

Take care in corridors.

> **⌐ ELDER-AID:**
> Paint door trim and moldings a deep color for drama or architectural interest only if the architecture is interesting! Dark for the sake of dark can be unsettling. Ditto for Venetian blind tapes.

visibility, be sure to maintain a sharp color contrast between the furnishings and the surrounding wall color, and illuminate objects well.

SHELVES AND BOOKCASES: These also can be dangerous in hallways. To prevent accidents, softly illuminate wall-hung shelves and shallow bookcases, round their corners, and paint or stain a tone that contrasts with the walls.

CORRIDOR DOORS: Doors should not open into hallways, blocking those who would enter rooms to help occupants, if needed.

CORRIDOR RAILINGS: Usually installed on one side only, corridor railings are helpful to seriously vision- or mobility-impaired people. Please see sections about railings on ramps and stairs in chapter 2.

> **ELDER-AID:**
> Existing ceramic tile can be treated with a coat of non-slip paint. Not as attractive, perhaps, but it beats falling!

CORRIDOR FLOORING

COLOR: Because corridors are crucial in emergency exit situations, floor colors should be in a medium shade, and maintain color contrast with the walls. For example, if the carpet is medium hued, the walls and woodwork should be light. Also, carpet or tile corridors in colors different from main areas.

MATERIALS: Carpeting is the first choice. It should be heavy-duty, high-density, tight weave, or loop pile not to exceed a half-inch, with dense firm padding to absorb sound, soften falls, and insulate. Be sure carpeting is securely fastened. Replace if worn to avoid tripping or insecure footing, resulting in falls. To avoid tripping, all flooring materials must be attached, joints flush, and floor levels must be even.

> **ELDER-AID:**
> Choose carpeting with a high fire retardation rating.

The next choice is resilient vinyl or linoleum, preferably in tile form because the grout, which should be flush, adds friction. The least preferable floor materials are wood and ceramic tile, because they tend to be slippery and dangerous if wet and lack the cushioning of carpet in case of a fall.

Dumb Mistakes

Despite accessibility regulations imposed by the Americans with Disabilities Act, you must take care *wherever* you go. Max and Marcia had a frightening experience at their local public library.

Getting to know their new neighborhood, they visited the beautiful modern building for the first time. They passed through the entrance level. Soon, the flooring changed, a design signal that visitors had entered another area. The levels were not even and Max tripped where the entrance tile met the carpet, and fell spread eagle on the floor. A later examination revealed no injuries save black and blue knees and belly. Lucky Max!

It was hard to believe that a public facility, careful to enforce all other ADA rulings, could overlook safe interior flooring for its patrons. A difference of at least an inch separated the flooring levels of the two areas. For safety, a quarter-inch is the maximum acceptable difference.

There's no moral to this story, other than to acknowledge that dumb mistakes can happen in the best of places. So take care; it could happen to you.

STAIRS

Precautions noted for corridors, above, also should be followed for stairways. But stairs require some additional considerations:

CLUTTER: *Important!* Keep stairs free of clutter. For safety's sake, items to take upstairs or down should not be on the steps. A small shelf or table at each end of the stairway would help. Some staircases have landings, and it's tempting and very attractive to place a potted plant or sculpture in the landing corner, but this may be hazardous.

RISERS AND TREADS: Risers higher than 6 to 7 inches are difficult to climb. Minimum tread depth is 11 inches, or deep enough for resting your entire foot. The nosings (front

Watch your step.

No door.

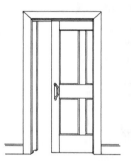

Pocket door.

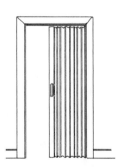

Accordian door.

corners of the steps) should be sloped, angled, or rounded. Avoid hazardous open risers.

RAILINGS: Please refer to the sections in chapter 2 about railings on ramps and stairs. Sturdy handrails should be on both sides of the stairs between 34 and 38 inches above the stair nosing, with one side securely attached to the wall, allowing about a 1½ inches for thumb space. Railings must not be interrupted by newel posts or missing segments, and should not rotate within their fittings.

HIGHLIGHTING: Contrast the color of stairs with surrounding floor covering. Steps can be attractively emphasized by carpeting or tiling treads and nosings in one color, the risers in a contrasting color. Edges of steps can be highlighted with vivid fluorescent or contrasting colored tape, but tape must be checked frequently lest it come loose and cause problems. Tiled treads can be dangerous if wet and lack the cushioning of carpet in case of a fall. Rubber stair treads can reduce slipping, but might cause tripping.

BENCH: Space permitting, without compromising safety, place a bench at the top or bottom of a stairway to serve as a resting place.

LIGHTING: Stairs and landings should be illuminated uniformly. Indirect lighting or cove lighting that does not shine directly down is best because it will not create glare or cause distractions. Please refer to lighting suggestions for corridors in this chapter.

ELIMINATING STAIRS: Would a ramp be feasible to replace present steps?

CHAIR LIFTS AND ELEVATORS: These are gaining popularity as more people decide to stay put and adapt their homes to ageless living. Space for a future elevator is often provided for in new residences, should it ever be desired. Closets located one above the other at the same location on each floor are readily converted. When an elevator cannot be installed, a good alternative may be a chair lift, an electrically driven chair attached to a staircase.

INTERIOR DOORS

It is important to be sure that all doors operate easily throughout your home. When wheelchairs or walkers are considerations, doorways should be widened to between 32 and 48 inches, depending on appliance width. Here are some ways to do it:

REMOVE DOORS: Remove the doors, if privacy is not a consideration, to add 1½ to 2 inches to the door opening, plus another ¾ inch if the doorstop is removed. Also remove double swinging doors and those that lead to traffic lanes, and replace them with wider ones. This may involve altering the structure of the home, so consult with a building contractor or architect before starting.

REPLACE HINGES: Replace existing hinges with swing-away hinges to widen door openings by 1½ inches to 1¾ inches, sometimes all that is needed for clearance.

CHANGE THE DOORS: Here are some options for different kinds of doors.

~ *Pocket doors,* which retract into the walls, can increase doorway width. Retracting doors can be inexpensively mounted on the surface of existing walls, although they are not as attractive as those that slide into the walls.

~ *Folding (accordion) doors,* multiple panels attached or hinged together, are good for infrequently used areas. They usually are lightweight, but can be flimsy and require lateral force to operate.

~ *Bi-fold doors,* which are a set of hinged panels that fold together when opened, are popular and space saving, but also require lateral force to operate.

~ *Double-leaf doors* are two narrow doors mounted in a single frame. They use less floor space, but may be a bit more difficult to open, and must clear 32 inches between door faces when open.

~ *Swinging (barroom) doors* should be avoided, because they can swing back and strike an unwary user.

~ *Sliding doors* also should be avoided, if possible. Although sliding doors are useful in tight spaces, their weight may be a problem, and their surface-mounted tracks can cause tripping. *Sliding glass doors* are particularly difficult for some folks to handle, and glass doors insulated against noise, such

Bi-fold door.

Double-leaf door.

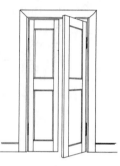

Sliding doors.

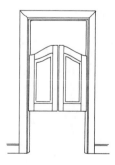

A no-no!

as those in buildings near airports, are especially heavy. Be sure to identify all glass doors clearly with brightly colored decals or suction-mounted suncatchers, to avoid walking into them. These decals often are used in public places to avoid accidents—and lawsuits.

> **ELDER-AID:**
> To secure sliding glass doors, simply insert a strong wood or metal tube in the inside floor track. Even a broom handle might work. Also affix the stationary panel to the door frame.

Draperies need to be totally cleared when the sliding glass doors are open. Decorative brackets or tie-backs are desirable not only to maintain door clearance, but also to prevent draperies from "flying" outdoors in a strong breeze or jamming the doors. Consider electric motors to operate the door or window coverings if a sliding glass door area is very wide, or is part of an entire window wall. Electrically operated outdoor storm shutters might also be worth considering. The disadvantage of this, however, is that they are inoperable during a power failure, so rig them for alternate manual operation.

Chapter Four

Food Preparation
What Fills Your Belly
Feeds Your Soul

If we had to choose between giving up sex and giving up food, the world would die from a lack of babies.

—Source unknown

Good food is one of life's great pleasures. So it is understandable that life, from times of cave cooking to today's nouveau cuisine, has evolved around the hearth, and kitchens have become our most favored of rooms. We salivate at the mere thought of a good meal and are warmed by breaking bread with loved ones. Yet, as we've grown older, kitchens may have lost their appeal because they've become too difficult, often painful, to use, and our interests now may have veered away from succulent pot roasts and perfect soufflés.

What do we make for dinner? Reservations. There's sweet irony here: When many of us now have the time and, often, the resources to entertain handsomely at home, the appeal has lost its glow. Yet that does not deter so many of us from chasing dream kitchens, touted by decorating magazines, only to find they do not work well for us.

That's because dream kitchens belong in dreams. There is no such thing as a one-size-fits-all kitchen, even for the Madison Avenue–calculated, equally nonexistent, "average" person. No one plan will be right for everybody every time. Kitchens can be U-shaped, galley, no-wall, island, peninsula, triangle, and every configuration imaginable, and all (or none) will work, depending on the needs and expectations of the cook, particularly when physical limitations are to be considered. A kitchen's most important design requirements are features that demand the least strain, are efficient, and make you feel good to work there—not necessarily state-of-the-art cabinets and appliances. Human intangibles such as conviviality, warmth, and joy cannot be factored into dream kitchens. A *real* dream kitchen is whatever *works* for you, *feels* right to you, and *brings pleasure* to you and those you love. Ambiance means a lot. That's probably why kitchens are called the soul of the home.

While kitchens should project your personal imprint, a fussy, cluttered kitchen can be confusing and cause accidents, even though the penchant for overdoing may have survived in your psyche since the days of following Mother's footsteps. Also keep in mind that today's kitchens tend to be "gender-free," no longer the domain of the lady of the house. It's time to pit habit against reality and look at what you *really* need. Are the food storage, food preparation, cooking, clean-up, and serving centers located within a few steps of each other, and comfortably accessible to where you dine? Is everything where it should be for easy reach, the most frequently used things easiest to find? Is the lighting, both natural and artificial, efficient and easily controlled?

Your kitchen requirements depend on how much and how often you cook, on your physical needs, and on your budget. Your kitchen may require only a few changes, such as adjusting the lighting, buying some new tools, refitting cabinet interiors with space-saving inserts, or readjusting shelf heights. Or you may need to modify present equipment by adding, changing, relocating, or refacing components, possibly moving or replacing some appliances. For those who can afford it, an entirely new age-proofed place to indulge your culinary skills once again may be in order.

Readapting a kitchen or creating a new one can be fun. Most folks have complained in the past that they've always had to cook in kitchens designed for somebody else by somebody else—women say by men; men say by women who can't cook. Okay, now's your chance!

No adaptation or accommodation is "too much trouble" to transform your kitchen back to the happy, manageable place it used to be. Bon appetit!

First, call up your can-do attitude; without this nothing goes right. Then make a list of your special

> **ELDER-AID:**
> Investigate all types of spice racks, shelves, and turntables for the one most adaptable to your needs, and place it at arm's reach. Then, to find your spices easily, place them in alphabetical order.

needs, such as lowered (or raised) cabinets or a place to work while sitting down. Plan the kitchen yourself on ¼-inch graph paper (please refer to part 3), and make that plan your bible; without good planning, nothing else will work.

You may want to present your list and kitchen measurements to a designer in a kitchen store or kitchen-planning department of a home-improvement emporium. Many are equipped to plan your kitchen by computer while you wait, including three-dimensional versions of the finished space. A caveat: Be sure the person who helps you is a qualified, trained kitchen planner, preferably one experienced in designing kitchens for the elderly. Ask to see her work and client list. The cost will depend on quality, size, and the number of changes needed. Another good idea is to have the kitchen designer do the site measurements, thus assuming responsibility for their accuracy.

The information that follows will help you to plan an elder-oriented kitchen, or evaluate one if you are looking for a new home. Alice and Craig didn't consider this a problem . . .

Alice's No-Cook Kitchen

Empty-nesters, Alice and Craig decided to sell their family home and buy a luxurious new townhouse. Facing a country club, it was itself beautifully landscaped and had several picture windows to bring indoors the serenity of the vista. Craig insisted that they refurnish, as well, so the interiors were executed in mellow woods and warm colors for their northern climate. The bath was equipped with all sorts of body-pampering devices, and the kitchen was state of the art.

Alice, who had always hated to cook, made her wishes known. She promptly placed a potted geranium atop each of the stove's burners! Craig got the message and became quite adept at preparing breakfasts of frozen orange juice, cold cereal, and instant coffee made with water from the automatic hot water dispenser.

What's for dinner?
Reservations.

UPPER CABINETS

HEIGHT: Adjustable height shelves are necessary. Mount them lower than normal for easy reach. Or make them adjustable by motorized or mechanical systems (expensive!). It's best to check with a professional kitchen planner.

ACCESSIBILITY: Include some cabinets without doors for immediate visibility and easy access.

DISH STORAGE: Choose vertical separators on shelves for dishes and platters to avoid stacking. Free-standing wire shelf inserts double shelf storage space, particularly in lower cabinets. Available in a variety of sizes, some with cup hooks, hangers for glassware, pot hooks, and the like, these shelves should be adjustable. Back-of-door shelves are handy for small items, but take care not to bump into them.

ORGANIZATION: Reserve top shelves of upper cabinets for seldom-used items, lower shelves for everyday things.

BASE CABINETS

HEIGHT: Provide two heights for base cabinets: for standing, 36 inches; for sitting, 29 to 30 inches from the floor. Lower heights also can be created with rolling carts or a "bridge" continuation of the countertop supported by sturdy legs or by a small cabinet on the unattached end, like a pedestal desk. Please note that suggested heights are for the so-called "average" person, and that you may want to adjust them to fit your needs. Also consider pull-out surfaces or placing a wooden or plastic slab like a cutting board atop an open drawer at the right height.

FULL-HEIGHT PANTRY CABINETS: These are convenient. Remember adjustable shelves, reserving top shelves for little-used items. It may be more efficient not to have doors on the lower shelves.

DRAWERS: Provide full-extension pull-out drawers. Replace some drawers with pull-out shelves or wire baskets for easy reach with little bending.

KNIFE BLOCK: Include a wooden block for knives, for safety, or a wall-mounted magnetic holder hung near the food preparation area.

CORNER CABINETS: Install Lazy Susans (turntables) in corner cabinets, and smaller ones on shelves, to find things easily, and also to save space.

UNDER-SINK SPACE: Consider fold-back doors under the kitchen sink to allow for knee space while sitting, and wheelchair accessibility, if needed. The open space can be closed with retractable doors or a simple curtain. Some folks prefer just to remove the doors and toe space. Install a temperature control valve to prevent scalding water from reaching the pipes, and insulate pipes to prevent burns.

CABINET HARDWARE

CABINET HANDLES: Should be large and easy to grasp; round knobs can be difficult to manage.

TOUCH-LATCHES: Work well with minimal effort, but may also spring open easily and cause accidents.

> **ELDER-AID:**
> If you can't change the hardware, loop strong cords around cabinet knobs to make them easy to pull.

COUNTERTOPS AND WORK SURFACES

STRETCHES OF CONTINUOUS COUNTER: Use for sliding heavy objects. For example, eliminate lifting pots of heavy water by placing the sink adjacent to the cooktop so you can fill pots with a sprayer and slide to the burners.

EDGES: Ideally, corners and edges should be rounded to avoid injury if you bump into them.

COLOR: Select a non-glare light-to-medium shade. White reflects the light and is hard on the eyes; very dark or intense tones, such as red, bright orange, or vivid green, also are poor choices. Choose a cheerful color as background for your equipment and dishes—and for yourself. Select your favorite color, but avoid yellow-green, lavender, and cool tan, which will tend to make your kitchen gloomy.

FINISH: For better visibility, insert a band of contrasting color on the facing edges of the countertops. (Remember the maxim—dark against light, light against dark for best contrast.) Also choose a matte (not shiny) finish to prevent glare in easy-care Formica or other plastic laminate, or a solid surface such as Corian or Fountainhead. Stone, such as marble and

🙌 ELDER-AID:
Keep a surgical glove handy for opening containers. Just lay it across the top and turn. Its mate can be placed under the container to keep it from slipping.

granite, while wonderfully glamorous, will stain. Tile, also beautiful, does not have an unbroken smooth surface and the grout can be problem to keep clean.

OUTLETS: Electric outlets for lights, exhaust fans, garbage disposal switch, and the like should be installed on the front of the counter edge for accessibility and safety.

CUTTING BOARDS: Use portable plastic ones, easily sterilized in the dishwasher, on the countertop near the sink to protect the finish from knife damage that can harbor germs. Wooden cutting boards require frequent scouring (there is some controversy over whether plastic or wooden cutting boards are more sanitary; I prefer plastic).

"FOUND" STORAGE SPACE

When you can't find room for a pantry, condiment shelf, or first-aid cabinet in a small kitchen, here are some places to look:

MIDWAY SPACE (SOMETIMES CALLED MARGIN SPACE): This is the area between the bottom of the upper cabinets and the countertop. It's a good place to install shallow open shelves to hold spices, medicine, or other small items that tend to get lost behind other objects. Usually, it is possible to built a 2- to 3-inch-deep "cap" on the top of the backsplash.

IN THE WALLS: Storage space sometimes can be recessed in the walls for canned goods, cereal boxes, brooms and brushes, and other slender items. Open an unused wall or portion of a wall, finish the inside, install shelves 3 to 6 inches deep, and frame it in. (This may be a job for a professional carpenter.)

INSIDE THE FRONT TOP PANEL OF THE SINK: Attach a shallow shelf or a readymade plastic tray in the open space, hinge the panel, and replace it. This space is great for keeping scrubbers, scrapers, and rubber gloves.

OPEN SPACE ABOVE UPPER CABINETS (SOFFIT): This space is good for keeping—and showing off—seldom-used or decorative items. If the soffit is closed, it may be possible either to open it up or add doors.

USE YOUR OWN EYES AND IMAGINATION! Does space under a stairway suggest a wealth of possibilities? Is there room above a doorway for a shelf? What else?

WALLS

VINYL OR VINYL-COATED WALL COVERINGS: Lots of people like to hang gay patterns on their kitchen walls. If you do, choose one that is scrubbable for easy spot removal and long life. Do not choose a dark color or a large or busy pattern; they will crowd you in.

PAINTED SURFACES: Use a non-reflecting matte finish. Choose a cheerful, becoming color. Because color affects physical comfort, play to the warm tones in cool climates and northern exposures; in the tropics, veer to the cool. It's been proven that room color affects body temperature.

CERAMIC TILE: This is considered the Cadillac of kitchen (and bathroom) walls. If you can afford it, it is shiny clean and easy to maintain. One caveat: Keep tile grout to the minimum for easy care. Most people love ceramic tile and stone, while other folks think they look cold and institutional. Much depends on color and texture, so carefully investigate your choices.

PEGBOARD: Install pegboard (or wire grids) in slivers of wall space or ends of cabinets for easy access to often-used small items such as special tools, or for message centers or revolving art such as grandkids' drawings and family snapshots. Some folks find a large pegboard area more useful (and less expensive) than cabinets.

> **ELDER-AID:** Buy an extra roll of wall covering for future repairs, if necessary, or for table coverings, to cover waste baskets, or make shelf liners or ceiling appliques. If you don't use it all, try it for gift wrap.

SMALL APPLIANCES

These are best kept on the counter tops for easy accessibility. Some cabinets are available with "disappearing" tambour doors (like those on old-fashioned roll-top desks) to conceal the appliances, if they are unsightly, cause too much clutter, or take up too much space. Some folks like to use washable ready-made covers for toasters, mixers, and the like.

> **ELDER-AID:** This from Julia Child's kitchen: Outline frequently used pans and cooking utensils on a pegboard, ready to find again without searching. Her outlines are white on a green pegboard, which is easy to see.

STOVES

Gas or electric ranges remain the most popular cooking devices, with burners, oven, exhaust, and sometimes microwave, all in one unit. However, as ecology-minded folks will remind you, electric heat for cooking is the most inefficient and wasteful use of energy—while those more safety-oriented maintain that cooking by electricity is the safest, particularly among elders. Whatever your choice, here are some thoughts to consider:

KNOBS: Control knobs should be side- or front-mounted to prevent reaching across hot burners. Stagger burners for the same reason. Select the special easy-to-grip knobs. Also, angle a mirror above the burners, if possible, to see what's going on in your pots without reaching across the burners. All controls should be clearly marked and easy to operate.

OVEN DOORS: Side-hinged doors are safer, but may be hard to find.

GAS SENSOR: Gas ranges should be fitted with a gas sensor for safety.

WALL OVENS: These have many advantages, such as being safer and easier to operate than all-in-one stoves, eliminating the need to bend over while the heat assaults your senses and the possibility of the door burning your leg. Foods can be seen easily without opening the door. The cabinet under the oven is a good place to store bulky items.

COOKTOPS: These can be placed away from the oven, usually to one side. They are safer and more convenient than burners located over a hot oven. Glass cooktops are easy to clean and operate, but automatic cooling controls are recommended. Glass cooktops also permit easy sliding of pots to countertops with less lifting.

MICROWAVES: These are best located on or at countertop level for easy reach. Ditto for those convenient, small toaster ovens.

SAFETY SUGGESTIONS: Curtains, pot holders, towels, loose-fitting garments, and other flammables should be kept away from cooking devices. Synthetic fabrics are known to catch fire and flash-burn quickly. Allow adequate approach in front of all appliances, optimally 30 inches long by 48 inches wide.

ELDER-AID:
If small appliances are difficult to pull forward, or stick to the countertop, place wide, smooth thumbtacks on their little "feet" for easier glide.

ELDER-AID:
Drop-front ovens are more useable when one oven rack is at the level of the adjacent countertop to shorten the distance when moving hot pans. A pull-out shelf installed next to the oven at rack height also reduces the need to lift and carry.

SINKS

ADJUSTABLE SINKS: Installed much the same way as adjustable cabinets, it is possible to locate them according to requirements.

OPEN SPACE UNDER THE SINK: Space is necessary for those who like to work sitting down, or for wheelchair users. Leave the sink cabinet empty and replace the normal doors with fold-back doors, retractable doors, a simple curtain, or eliminate the doors and kickplate completely, if it's easier. Insulate pipes to prevent burns, and install a temperature control valve to prevent scalding hot water from reaching the pipes.

SHALLOW SINK BOWLS: 5 to 6 inches deep, shallow bowls will provide more knee space and reduce strain on the back and arms.

SINK RACKS: Available in metal, plastic, or wood, these also raise the working level and ease strain. Rubber-coated racks are kind to tableware.

An accessible sink.

CORNER SINKS: These utilize an awkward storage space. They should have spread space on both sides.

↪ ELDER-AID: Store pot lids in vertical files, which can be bought in kitchen, music, or office supply stores.

FAUCETS: Single levers and paddle handles are best on faucets. Choose a model with pull-out, hand-held hose and spray, and install it next to the stovetop, if possible, to fill containers and move them without lifting.

WATER TEMPERATURE: To avoid burns, set the water temperature at 110 to 120 degrees Fahrenheit or "low" setting.

AUTOMATIC HOT WATER DISPENSERS ("INSTANT-HOT"): These are handy for a quick cup of tea and to avoid lifting boiling kettles. But be careful; the water temperature is 190 degrees! Not usually recommended for elder kitchens.

ON-DEMAND OR "TANKLESS" WATER HEATERS: The most energy-efficient type, these are installed under the sink and come on instantaneously as you use the hot water tap.

REFRIGERATORS AND FREEZERS

Side-by-side units afford easier access than standard upright or chest models. Opt for one with an automatic ice cube maker, chilled water spigot and, ideally, equipped with a small outside door that gives you access to cold drinks without opening the refrigerator. Under-the-counter models should be avoided unless you are a wheelchair user. They usually are difficult to access and can cause undue physical strain.

DISHWASHERS

SIZE: Dishwashers now are available in many different sizes, some designed to be installed under lowered counter tops. Be sure to measure your space; they appear smaller in large showrooms. Also, consider installing a normal-size dishwasher a few inches higher if bending is a problem.

↪ ELDER-AID: Another way to lower a dishwasher is to remove some or all of the toe-space under the base cabinets.

NOISE LEVEL AND WATER CONSUMPTION: Choose a model for which both are low. You may pay a bit more up front, but the ultimate payback in comfort and energy savings will be justified.

GARBAGE/TRASH DISPOSAL

BEWARE: Garbage disposals are known to thrive on jewelry and fingers!

NOISE: Some models are quieter than others. If possible, ask to see one in operation before purchasing.

LOCATION: Place the disposer toward the side of the sink, should you need to sit at the sink while working.

TRASH COMPACTORS: These are handy to save trips to the trash can, although they don't save trash weight. Consider whether the space could be put to better use, perhaps for storage of large trays or frequently used pots.

COMPOSTING: Collect your kitchen scraps in a container and use them to make compost for your garden, along with weeds, grass clippings, dried-up cut flowers. Mother Nature does the work of disposing of the garbage, and it makes excellent fertilizer for your vegetable and flower beds. Compost piles are easy to make and require very little care and maintenance. Look at any gardening book for details. Of course, composting may be impractical or difficult in some locations.

> **ᴄᴐ ELDER-AID:**
> To avoid garbage odors, if you do not have a disposal in your sink, or cannot go outdoors in inclement weather, place garbage in plastic bags (newspaper sleeves or supermarket bags are fine) and store in the freezer until garbage collection days. Don't forget to include smelly fish cans, flattened to save space.

KITCHEN FLOORING

SURFACE: The surface should be slip-resistant and resilient, in a medium color that neither shows every speck nor hides potentially slippery material.

CARPET: Kitchen carpet works well, but is more difficult to keep clean and often needs to be replaced because it retains odors and sometimes mold.

PATTERNS: Patterns can be disturbing and also tend to conceal slippery material.

BORDERS: Perimeter borders should be a contrasting color to help define the kitchen area for the sight-impaired.

KITCHEN ELECTRICAL

LOCATION: Install appliance controls, and possibly light controls and telephone on the countertops, for easy access, away from water source and hot surfaces.

OUTLET STRIPS: Often a good alternative, install cable raceways to the rear of countertops or under upper cabinets for maximum convenience.

GROUND-FAULT-INTERRUPT (GFI) OUTLETS: Install GFI if outlets are near water. All outlets should be properly grounded. Check with your electrician.

THERMOSTATS: Install thermostats at approximately eye level. Choose those with large number displays with "click-stop" dials that allow heat/cool adjustments by touch. Ideally, they should be programmable.

APPLIANCE CONTROLS: Ideally, appliance controls should contrast with the color behind them to be more easily seen. Folks with limited eyesight should consider controls that can be identified by touch, or that make special sounds. Special lights should tell you when an appliance is on or off, and there are some that disengage themselves automatically after a preset period of time.

WALL OUTLETS AND SWITCHES: Install switches about 42 to 48 inches from the floor, or whatever height is comfortable to reach. Wall light switch extension handles make switches accessible from a sitting position. Touch-sensitive and rocker switches are easier to operate than toggle switches.

UPGRADING: When renovating a kitchen, upgrade electrical power and replace worn insulation. Relocate the service panel and/or fuse box, if necessary. And don't forget to check for worn-out appliance cords.

FOR OLDER EYES: If your vision has become less keen, you may require double or triple the wattage of common incandescent light bulbs in existing kitchen fixtures. If heat becomes a problem, try compact fluorescent lighting to lower the heat, increase brightness, reduce energy costs, and avoid injury from possible burns and fires caused by high wattage—even though fluorescent lighting is not preferred for older eyes.

HALOGEN LIGHTS: Best to avoid them because they are heat-intensive.

Task Lighting: Consider installing special under-cabinet lighting and baseboard lighting to guide you, if necessary. Glare-free task lighting for work areas is a must.

KITCHEN COLOR

Plain or fancy, color it light, bright, warm, and happy. Nobody wants to work in a grim kitchen. For visual ease and safety, the trick is contrast, lots of contrast.

Broad surfaces: When countertops, cabinets, and large appliances are light to medium in tone (ideally, soft blue, peach, warm yellow, light wood tones, etc.), darken the walls enough to make the others easily seen. If cabinets are dark wood and cannot be changed, use light (not white) walls that will not reflect light and cause unwanted glare.

Floors: Cover floors in medium to medium-dark colors. Very dark floors are as difficult to keep clean as very light ones. Pattern is a personal choice, but keep in mind that a lot of pattern can cause unrest and, in extreme cases, disorientation.

Accessories: Use gay colorful dishes and objects that play up the colors of your room; again, light against dark, dark against light for sharp delineation. Mix and match, alternate dishes, accessories, and mats for fun and to avoid tedium.

> **ELDER-AID:**
> A stepstool can serve as a handy plant stand in the kitchen or balcony. Simply paint it an attractive color and decorative plants will do the rest. Two stepstools or short ladders fitted with boards between them can double as a bookcase or curio/plant catchall: a good place to grow herbs.

Other kitchenware and equipment: Purchase the best-looking, best-quality tools and utensils you can afford. Daily use of fine and beautiful things make you feel special, too. Nothing is "too good" for you to use!

Bring the outdoors in: Flowering plants such as African violets, herbs, potted seasonal annuals—even pineapple tops and sweet potato vines—caress the eye and feed the soul, and indoor gardening can be a satisfying hobby. An aloe vera is the perfect kitchen plant, because the juice from this easy-to-grow succulent is a wonderful burn ointment, applied directly to unbroken skin.

OTHER HELPFUL ITEMS

All sorts of gadgets and helpers are available for the kitchen—special openers for jars, bottles, and cans and special glassware, plates, and flatware, for example—and more are being introduced each day. Ask the clerks of kitchen stores to help you find what you need—and don't forget to check the Internet.

> **ᗌ ELDER-AID:**
> To prevent bowls, plates, and pots from slipping on the countertop while you're working with them, place a damp dish cloth or a non-skid rubber pad underneath. Also look for non-skid cutting boards and bowls.

FIRST-AID KIT: It is *very important* that your kitchen include a first-aid kit and a chart with first-aid procedures.

FIRE EXTINGUISHER: A multi-purpose extinguisher usually is best not only for paper and wood, but also for plastic, flammable liquids, and electrical fires.

KITCHEN STEPSTOOLS: These are handy for reaching high objects. They should be very sturdy and in good repair. Those with handrails are safest.

SPECIAL TOOLS: The following are but a few of scores of tools that make life easier in the kitchen:

> **ᗌ ELDER-AID:**
> This from a washer repairman: Use about half the amount of laundry detergent recommended by the manufacturer. The agitation cleans clothes as much as or more than the detergent. Add it as the water is going in, before the clothes, to assure good circulation through clothes.

~ Plastic handle grips safely replace pot holders for handling hot and cold dishes and cookware. Be sure, though, that pot handles do not protrude past the stove edge.

~ Elbow-length, flame-retardant oven mitts to reduce burn potential.

~ Easy-grip kitchen tools are easier to hold and use than normal ones.

~ Wooden oven sticks, notched and lightweight, will safely pull oven racks. Plastic or wooden 15-inch tongs will safely move food in or out of the oven.

~ A "reacher" provides easy access to objects on shelves or floors. Usually, these are 2 to 3 feet long with trigger-action grips, serrated ends, and magnetic tips, similar to the old-fashioned gadgets grocers used for reaching items on high shelves.

Cleo's Third Reacher

Cleo was in a bind. She couldn't bend over to feed her cat, and she couldn't stretch high enough to reach a cereal bowl on an upper cabinet shelf, all thanks to a recent back injury. Well, she figured, she could always feed her cat on a countertop, but that wasn't so sanitary. And she could always rearrange her kitchen cabinet, but that was an awful lot of trouble for a cereal bowl!

What to do?

A friend suggested she purchase a "reacher," one of those gadgets that grab things for you, so you don't have to bend over or stretch so high, similar to what old-time grocers used to retrieve things from high shelves. "Sure," she figured, "that should do it!"

The reacher worked for a while—when she didn't drop it while reaching. So Cleo purchased another reacher to reach the reacher she'd dropped while reaching. And that worked for a while, too—until she forgot where she'd put her reachers. So Cleo bought a third reacher to use while she hunted for the other two.

The friend who had initially suggested a reacher thought having three reachers was strange, and said to Cleo, "Well, I wouldn't do that, but you know what they say, 'Whatever works . . . '"

Cleo, who felt her good sense was being challenged, responded, "Listen, this is no different from my glasses. I have three pairs of them, too: my good glasses, and the drugstore glasses to help me find my good glasses when I misplace them . . . and another pair to help me find the first two!"

LAUNDRY FACILITIES

Many folks prefer the washer and dryer to be located in the kitchen when they have no separate laundry room, to avoid treks to the garage or basement. However, laundry odors are not very appealing where food is served. Others feel that laundries should be located where clothes are kept, near the sleeping/dressing areas, for convenience and, in a two-story house, to avoid steps. Wherever your laundry room is located, here are some suggestions for making your laundering chores easier and more pleasant:

SORTING TABLE: If there is room, try to include a dining-height table for sorting, folding, repairing clothes, and for other household chores.

ELDER-AID:

A retractable clothes-line in the bathtub is handy. To avoid slipping and stretching, install the line 4 to 5 feet from the floor, instead of at the usual shower curtain height.

IRONING BOARD: A folding ironing board, hung on the wall or behind a door, saves space. Those that are built into the wall are easy to open, are lower for ironing sitting down, and usually are lightweight—but remember they generally are anchored to the laundry room and cannot be moved elsewhere, to a room overlooking a garden, for example.

WASHER/DRYER HEIGHT: A 4- to 6-inch platform makes washers and dryers easier to reach. Both should be front-loading, and the tops can then be used for folding if you don't have a separate table.

CLOSET STORAGE: If you have limited space, stack the front-loading washer and dryer in a hall closet, accessible to all rooms. Appropriate the dryer as a clothes hamper when it's not in use. However, this is not a good idea for wheelchair users.

ELDER-AID:

For safety's sake, consider purchasing an iron with a retractable cord—no dangling cord to trip over or to pull the iron off the ironing board. Also, be sure to let the iron cool off in a safe place away from traffic.

MODELS: Choose models with simple controls. Too many settings are confusing, and we rarely, if ever, use them all.

APPLIANCE SIZE: Select the proper size appliance for your space. Remember that models appear smaller in the vastness of the store than in your home. Measure . . . measure!

STORAGE: Store laundry products on accessible shelves or cabinets near the units.

CLOTHES HAMPER: Space permitting, stacked plastic or wire baskets (instead of a clothes hamper) are good automatic clothes sorters (one for clothes to be bleached, another for delicates, etc.)

If You're Physically Challenged

Accessible reach and accessible operation ranges are important to wheelchair users and can make the difference between user-friendly kitchens and those out of limits. This includes cabinets, shelves, closets, drawers, and major appliances, but not moveable appliances such as microwave and toaster ovens. Please note that the following guidelines were developed by the ADA for public use; adapt or adjust them as needed for private dwellings.

- UNDER-THE-COUNTER REFRIGERATORS: Those made with pull-out shelves for easy access are convenient, in addition to upright models for other members of the family, if possible.
- SEATED WORKSPACE: Allow knee space for folks who must work sitting down, possibly under sinks and countertop segments. Minimum knee space dimensions are 30 inches wide, 27 inches high, and 19 inches deep. It is best unobstructed, insulated or padded, if necessary. Swinging retractable cabinet door hardware will make it possible to conceal knee space when not in use and doors can be pushed under the counter, out of the way.
- CABINET DOORS: For the visually impaired, swinging doors can be dangerous. Install hardware that allows doors to swing up rather than out and remain open to provide full view of cabinet contents.
- FORWARD REACH: This should not be *less* than 15 inches high, and not *more* than 48 inches high without obstruction. Where the obstruction is less than 20 inches deep, no forward reach can be higher than 44 inches.
- SIDE REACH: This should not be *less* than 9 inches high and not *more* than 54 inches high. For obstructions that are not more than 34 inches high or 24 inches deep, maximum reach should not be higher than 46 inches.
- FLOOR SPACE: Clear floor space, at least 30 inches by 48 inches, should be provided at fixed or built-in storage units, and allow for either a forward or side approach.
- CLOSETS: The door width should be at least 20 inches and the horizontal reach range not more than 21 inches from the opening. The shelf reach, if it is over 10 inches deep, should not be less than 9 inches high, or more than 48 inches high.
- HARDWARE: This should be operable with one hand without tight grasping, pinching or wrist twisting, and require no more than five pounds of force.
- CONTROLS: Verify that controls on stoves, cooktops, ventilation fans, dishwashers, refrigerator, freezer, and other appliances are accessible.
- STORAGE SPACE: Storage space in refrigerators, freezers, and cabinet shelves must be at least 50 percent within accessible ranges.

Chapter Five

DINING FACILITIES
Setting Pretty

We may live without friends. We may live without books. But civilized man cannot live without cooks.

—OWEN MEREDITH

IT HAS BEEN SAID that humankind's most traveled artery is the alimentary canal. How true! Eating, feasting, even fasting, are ritualistic parts of life, often requiring separate places to be observed and enjoyed. Even today, many folks feel they must maintain numerous places in their homes to dine, with special table appointments for each area. Old habits die hard. Yet lots of other people are discovering they prefer simplicity, and going . . . going . . . gone! are the separate dining rooms, the buffets laden with "company" china, silverware they rarely use that takes a whole day to polish. Present, less demanding needs may require only a dining alcove in the living room, a breakfast area, or an eat-in kitchen. Being guests in our children's homes is becoming more frequent (and often more pleasurable) than having large family dinners in our own homes and maintaining all the paraphernalia that goes with it.

Elinor didn't think so, and Milton, well . . . he wasn't so sure.

Elinor and Milton's Moveable Feast

Elinor and Milton, a retired couple, had sold both their family property in the north and their winter vacation condo, and built a custom lakefront home in South Florida, which they promptly called "The Last Hurrah." (And Milton soon began to call his wife "Elinor the Acquisitor.")

Space and upkeep apparently were not immediate considerations. They constructed an oversized his-and-her kitchen with two work stations, two sinks, two stoves, double almost everything. When they weren't cooking, they frequented area restaurants, of which there was a copious supply, and became well known at the local culinary institute. Food—buying, preparing, tasting, serving, eating, everything that had to do with a beautiful cuisine—was their thing.

The kitchen occupied less than half of a cavernous space, which easily could have been a great room itself. The balance of this area was comprised of a well-equipped lounging space and bar with adjacent TV viewing and four places to eat: a breakfast bar and dinette indoors, plus poolside and side patio dining accommodations. A guest room (with breakfast trays in the closet) and full bath were tucked behind this area near the pool and patio. There also was a formal dining room. And the master suite contained a dining table and chairs and a wrought iron dining ensemble on the breakfast patio. In all, Elinor and Milton had seven places to dine—not including their bed!

While Elinor was fussing one day with serving pieces in the storage room off the kitchen, Milton confided, "I wish our old condo had been just a little bit bigger. Then she wouldn't have insisted on all this (blip). Somehow, it just grew, and grew, and grew . . ."

It's easy to get swept away by the mood of the times, or the pressure of your peers, but it doesn't have to be that way, if you think it through beforehand. When planning your own home, consider how often you will entertain and the number of people you will need to seat. In these days of crowded schedules, many people prefer light buffet dinners or "finger food." Nevertheless, this chapter contains some thoughts on sit-down dining.

TABLES

Those slabs of something raised and supported by something else, commonly known as tables, can be made from almost anything—from cave dwellers' rocks, to pioneers' planks and logs, to sleek steel and glass, to mellow woods. Tables have served as many

> **ELDER-AID:**
> Keep on hand scratch-sticks or scratch removers from your paint store to repair damage to wood furniture, or a bottle of iodine to camouflage the scrapes on dark wood.

uses as there have been civilizations: as religious altars and dining tables; in conference rooms and libraries, and laboratories and medical examining rooms, to name but a few examples. Sizes and heights have varied widely, as well. There are stand-up tables such as those of Dickensonian scribes, emulated by today's architects, Japanese tables at which you sit on the floor, those that fold up in a wall. In every possible style or period, the ubiquitous table can be purchased at any furniture store, while unusual creations continue to pop up at art galleries and craft shows—or, perchance, proudly in your own dining room. Yet, as sophisticated and grandiose as some tables have become, there probably is no such thing as a "new" table or a new use. Here are some suggestions for yours.

SPACE: Allow a minimum of 2 feet behind a chair for comfortable maneuvering at the table.

SHAPE: Square or rectangular tables on legs, while the most popular, can cause seating problems because guests must either straddle the legs or be seated on either side of them. Oval tables seem (but may not actually be) more comfortable, and eliminate corners that can cause painful bruises. Pedestal tables work better than those with legs. If space permits, choose a round pedestal dining table to circumvent the legs problem, encourage conversation, and feel more friendly. Expect scuff marks and scratches from shoes to appear on your pedestal. For some unknown reason, people seem to be more comfortable dining with their feet any place but flat on the floor.

TABLE TOPS: Glass tops are very popular, but not practical for many folks. Glass can be wiped down with glass cleaner, but tends to smear easily and require frequent cleaning. Be sure to round the corners and mark, tint, and accessorize them for clear visual delineation. Choose ⅜-inch to ¾-inch glass with beveled edges. The glass can be etched with decorative motifs, but it's expensive.

~ Plastic laminate (Formica, for example) or wood coated with urethane are best for easy care. Normal wood tabletops usually can be coated. Many people choose to cover the tops—and the beauty—with table pads.

~ Clear acrylic tops scratch easily, attract static electricity, and are best to be avoided.
~ Marble, granite, and most stone, while handsome and luxurious, are not as carefree as they look, requiring quick mop-ups to prevent staining. They usually need repolishing after a while, depending on use.

> ✌ **ELDER-AID:**
> Remember that acrylic is not glass and should be cleaned with a wax spray—not a glass cleaner—to protect and shine it, and reduce static electricity.

TABLE SETTING

Table setting is another place in your home to express your personal style and taste. The stores teem with all sorts of table accouterments: China, flatware, hollow ware, glassware, table linens, and an unlimited range of decorations, in all colors and practically all possible shapes and sizes, in all price ranges. Take your choice, and remember that dining always is enhanced by attractive presentations. Here are some tips:

STYLE: "Dress" your table much the way you dress yourself: formal or informal, plain or fancy, blending colors and objects to complement each other. Some folks purchase sets of matching patterned dishes, cloths or placemats in colors adapted from the China, some glassware—and that's it, a simple formula. Others like solid-color sets of dishes, such as plain white or warm earth colors, and are then able to mix them with other patterns and colors, contemporary or antique, and change the "look" at will. It's a matter of personal taste, and the time available to devote to it.

DISPOSABLES: For the sake of reducing work and for simplicity of presentation, do consider the attractive paper plates and products available today, in soft or bright colors and designs, in all sizes and most price ranges. Be sure they are disposable (and biodegradable), or you will have defeated the purpose of no dishes to wash.

SPACE: Each place setting needs to be a minimum of 22 inches wide, but 30 inches is optimum; minimum depth should be 16 inches; optimum 18 inches; space between settings should be 10 to 18 inches. All measurements depend on how elaborate your settings are and the number (and physical size) of diners at your table.

WHEELCHAIR SPACE: If a wheelchair is to be considered, the above measurements will change to minimum width, 30 inches; minimum depth, 19 inches; minimum space from floor to underside of table, 27 inches; minimum 23 inches from the edge of table to the back of the wheelchair, or

42 inches clearance to the wall. It may be necessary to consider turnaround space, as well as height and reach ranges, depending on the size of the vehicle and the person's abilities.

SERVING FACILITIES

BUFFETS: A buffet, ledge, counter, or movable cart, should be located near the table, with appropriate electrical outlets installed at table height for items such as toasters, chafing dishes, and coffee pots. Special serving carts equipped with heating elements will keep food warm and eliminate extra trips to the kitchen.

SHELVES: Wall-mounted, drop-leaf ledges are useful for serving in limited space, and can be folded out of the way when not in use. In general,

Make space for a wheelchair.

shelves or ledges are space-saving conveniences, hung singly or one above another.

PLATE RAILS: Plate rails (grooved shelves wall-hung 12 to 15 inches from the ceiling) are good places to display decorative items and seldom-used serving pieces. Be careful when you collect or return them, or, preferably, get someone else to do it for you.

LIGHTING FOR DINING

CANDLES: Candles are always glamorous and flattering, but be sure they do not become fire hazards. Diners should not need to reach across candles, and candles should be placed in tight-fitting holders to avoid spills. Don't leave candles unattended, and keep them away from drafts.

> **ELDER-AID:**
> To make candle-holders smaller and tighter, line them with aluminum foil.

DIMMERS: Dimmer switches on chandeliers or sconces help to achieve the desired level of illumination without sacrificing clarity. Bulbs in chandeliers and sconces should be frosted or fitted with shades to avoid glare from direct view of the light source.

GLARE PREVENTION: Light from auxiliary lamps should reflect on the ceiling or walls. This will prevent glare, harsh shadows, and special light-refracting problems for people who wear glasses. And lest we forget, reflected light is flattering.

Food, to many people, is a mere necessity; to others, it is a consummate passion, as stated in the old saw, "Live to eat, or eat to live." On both counts, that's too bad, because sensible, leisurely dining in a pleasant atmosphere can highlight anyone's day. Even in a busy, hurried household, taking the time at least once during the day to savor the tastes, the smells, the look and touch of good food, and hopefully, to enjoy the camaraderie of friends or family, offers many dividends. Eating well is nourishment for the body, sustenance for the soul.

Chapter Six

COMMUNAL SPACES
Sitting Pretty

For the unlearned, old age is winter; for the learned, it is the season of the harvest.

—OLD HASIDIC SAYING

WHAT IS A LIVING ROOM? These days, that's not always so clear-cut. We *live* in many places all over the house—the family room, the den, the study, the bedroom sitting area, the front porch, the patio and, once in a while, the *real* living room that's become like a Victorian parlor, opened only for special occasions. And lots of us live in only one room. In fact, many people have given up the living-room concept, opting instead for an everything-in-one "great room," as it's called (see chapter 23), or paring down to smaller quarters where the living room is really *lived in*. Whatever you call them, wherever they are, your communal spaces need special safety and comfort considerations.

These areas do not mandate that genre of furnishings we've come to call "casual," or "period," just things that are easy to live with and easy to maintain, old or new, in whatever style or mix of styles you choose. Warm and familiar things are always welcome. Taste is your choice. Keep in mind that the general ambiance of your home should calm you and lift your spirits. Homes "talk" to you, they really do! Cheerful, inviting, very personal spaces are what homes are all about. The following information will help you to achieve them.

> **⌒ ELDER-AID:**
> Strips of clear double-faced tape on furniture edges will keep cats from clawing them. Commercial versions also are available: clear tape for furniture, brown tape for plants.

SEATING

FLAME RETARDATION: Upholstery fabrics and cushioning should be flame-resistant and fire-retardant. According to the Consumer Products Safety Commission, petroleum-based polyurethane foam, used in most upholstered goods, is highly flammable, emits deadly gases such as carbon monoxide and cyanide when it burns, and radiates an intense heat that can roast flesh. It can be a killer!

Check labels attached to the underside of the furniture for fire retardation processing. Ask for help if the meaning is unclear. Fire protection can be enhanced by spraying chemicals on fabrics, treating the foam, or placing a fireproof barrier between them. Be aware that most manufacturers are fighting these precautions because of price considerations.

> **⁓ ELDER-AID:**
> To aid conversation among sight- or hearing-impaired people, place comfortable chairs face-to-face, and cut off distracting background noise, light, and motion such as TV or radio. And move closer. Halving the distance quadruples the sound.

SUPPORT AND COMFORT: Do not select low, marshmallow-soft chairs and sofas, even though they may look inviting. Deep, cushiony pieces provide little or no support, and are also hard to get out of. Firm backs and seats that are hard-edged, as opposed to spring-edged, facilitate easier rising. If you select a reclining chair, be sure the mechanisms are easy to operate.

ARMS ON SOFAS AND CHAIRS: These are real necessities, and should extend forward of the seats to help users rise. Try to avoid arms that are the same height as the backs; they may be difficult to use. Opt instead for arm heights about the same as end tables, about 22 inches from the floor. Wooden arms or ends of arms are the best choice. An automatic device that assists in rising may be in order.

STURDY CONSTRUCTION: This is important. Light, pretty little chairs, charming as they are, may cause accidents. Chairs should be non-slip, resistant to tipping over or breaking when leaned on, and large enough for heavy or less agile people. We may have gained a few pounds, and may now sit down more heavily, and need seating to accommodate these changes.

TRY-OUTS: Always test the sofas and chairs you intend to purchase. Many retailers will offer to sell you items from catalogues. Just remember that you can't sit on a photograph. You'd be risking your comfort, money, and possibly your safety.

FABRICS: Many visually-impaired people identify by touch. Use various textured surfaces on furniture (and walls) to aid in orientation and direction. Textures also provide auditory clues by absorption and deflection of sound.

FURNITURE PLACEMENT

TRAFFIC PATTERNS: Tacit directions for moving about your home should be well defined by furniture, change in colors, and often lighting.

EASY ACCESS: Keep furniture and accessories out of traffic paths. Stumbling over furniture on the way to an easy chair is no fun.

FREE-STANDING OR "FLOATING" ARRANGEMENTS: Although placing furniture away from walls may be fashionable—free-standing chairs facing a sofa, for example—be sure they will not create passage problems. An exception would be using furniture to divide areas, such as a sofa placed at right angles to the wall to define a dining area.

ADEQUATE SPACE TO MOVE AROUND: A rule of thumb is about a 4-foot path. Extra space usually is better than an extra chair.

VISUAL (NEGATIVE) SPACE: Too many small objects and free-standing pieces, attractive though they may be individually, get in the way of safe passage, cause clutter and confusion, and rob you of feelings of serenity. It's better to group bric-a-brac together. (Please refer to chapter 17 on Clutter and Collectibles.)

OFTEN-USED EQUIPMENT AND ITEMS: Telephone tables and craft cabinets, for example, should be placed at approximately hip or waist height for less strain and easy accessibility.

LAMPS: Place movable lamps near electrical outlets to avoid long cords to trip over and overloading outlets. Or install additional outlets.

- ~ Provide task lighting for special activities, such as sewing or piano playing.
- ~ Treat table and lamp together as one object when determining proper placement for reading or other activities.
- ~ Consider wall mounted lamps to free table tops and eliminate the possibility of knocking over the lamps.

AUTOMATIC LUMINAIRES: Auditory signal (such as a clap), light-sensitive (ones that go on automatically when it gets dark), or touch-activated lamps, ceiling, and wall fixtures are easier to use than switches.

TABLES AND CABINETS

CORNERS: All corners should be rounded, about the curve of a half-dollar, to avoid bruising.

APPROPRIATE HEIGHTS: Tables of armchair height, about 22 inches, are good for smooth transfer of objects between the hand and the table, and also to hold reading lamps. Cocktail tables are seat height, about 18 inches. Dining tables vary between 28 to about 30 inches high, the lower height generally relegated to game tables. Low coffee tables and ottomans (15 to 18 inches high) often cause falls by people bumping into them. Consider using a tea table (about 24 or so inches high) for normal height seating.

GLASS-TOPPED TABLES: Clearly define such tables with large, brightly colored objects, chairs placed nearby.

ELECTRONIC EQUIPMENT: TV and stereo storage cabinets should be placed within easy reach. Remove trailing and dangling cords. If extension cords are necessary, choose those of the proper gauge; that is, lightweight for lamps and such, heavyweight for TV. The gauge is printed on labels attached to the cords. Use only those with built-in circuit breakers.

> **ELDER-AID:**
> If a needed outlet is behind a piece of heavy furniture, have someone move the piece for you and add an extension cord to the outlet, just long enough to be accessible, not to trip over, and replace the furniture. To avoid stooping, fasten the extension cord to the wall (tape or staples often will do) at a comfortable height.

TELEPHONE

Always have a cellular or cordless phone nearby. Also advisable is an emergency response device. Some models can be worn on one's person. The cord from the telephone to the handset should be at least 29 inches long. Check to see if the telephone is hearing-aid compatible and equipped with a volume control, if necessary.

> **ELDER-AID:**
> Drape newspapers and magazines over a towel or quilt rack for easy access and easy disposal.

If You're Hearing-Impaired

- LIGHTING: Deaf people prefer recessed ceiling lights to aid communication by making it easier to see each other clearly. Light should be directed to sitting or TV areas. Avoid table lamps because they cause glare on the TV screen, distract from the TV captions, and also get in the way of conversations in sign language.
- END TABLES: End table heights should be the same as arm heights on sofas and chairs for easy placement or removal of articles, so you can rely on tactile rather than aural cues when setting down a cup of tea, for example.
- EMERGENCY SYSTEMS: Install a light-relay system to help the hearing-impaired respond to sounds such as fire detectors, telephones, door bells, and other sounds around the house.

Chapter Seven

SLEEPING AND DRESSING
Sweet (and Safe) Dreams

Ever since man first stood erect, he has wanted to lie down.

—MARK DITTRICK

BECAUSE PEOPLE SPEND MORE than a third of their lives—about 195,000 hours in a 70-year lifetime—sleeping, ailing, lounging, loving, and reproducing in bed, the bedroom, more than any other room in the home, symbolizes life's cycle. And if we were told we must give up every stick of furniture we own except one, which would we choose to keep? Most folks would opt for their beds. But not everyone . . .

Louis I. Kahn, the famous architect, once told an auditorium of students in Philadelphia about his own lean student days, when he almost chose to become a concert pianist instead of an architect. He could afford only a tiny efficiency apartment, where there was room for either a bed or his baby grand piano, not both. So he slept on the piano, he said.

Archaeologists tell us that beds as we know them date back to the ancient Egyptians, from about 3200 B.C. onward, evolving from simple rectangular frames lashed to short legs to grand affairs around King Tutankhamen's time, 1350 B.C., sheathed in gold or carved entirely of ivory. Some had mosquito-netted canopies, but none, it seems, had pillows. Wood, sometimes ivory or glass, headrests were used, and still are used today in certain parts of the world.

On the heels of the Egyptians came the couch-cum-bed of the ancient Greeks, and the Romans' sleeping accommodations that varied from shelves and alcoves in the walls to roughly hewn wood beds laid close to the ground to elaborate higher ones designed for one, two, or three people, inlaid in tortoise shell, silver, ivory, and the like, contrived according to one's station in life. We never change.

And so it went, from those early times to now, each era offering its own versions of dreamland.

There are literally thousands of varieties of beds worldwide, all expressing humankind's need to rest, regroup, and reinvigorate itself. So take your pick—but be sure to select the best you can afford. To give yourself the comfort, luxury, and beauty of a well-made bed is one of life's true pleasures.

> **ELDER-AID:**
> Hospital-type beds do not have to look like hospital beds. Apply a decorative fabric used elsewhere in the room to the base or bedskirt, with a matching or contrasting spread and throw pillows.

BEDS AND MATTRESSES

Choose the bed size best for you and compatible with the size of your room. Many people want king-sized beds because they look glamorous and are fashionable, only to find they sleep on only one side. On the other hand, 78-inch length on any width bed is a blessing to anyone 6 feet and taller.

STANDARD SIZES: Twin, 39 by 72 inches; double, 54 by 72 inches; queen, 60 by 78 inches; king, 66 by 78 inches, often comprised of twin-sized beds pushed together, or two box springs or a platform under a single mattress. Extra-long, extra-wide, odd-shaped mattresses can be custom made, as can those for built-in beds.

BED HEIGHT: Your bed height should be neither too high (some four-poster beds) nor too low (some platform or water beds) for your physical size. Bed height should be the same as wheelchair seat for easy transfer. Beds can be lowered by shortening their legs, raised by placing them on large wood blocks or platform. To avoid dizziness that sometimes occurs when changing from lying to standing positions, or that is brought on by certain medications, sit on the edge of the bed for a few moments before standing up.

> **ELDER-AID:**
> Queen-sized top sheets and blankets generally will fit king-sized platform beds where less tuck-in is required, and may cost less.

MATTRESSES: The degree of firmness is an individual choice. Although firm mattresses generally are considered necessary for better back support, especially easing lower back pain, new findings indicate that they may aggravate neck, shoulder, and back pain. Judge a mattress for its "feel" and comfort and proper alignment of your spinal column. It should be low enough to rest your feet on the floor when seated. Be aware that while most mattresses are "inner-spring," containing metal coils, other types are available.

BOX SPRINGS: Box springs, invented for extra bounce and a luxurious look (and extra cost), are not really necessary for a good night's sleep. If rising from bed is not a problem, a mattress can be placed on a standard platform-bed frame, or any suitable platform, anywhere, including the floor.

WATER BEDS: Generally not recommended for elders, unless prescribed by a medical professional for special conditions such as burns and skin problems. Possible leakage is also considered a risk.

AIR MATTRESSES: Because they put less pressure on the body, air mattresses often are used to prevent bed sores. They can be adjusted for firmness.

FOAM MATTRESSES: These distribute body weight more evenly and sometimes can ease pain, but generally do not provide firm support.

ELECTRICALLY OPERATED CONTOUR BEDS: These marvels are extremely comfortable and adaptable. Many people are opting for actual hospital beds that are then converted to residential use and decor. These are the optimum in comfort and convenience, but usually are quite costly.

BED RAILS: These may be necessary for the safety of restless sleepers, or to provide extra support for getting in and out of bed. They are adjustable and can swivel or be locked in place. Locking in place is an important feature to avoid losing your balance if the bed should shift, especially important on hard-surfaced flooring.

BEDCLOTHES

MATTRESS PADS AND COVERS: In addition to protecting the mattress, pads and covers provide some degree of comfort. In addition to quilted cotton and cotton flannel, they are available in chenille, fluffy wool, and flat wool over copper-wire mesh that's supposed to ease aches and pains. "Egg-crate" foam or air-filled mattress pads relieve pressure. These are placed directly on top of existing mattresses. Allergy sufferers should consider special "allergy-proof" covers that totally envelop the mattress and block out irritants. Organic cotton items also are available for people with chemical sensitivities.

> **∽ ELDER-AID:** To avoid hitting your toes on bedframe rollers, attach a foam-rubber cold drink holder to each roller.

PILLOWS: Always a very personal choice, pillows are available in all manner of fillings—goose down, duck feathers, Dacron, foam rubber, kapok, and other exotic fillings, even moss and leaves—and in all imaginable shapes, sizes, and degrees of firmness. (Many Japanese use wooden blocks and ceramic figures!)

If you have allergies, beware of down and foam-rubber fillings, and look at pillow covers similar to mattress covers mentioned above. To ease pain, investigate orthopedic neck and back pillows, and those made especially for reading in bed. Pillow protectors, simple washable zippered cases, will absorb body oil and odor and lengthen pillows' lives.

BLANKETS AND HEATING PADS: To prevent burns and fires in bed, do not tuck in electric blankets, nor put other blankets on top of them. Also be sure heating pads are turned off before you fall asleep.

LIGHTING

PLACEMENT: Lamps, switches, intercoms, and master electrical house controls should be near your bed for convenience when rising at night, and also for safety, along with a phone with glow-in-the-dark numerals, at arm's length, programmed with emergency numbers.

> **∽ ELDER-AID:** Add storage to a round bedside table with a cloth with pockets for TV clicker, reading glasses, medications, nail-care items—whatever you need close by.

SAFETY: Motion-activated lights (sensors) installed at floor level near bedroom, bath and hallway can light your way. Install a bedroom nightlight. Keep a flashlight handy for emergencies.

SAVING SPACE

When bedrooms cannot accommodate the size bed you want, sometimes crucial inches can be found elsewhere.

REDUCING FURNITURE: Eliminate an extra chest of drawers by flanking your bed with night tables that provide good storage space, or place your writing table on one side of the bed, and a bachelor-type chest on the other. Surfaces of bed tables should accommodate nighttime needs. Wall-hung lamps (with switches on the cords) free tabletops and cannot be knocked over during the night.

BED-SIDE TABLES: Are two bed tables necessary? Perhaps one is all you really need. If your eye requires symmetry, replace the matching bed table with a tall and narrow potted plant, sculpture, or wall art, or a small telephone table, for example. The unused table might be utilized next to a chair elsewhere.

REDUCE SIZE: Smaller storage pieces—chests, dressers, etc.—22 inches deep instead of the normal 24 inches deep, and not as wide as standard size, may be adequate.

BUILT-INS AND WALL UNITS: Wall units will utilize wall space instead of floor space. Think of cities where skyscrapers reach up when there is no room to spread out. Custom built-in cabinetry will utilize the odd corners and spaces for added storage.

UNDER-BED STORAGE: Under-the-bed storage boxes are fine for seldom-used items, but difficult to use on a daily basis.

CLOSETS: Closets can be engineered to take the place of bulky furniture; that is, accessible trays, shelves and drawers can be built in along with multi-level hanging and storage facilities; or, in some cases, small free-standing storage pieces can be added. (Please see Closets, below, and sketches.)

Good bedside storage.

CLOSETS

Messy closets waste your time because you can't find what you're looking for; *inaccessible* messy closets cause accidents, waste even more time, try your patience, and defeat their purpose, especially if you're motion impaired. It's very rewarding, but not difficult, to create neat, efficient closets. Here are some tips:

DOORS: Install doors that permit full view of closet interiors, such as double-wide or bi-fold doors that eliminate unreachable dead space at the ends of closets. Sliding doors also reveal closet interiors, but only half at a time, and they require frequent switching. Doors on walk-in closets must be wide enough to permit easy entry. In-swinging doors that block access to clothes storage should be reversed.

ADJUSTABLE-HEIGHT CLOSET RODS AND STORAGE SHELVES: These are best, ranging from 3 feet to 5 feet 6 inches above the floor, to be raised or lowered as needed. Notched mounting blocks (usually custom-made) on either side of the closet will allow for adjustments.

DOUBLE-HUNG CLOTHES RODS: They double your hanging space. Simply measure your clothing and install rods at appropriate heights.

HIGH SHELVES: Add a shelf above the standard closet shelf for storage of less-used items. It should be 2 to 3 inches shallower than the normal closet shelf.

MODULAR SYSTEMS: Ventilated, vinyl-coated shelving units are available at most hardware outlets and stores that specialize in storage systems. These systems provide versatile storage units including shelves, rods, hooks, and baskets to be positioned as best suit your needs.

DRAWERS: Storage drawers should be hung on full-extension drawer slides for unobstructed viewing of

Standard closet

A   sliding doors prevent entrance and obscure contents
B   recessed finger slots, hard to use
C   no light
D, E   shelf and rod too high
F   wasted space
G   track dangerous

Accessible closet

A   folding doors provide easy access and visibility
B   loop handles, easy to hold
C   no track
D   automatic light
E, F   adjustable shelves
G   optional wire baskets
H, I   adjustable clothes rods

ELDER-AID:
If you hang cloth-
ing according to
use and color, items
will be easier to
find. For example,
blouses hung to-
gether in one part
of your closet can
be further divided
by color: white,
gray, black; red,
pink, coral, etc. The
same for pants,
skirts, and so on.

drawer contents. Wire basket drawers also allow full viewing of contents.

GRAB BARS: Install these outside of closet doors and inside walk-in closets at convenient places, to help avoid accidents.

CLOSET LIGHTS: Install those that are automatically activated when the door is opened; some are battery operated and easy to install yourself. Daylight compact fluorescent bulbs are cooler inside closets than incandescent, although not good for your eyes over long periods of time. (Fluorescent light bulbs can be found in shapes other than the elongated bulbs we've become accustomed to seeing.)

LAZY SUSANS: Small turntables make items on shelves more accessible.

If You're Physically Challenged

If you are physically challenged, special attention may be required in your bedroom, such as wheelchair maneuvering space and clearances, including a 60-inch diameter turnaround space and transfers, and an accessible (direct, unobstructed) route to the outside. A hospital-type bed with a special mattress, as noted above, may by needed. Please note that the bed height should be the same as the height of your wheelchair for easy transfer. Bed height is simple to adjust (see page 57). Folks with mobility impairment may require the following guidelines from the ADA to access closets, cabinets, shelves, and drawers, particularly built-ins.

- APPROACH: Floor space of at least 30 by 48 inches that allows for either forward or side approach is needed.
- TURNAROUND SPACE: Walk-in closets must allow for turnaround space for wheelchairs.
- MEASUREMENTS: Closets where passage is not required to access must be 32 inches deep maximum; horizontal reach, not more than 21 inches from the opening; rod and/or shelf reach, not more than 48 inches, if over 10 inches deep.
- DOORS: Hardware and doors must be operable with one hand without tight grasping, wrist twisting, or pinching, and require no more than 5 pounds of force to operate.

Chapter Eight

SELF-CARE
Getting Personal

*The bath is the cradle for communion with life, because water is
the source of all that lives.*

—DIANE VON FURSTENBERG

A positive mental health resource.

ADVICE FOR THE BATHROOM is easy: Buy the best, safety-oriented,
downright Sybaritic equipment you can afford. The marrying of the pri-
mal needs for cleanliness with modern technological wizardry has begot-
ten bath luxuries such as we've never before known, from spas, saunas,
and waterfalls to the simple pleasure of hot water at the turn of a tap. So
indulge your senses; the peace and pleasure of the bath can be yours. Retreat . . . regroup . . . relax! This is your time of life to *enjoy.*

Don't think of your bath equipment merely as pampering devices.
Over the centuries hydrotherapy (water therapy) has been found to be a

constant source of healing and renewal. Plumbing systems five thousand years old have been discovered in Crete, and bathrooms from 1800 B.C. were unearthed in Mesopotamia. Benefits of the bath have been documented by the ancient Egyptians, Greeks, and Persians, and the Romans are known to have bathed together in regular health rituals; the Japanese still do. Psychologically, hydrotherapy signals the body to relax and unwind. The bath is a positive mental as well as physical health resource, a refuge from daily stress, a place of serenity, privacy, and pleasure.

> **⤴ ELDER-AID:**
> If it is difficult for you to remove the empty toilet paper tube from a spring-loaded holder, just slit the empty tube with a scissors. Better yet, replace the holder with a newer open-end model that allows you to slide the tube on or off easily.

Some baths utilize technology such as modern exercise equipment, saunas, rain-makers, and the like. A new concept, a prefabricated modular bathroom for elders, bears watching. It contains a built-in seat and recesses to hold bath items, a hand-held shower, grab bars, and other amenities.

Many folks enjoy the luxury of bathrooms that emulate sitting rooms, where bathing paraphernalia mix with chaise longues, carpets, fine art, and books. Style, as always, varies with people, from a steamy tropical ambiance, with vibrant floral wall covering and live orchids, to svelte sterile white and chrome. And if you've attended to energy conservation strategies in the overall plan of your home, you will enjoy your bath luxury even more!

> **⤴ ELDER-AID:**
> A continuous trickle of water will help to keep the bath water warm and provide the tranquil effect of a running stream.

Whatever your preference, do provide yourself with as good a bathroom as you can afford. Most importantly, be sure it is a safe facility. *Bathrooms probably are the most hazardous rooms of the house.* The U.S. Consumer Product Safety Commission reported that more than 156,000 bathroom accidents occurred in 1999, and, as our longevity increases, so does the probability of accidents. This is broadly attributed to the inflexibility of the placement of bathroom fixtures, again highlighting that design should be dictated by personal requirements, not the bottom line. Since mass building development makes this impossible, here are some safety tips:

~ Are *all* working parts of your bath are in good working condition.
~ Do the toilet, sink, and tub flush, fill, flow, and drain properly?

Love Doesn't Know about Burdens

Marge had been sick for years, with some bad days, some good. On one particularly good one, she took herself into the bathroom to fix her hair, put on a little lipstick, and use the toilet. It felt good that morning to move about and stretch a bit. She turned when on the toilet seat to reach the paper with her left hand instead of her right because her shoulder hurt. She grabbed for the toilet paper holder for support. It pulled out of the wall, hurling her forward against the tub. She injured her head and was rushed, bleeding, to the hospital.

Several days later, Marge was awake and alert when her husband, Wally, arrived to see her. "What happened?" she asked. He explained.

"Y'mean a little thing like that did this? Stupid, stupid me. Should've looked first." She dropped her eyes and shook her head mumbling. "Ay, yi, yi, yi." After a few moments, she asked, painfully, "Do you still love me?"

"Love you?" Wally looked at her for what seemed a very long time, and slowly, carefully, answered, "Yes, I still love you. Just like when we were kids. Only more. Your life is my life." He took her small hand into his large one and gently squeezed it.

"Oh, thank God," she said, tears falling freely. They sat in silence for a while, warm in each other's presence. Then she said, "I had it all figured out before you came." She took a deep breath. "Go open the drawer, and take out from the back a little bundle wrapped in Kleenex."

He found the little bundle and opened it. Some pills spilled out.

"Sleeping pills," she said. "I've been up nights, so they gave these to me. I saved them to swallow all at once so I wouldn't burden you anymore."

Wally hurled the pill packet into the waste basket, and firmly said, "You're not a burden. Love doesn't know about burdens. I love you. Like I told you, your life is my life. Always will be."

~ Do knobs and handles operate easily and logically?
~ Are small conveniences such as the toilet paper holder, hooks, soap dish, and toothbrush holder firmly in place and conveniently located? Neglect of small things causes accidents, too.

BATHTUBS

Most importantly, remember the ABCs of safety: Always Be Careful. Many helpful devices are available for improving the safety of your bath.

FAUCETS: Front-mounted faucets prevent precarious stretching to check water temperature.

TRANSFER CHAIRS: The transfer chair/safety seat facilitates easy entrance and exit. It has short legs to position inside the tub, longer legs outside, and allows you to sit on the bench, then slide over to the tub side. Be careful, though, that the water does not spill out of the tub; wet floors are dangerous.

LIFTS: A bath lift, battery or hydraulically operated, lifts you from the outside of the tub to the inside for tub soaks, should this be necessary.

TUB BENCH: A tub chair or built-in bench (preferred) or swivel tub chair enables you to shower when seated, which is convenient when using a hand-held shower.

SHOWER SEAT: A fold-down seat, used for inside the shower and outside, should be *rust-resistant* and *lightweight* for easy removal. It should have a back for comfort and rubber feet for safety, and be at least 15 inches wide.

"SOFT BATHTUBS": Ideal for cushioning falls, should they happen, the interior is cushioned and slip-resistant. Expensive.

TUB MATS: Nonskid bath mats, rough-surfaced strips, or appliques added to the bottom of an ordinary tub can prevent slipping. Check frequently to be sure the adhesive is holding. Mats should be machine washable and should be changed frequently to clean both mats and tub thoroughly to remove mold and accumulated body oil and soap residue.

TEMPERATURE CONTROLS: Anti-scalding devices should be installed on tubs and showers. Water temperature controls, set at 110 to 120 degrees or "low," and drain should be easily accessible from both inside and outside the tub. If you have no controls, test the water by hand or thermometer before entering (the old "elbow test" is not reliable).

BATH SUPPLIES: A rust-proof shelf should be installed over the tub, or within arm's reach in the shower, to hold bath supplies for convenience and to help avoid accidents. A better idea: If possible, recess faucets, handles, soap, and bath products receptacles into the wall to avoid injury. Keep all glass bottles, jars, or tumblers out of the bathroom; use plastic or paper products instead.

BATH OILS: Certain herbs and additives for the tub are associated with special qualities to heal, relax, and energize you. Try some, but do *avoid oils,* which are slippery. Music, soft and calming, is delightful. But be sure radios and cords are away from the water, out of reach.

BATH MATS: Floor mats in the bathroom that are not fastened to the floor—beware! At the very least, they should have non-skid rubberized backs. To avoid tripping, it's best not to have them at all. Bathroom carpeting may be a wiser choice, even if it means replacing it from time to time.

> **ᔕ ELDER-AID:**
> Handles that are difficult to turn often can be improved by replacing faucet washers.

SHOWERS

A good shower head and/or a hand-held shower, which allows you to shower while sitting down, are necessities. They also allow you to rinse off soap from the tub and shower to avoid slipping.

An elder-friendly bathroom.

SHOWER STALLS: Pre-fab molded shower stalls with seats are available. Also check for those without curbs to prevent tripping, and to allow for wheelchairs, at least 3 feet by 4 feet, if necessary. The drain should be recessed and the floor sloped to aid drainage.

FAUCETS: Controls should have levers instead of knobs for easy grip, and should be reachable from both sitting and standing positions. Sometimes it is safer to locate shower controls outside the stall. Existing faucet knobs can be covered with plastic lever-type tap turners for ease of handling.

GRAB BARS

Grab bars probably have helped to avoid more accidents than any other safety appliance in the home! Remember, though, that grab bars are not towel bars; you need both.

SIZE: Grab bars should be $1\frac{1}{4}$ to $1\frac{1}{2}$ inches in diameter and allow at least $1\frac{1}{2}$ inches of clearance between the bar and the wall.

PLACEMENT: Grab bars should be installed at the entrance to the shower stall, inside the shower stall, on toilet walls, and wherever there is a chance of falling, including outside the bathroom near the threshold lip (remove, if possible), a danger spot. Attach grab bars to tub walls, one at a comfortable slant starting a few inches above the tub; the other, vertically or slanted beginning at 33 inches from the floor, or at shoulder height, for a tub shower.

ATTACHMENT: Attach to wall studs, or wood blocking between studs, for stability and strength; they should be capable of supporting 250 pounds.

VISIBILITY: Available in a wide color range, grab bars should contrast with the walls for easy visibility.

MATERIAL: Look for those with a rough surface texture or that are treated to be slip-proof, for easy grasp. Avoid stainless steel or chrome bars because they are slippery and have an institutional appearance many people dislike.

PORTABLE GRAB BARS: These can be attached to the tub edge for steadiness when entering or leaving the tub, as can pivoting grab bars that can be moved out of the way. Sheltering arm grab bars that surround users provide the best support for rising and sitting on a toilet.

DOORS

MATERIAL: Shower doors must be made of tempered or laminated safety glass or acrylic to avoid injury caused by falling through the glass.

TYPE: Select a fold-out model, rather than one with sliding doors, or an extra-wide model, to allow entering with walking aids.

CURTAINS: Shower curtains are preferred to shower doors by many people because they are not as cumbersome. Be sure they have magnets to hold them in place. Avoid dark-colored curtains because they block out the light and tend to invite mold. Look, instead, for a curtain with a clear 2-foot plastic border across the top to allow light in. The rod should be screwed securely into the wall; avoid tension rods, which tend to slip down. Never place any weight on the shower rod.

THRESHOLDS: Shower thresholds benefit from application of an abrasive tape of a contrasting color for safety and clear delineation.

BATHROOM DOORS: Pocket doors (those that slide into the wall) or doors that open out are best to prevent the user from blocking the door in an emergency. Leave the bathroom door unlocked for access from both sides.

BATHROOM LIGHTING

Plenty of good light in the bathroom is the first consideration for avoiding accidents, facilitating grooming, and finding the right medicine bottle.

CROSS-ILLUMINATION: Locate lighting fixtures on both sides of the mirror. A single light over the sink illuminates only the top of your head, and long shadows will appear under your eyes, nose, and chin. Place lights about 60 inches above the floor, or according to your height, and about 30 inches apart.

> **ELDER-AID:**
> If your shower curtain is too short, loop a set or two of identical shower curtain rings through each other to lengthen it. Too long? Shorten it with a pinking shears or with iron-on tape.

> **ELDER-AID:**
> Hang a magnifying glass on a hook near the medicine chest to solve the problem of reading small print on prescriptions and over-the-counter preparations.

Many variations of cross-illumination are available, such as mirror-mounted lights, theater-type channel lights hung on either side of and above the mirror, and single decorative lights on either side of the sink, to name a few.

DIMMER SWITCHES: Reostats will cut glare and heat when lights are not being used for close work.

SAFETY: Look for the blue UL labels on lighting fixtures. They denote that the lights have been approved by the Underwriters Laboratory for use close to a water source. For extra safety, also check with an electrician for a ground fault interrupter (GFI)—that is, an instantaneous circuit cut-off in emergencies. Always hire a licensed professional electrician.

> ✍ **ELDER-AID:**
> Buy bath preparations that have flat-topped containers, and store them upside-down to squeeze out every last drop. They can be expensive.

TUB AND SHOWER LIGHTING: A light over the tub and shower is important. A central bathroom ceiling fixture generally is not enough. Install the fixture with white opal diffusers flush with the ceiling to avoid visual discomfort.

NIGHT-LIGHTS: Install one in the bathroom and keep it on at all times.

SKYLIGHTS: Skylights should be made of white opal acrylic that diffuses and softens the light, as opposed to clear glass or Plexiglas that project a hard light. Ultra-violet filters or an easily operated louvered shade prevents sun damage and reduces sun-generated heat, of great concern in warm climates. Check frequently for mold build-up.

BATHROOM STORAGE

Accessible is the key word here, including lots of open shelves.

MEDICINE CABINETS: Install at an easily reached height, preferably to the side of the sink.

VANITIES: Vanities should contain pull-out shelves, some with wire bins. Lazy Susans on shelves increase accessibility. (Please refer to some of the cabinet features outlined in accessible kitchens.) Install them 34 to 36 inches from the floor to avoid back strain, similar to kitchen cabinet height, not the common 29 to 30 inches. (You may have to purchase the cabinet in the kitchen-planning department.)

BATHROOM FLOORING

Every floor close to water sources needs special attention. Bathroom floors should have slip-resistant surfaces such as non-skid ceramic or vinyl tiles (which are *not* non-skid when wet, so be careful!) or indoor/outdoor carpeting. While carpeting softens falls, it also tends to collect mildew and retain odors, and is best changed frequently, especially in warm climates. Spills from the shower, lotion, and powders create instant danger of falling. Clean them up immediately!

DECORATIVE ACCESSORIES

Attractive, personalized accessories in your bathroom, whatever size it is, make you feel special. Hang good art or reproductions or items of personal interest on the walls instead of everyday wallpaper. One friend hung photo portraits of flowers; another, nudes; someone else, pastoral scenes. An art teacher hung a collection of covers from *The New Yorker* magazines; a music teacher, old sheet music; a racetrack habitué, tickets for horses that never won. Ideas abound. Don't be afraid of looking "silly"—the loo is a good place for a good laugh. Nonglare glass on art does reduce glare, but distorts the art when viewed from an angle.

> **ELDER-AID:**
> If using a watering can is a problem, especially for hanging plants, try watering them with ice cubes.

Unusual accessories might include exotic shells as soap dishes, pretty flagons and jars for bath paraphernalia (but avoid glass and easily broken ceramics), a basket with potpourri, for example. Or, again, go for the humor! How about some funny "bathroom" books?

~ Personal appliances such as hair and body dryers, electric toothbrush, and such are easier to reach and use when wall mounted to fit your height and reach.

~ Plants at the window, sitting on the floor (be sure that you won't stumble over them), or hanging from the ceiling (out of your way) over the tub will create your own indoor garden, when you don't have a good—or any—view outside. Plants help to block out noise while you relax, and also help to purify the air. Certain indoor varieties, such as philodendron and spider plants, are said to remove chemicals, smoke, and other unwanted substances from the air. Read up on it.

~ Towels in beautiful colors help to dress up any bathroom. For easy visibility, be sure they contrast with the color of your walls. The same for shower curtains.

SPECIAL CONSIDERATIONS

Given the hazards in the bathroom, you may wish to install a telephone extension there, or carry a cell or portable phone with you. People who are physically challenged might need to include:

TOILET SEATS: A raised toilet seat, preferably wall hung, should be 18 to 19 inches from floor (the average toilet is about 16 inches), centered 18 inches from the side wall, with grab bars to the back and sides, and bathroom tissue, telephone, and other necessities within reach. Look for models that include arms for additional support. Raised toilet seat attachments also are available.

STORAGE: Towel bars/racks, medicine cabinet, and adequate storage need to be within reach. Similarly, electrical outlets, light switches, and telephone should be conveniently located.

SINKS: The sink should be wall-hung or "floated" 27 to 30 inches from floor to underside, with no cabinets underneath, to allow for leg space for those in wheelchairs. Insulate pipes to prevent burns.

MIRRORS: Hang the mirror at an appropriate height.

FAUCETS: Use single lever faucets, the easiest type to handle.

TUB LIFT: Install a lift to provide easy transfer in and out of the tub, if needed.

APPROACH AND TURN-AROUND: Make sure to include ample turn-around space, 60 inches for a wheelchair, somewhat less for walkers, and 18 inches maneuvering space at both ends of tub or shower. A 30-by-48-inch front approach is necessary to all bathroom fixtures.

From the ADA

- SEPARATE TOILET ALCOVES (OR STALLS): Minimum width, 42 inches at front; minimum depth, 42 to 48 inches from front; toilet seat height, 17 to 19 inches; grab bar height, 33 inches; minimum wheelchair turning space, 60 inches.
- TOILET FLOOR SPACE: Front accessible approach, at least 48 inches wide and 66 inches deep; lavatory may encroach up

to 12 inches. Side accessible approach, at least 48 inches wide and 56 inches deep; lavatory may encroach up to 12 inches.

- TOILET TISSUE DISPENSER: Locate not less than 19 inches from floor, not more than 36 inches from back wall. Must permit continuous paper flow.
- GRAB BARS: Rear wall, not less than 36 inches long starting no more than 6 inches from the side wall. Side wall, not less than 42 inches starting no more than 12 inches from the rear wall. Mounting height, 33 to 36 inches above the floor, mounted horizontally.

The Very Long Nose

Ellie, who is hearing impaired, likes to tell tales. One of her favorites—husband John was good-natured about this—had to do with the reason for changing the bathroom lighting in their retirement condo.

He was standing in front of the sink one day, she said, gazing into the mirror and mumbling. "I'm growing a long nose."

"Wrong clothes? Which clothes?" she asked. "And why are you making faces at yourself?"

"Not wrong clothes, Ellie, long nose! And I'm not making faces. That's the way I look. Can't you see how long my nose has grown?"

"Hadn't noticed," she answered. Which didn't make him at all happy. Not to notice, after all these years! He switched off the light and stomped into the bedroom, continuing to mumble about his long nose.

"Stop mumbling. You know I can't hear you when you mumble. Were you complaining again about my wearing the wrong clothes? When?"

John gave up, until the day after the electrician finished installing channel lights on either side of the bathroom mirror, where he was standing. "Ellie, Ellie, come quick," he shouted. "See what happened! A miracle in our own time. The electrician fixed my nose!"

"John, you're making me crazy. I told you before I don't know what clothes you're talking about."

EXERCISE FACILITIES

As Senator John Glenn has stated, "You are never too old to get in shape."

In this vein, our thinking about exercise has changed dramatically over the years. We have learned that even small amounts of exercise done regularly and consistently will help to reverse the aging process. Those who are able to work out vigorously at least five times a week have an even better edge. The American College of Sports Medicine recommends a minimum requirement of 30 minutes of moderate exercise three times a week, to reduce stress, burn calories, raise your metabolic rate, and strengthen your immune system. Also, it's been proven that working out with weights to increase muscle mass (and avoid osteoporosis) is not just for youngsters.

With this in mind, many people now are incorporating exercise facilities into their own homes, if they have the space and the resources. A wide variety of exercise equipment is available. For best and safest results, select equipment and exercise routines under the guidance of an expert trainer or physical therapist. They are well worth their fees. Also, the following suggestions are recommended for exercising at home and/or outdoors.

The U.S. Consumer Product Safety Commission and the American Academy of Orthopaedic Surgeons say that staying fit is one of the most important ways to enhance your life as you age. Exercise will lower the risk of falls, serious injuries such as hip fractures, and many common diseases; it may relieve pain and lessen recovery time when you do get sick. But it must be done safely. Small precautions have big pay-offs.

~ Always wear appropriate safety gear such as appropriate shoes and safety helmets.

~ When working out with exercise equipment, read instructions carefully and ask someone qualified to help you.

~ Check treadmills and other equipment to be sure they are in good working order.

~ Be sure to get the proper information about weight-training before you start. Check with your doctor for guidelines, if necessary.

~ Stop exercising if pain or swelling persists, and seek a medical evaluation.

Chapter Nine

ACTIVITY ROOMS
For Busy Brains and Happy Hands

*Doctor, I haven't asked you to make me young again. All I want is
to go on getting older.*

— KONRAD ADENAUER

"USE IT OR LOSE IT" is a message of merit. Studies have found
that hobbies, outside interests, and ongoing mental challenges do, indeed, help to keep us young. It has been proven that creativity does not
diminish with age, that, in fact, stimulating activity causes brain cells to
grow more branches.

The Best Seat in the House

Tovvy solved two cryptograms and a crossword puzzle every
morning after coffee, while on the john. His wife complained that
he spent too much time in the bathroom.

"My puzzles keep me sharp," he snapped back.

"Wrong end. Sitting so long will give you hemorrhoids," she
warned.

"This is mental stimulation. If I use it, I won't lose it," he insisted,
pointing to his head.

"Mental stimulation?"

"You bet!"

"Well, dear," she answered slowly, "in that case, I'll take the toilet seat to the upholsterer first thing in the morning!"

But it wasn't necessary. She found a padded toilet seat at the
local linen store, and gave it to him for Christmas.

Many authorities believe that retirement doesn't work and that the transition to retirement is one of the most stressful times of life. Retiring to something else, not from life, is the highly held answer for many people. Activity rooms, from closets-turned-offices to recycled cellars to fully equipped workrooms, have become essential.

We make space wherever we can, in basements, garages, porches, storage rooms, sometimes attics, and, often, laundry rooms. An extra bedroom, if you're lucky enough to have one, is ideal, and can double for guests or caregivers when needed. Elders utilize activity spaces for all sorts of pursuits such as painting, sewing, model building, conducting home-based businesses, following the stock market, studying, or social activities, to name but a few—and for computers. Ah, yes, computers . . .

COMPUTERS

These new-fangled, frustrating, complicated, I-love/hate-you machines are rapidly claiming the passion of elders everywhere. Cyber-savvy seniors—which all of you currently in your twenties, thirties, forties, and fifties certainly will be—are connecting with friends and family, using computers for fun and games and for education, in home offices, pursuing special interests, even earning extra income. Many are taking advantage of adult education centers for computer training, yet few classes include instruction for basic health and comfort needs when using them, especially instruction for elders.

AVOID OVERUSE: Staring at a glary computer screen for hours is difficult for everyone, but especially so for elders. Take a break every 30 to 60 minutes, set your eyes on a wider view, such as your garden, the house across the street, the sky, whatever. Also get up and stretch. Changing positions is good for the body and keeps blood flowing to the brain. A body in motion is the most healthy posture, the docs say.

LIGHTING: Balance the light, that is, locate light sources on both sides of the screen. Lamps should be adjustable, with louvers to direct the light and cut glare. Use with full-spectrum bulbs. Overhead lighting, especially fluorescent lighting, often causes additional glare. Be sure to adjust the screen position so that it does not reflect light sources such as desk lamps or ceiling fixtures. Natural light from windows can reflect on computer screens, creating more glare. Adjustable shades or window film is advised, if this is a problem.

GLARE REDUCTION: Computer shields, anti-glare or anti-reflection screens are worth investigating, to block out glare and cut radiation. They are available at most computer and office supply stores. Also check out power magnification systems, if you have low vision.

WALL COLOR: Darker tones such as medium rose, green, or blue work well to cut glare by absorbing light, as opposed to white, pale beige, or light yellow, which reflect light, dimming the characters on the screen and straining your eyes. Final color selection should depend on the location and light sources in the room and your sensitivity to it. Try it first. A little time and a quart of paint are nothing compared to your vision.

> **⌇ ELDER-AID:**
> Hearing-impaired folks say that nonglare ceiling or recessed lighting in a computer room or other activity spac, is best for deaf people, who depend heavily on their vision for reading, paperwork, and communicating with others in the room.

FURNISHINGS COLOR: Colors of surrounding equipment and furnishings also should be muted, desk tops in particular. White or pale yellow not only reflect light on the screen, but also bounce overhead light into your eyes as you work.

COMPUTER POSITIONING: Proper positioning of your computer components is important to avoid arm, neck, eye, and back strain. Keyboards need to be at typing height, 25 to 26 inches from the floor. A keyboard on top of a desk or table, 29 to 30 inches from the floor, generally is too high for longtime comfort. If you can't adjust keyboard height, try adjusting the chair. Also investigate voice-controlled machines.

MONITORS: For most people, these should be placed approximately 22 to 25 inches from your eyes to the center of the screen, and about 38 to 41 inches from the floor, or what is comfortable for you. The top of the computer screen should be below eye level to avoid strain on the neck and spine. Choose a model with tilt/swivel adjustments. Although most so-called computer furniture purports to take these requirements into consideration, you must check for yourself, putting comfort first, and aesthetic considerations second.

LAP-TOP COMPUTERS: Lap-tops are portable and convenient, and require much less space than the average PC. However, keyboards generally are smaller than full-sized models, and the placement of keys may be different. Since the monitor is attached immediately above the keyboard, it may be necessary to raise the surface on which you rest the laptop.

ELDER-AID:
You can remind yourself to get up and stretch from time to time by placing your printer away from your desk, across the room, say. Space usually baffles the noise, as well.

However, this may place the keyboard at an uncomfortable height. You may need to adjust the lighting and angle of the monitor.

CARPEL TUNNEL SYNDROME: This wrist problem affects many people who spend long hours using a keyboard or mouse—or performing any repetitive movement with the hands. Stretch your wrists, hands, and fingers frequently to relieve stiffness that, in turn, may cause muscle and joint inflammation. Also place padding under your wrists to relieve the pressure. You may want to use special wrist supports and/or seek medical advice.

COMPUTER CHAIRS: We hear the word "ergonomic" bantered about quite a bit, used interchangeably with comfort. Not so. Ergonomic refers to the interplay of mechanics with the human body. Simply put, an ergonomic chair is one that has been carefully designed to curve where you curve, support you where you need support. Select an adjustable chair. One size does not fit all! Adjustments make customizing possible, often at low cost. Try out several chairs before purchasing, and never buy from a photograph! Headrests and armrests on expensive models can get in the way, most people find.

Connect with the world!

Fabric should be medium to dark in color and very sturdy and wear-resistant, such as a tightly woven wool or acrylic. Leather and vinyl tend to be sticky and warm in the summer, cold in the winter and in air-conditioned rooms. Advantages are long wear and easy care.

FOOTRESTS: Separate footrests are useful for short people, and relieve leg strain. Your feet should rest fully on the floor or footrest when you are seated.

COMPUTER LOCATION: People without special computer rooms learn to find the space elsewhere, such as on a desk in the bedroom (be sure the height is comfortable), in a clean air-conditioned garage or basement, even on a large stairway landing or wide hall. The most favored spot seems to be a corner of the kitchen. Some new model apartments have ready-made computer stations built in. If you're into this most fascinating activity, you'll find a place. It's a fantastic way to keep in touch with the world!

There's a world of information available on such sites as Yahoo! Seniors' Guide (http://seniors.yahoo.com), SeniorNet (www.seniornet.org), Senior Resources (www.seniorresource.com), and others. Check them out—and ask your grandkids to teach you how, if you need to. You will find Web sites devoted to every conceivable activity in which one might be interested: gardening, cooking, travel, the stock market, film, travel—the sky's the limit. You might want to establish your own Web site to get in touch with relatives or old friends. Many people have renewed, or made, valuable friendships. A caveat: Know with whom you're chatting; villains lurk in cyberspace.

An Incidental Income

Pat and Paul, a retired couple in their seventies, input and edit crossword puzzles on their home computers. It all began when Pat, a crossword buff, was so disturbed by all the errors she found in books of crossword puzzles that she wrote to the publisher. He was delighted to hear from her and offered her a job proofreading puzzles for his company.

Now Pat and Paul receive packets of puzzles to enter into a computer program with both the clues and the answer grid. Later, they again receive the puzzles in proof form to edit for typos and errors. They have a great time doing it—and are well paid for their pleasure!

BASEMENTS, GARAGES, AND STORAGE AREAS

Are these areas your sanctums sanctorum, or are they booby traps? For some unknown reason, many folks don't consider basements, garages, or storage areas worthy of much attention. Yet they may appropriate them as workshops, hobby and art studios, places to keep gardening equipment and grow seedlings . . . places to putter . . . or maybe just to be by themselves—and spend more time there than they think. Although it's probably true that they needn't be decorated like the rest of the house, they do, indeed, need to be clean and safe.

Lack of safety provisions is the reason for the many of the accidents that happen in these areas. Incorrect handling of power tools, for example, is blamed for most hand injuries; improperly stored insecticides and other chemicals can be responsible for respiratory problems.

It pays to check basements, garages, attics, and other storage areas for possible trouble spots, and for ways to make working there more pleasant and productive. Information about safety in other parts of the home (elsewhere in this book) is applicable in any activity area. For relevant accessibility requirements from the ADA, see pages 18, 45, and 62.

LIGHTING: Good lighting is essential in these out-of-the-way parts of your home, especially near power tools, to reduce the possibility of accidents.

Painting in Salt Air

Bob and Bobbie had retired to a Florida oceanfront condominium. Now Bob would have time to paint, his lifetime hobby. As vice president of an internationally famous corporation, he had had little or no opportunity to indulge his talent. But where could he paint? A place for his hobby had been given less consideration than the cost and location of the condo—and Bobbie's passion for decorating.

The condo had two bedrooms, one often occupied by a visiting family member. There was no den, and Bob wouldn't dream of painting in Bobbie's living room! The rest of the apartment was comprised of a large kitchen, formal dining room (no paints here, either), a balcony, and one of the four storage rooms provided for unit owners on the same floor. So Bob painted in a vacant storage room.

It was difficult. The lighting was poor, the ventilation worse. So he brought in some portable lamps and an electric fan. Period. And he developed a cough that he blamed on the "salt air." It grew worse.

Meanwhile, Bobbie was planning an "outdoor living room" on the spacious balcony. When they talked about it one evening, Bobbie suggested that part of the area could be utilized as Bob's studio, with a portable aluminum easel and small chest on wheels for supplies. They set off the space with trellises planted with beach vines and roll-down heavy plastic shades for protection from the sea wind. An extra cart was always available to take his work indoors, if the weather turned bad. Outdoors, Bob produced many beautiful sea- and skyscapes and other works. His cough disappeared.

LIGHT SWITCHES: Switches should be installed at each entrance of a dark area, eliminating the need to cross a dimly lit place to reach them. Sharp and pointed tools make a fall more hazardous.

EMERGENCIES: Keep a flashlight handy. Have a phone and/or intercom nearby.

PROFESSIONAL HELP: Ask a licensed electrician to check the condition and performance of fuse boxes, circuit breakers, electrical cords, and, possibly, your equipment, if you cannot do it yourself.

POWER TOOLS: Improperly grounded equipment can lead to electric shock. Replace old tools that are not double-insulated or have become safety hazards. Be sure your tools have safety guards; replace missing ones. Also be sure you understand manufacturers' guides and instructions. Get help if you need it.

VOLATILE AND FLAMMABLE LIQUIDS: Check containers periodically to be sure they are clearly marked and tightly closed. Toxic vapors may escape and be inhaled; vapors from flammables can be ignited by pilot lights, as a case in point. Never store gasoline, kerosene, and other flammable liquids in your home. Paints and solvents should not be stored in your living areas, nor near heaters, furnaces, water heaters, and other ignition sources. Artists should not store paints, turpentine, and such, in a hot garage or attic. Never pour flammable or volatile liquids down your drain.

SPILLS: Clean up spills immediately, before walking on them, especially oil or grease on cement floors, or cover them with sawdust or other absorbant materials and sweep them up when the oil has been absorbed. Redo slippery surfaces.

VENTILATION: Adequate ventilation is important everywhere, but especially if your hobby requires volatile chemicals, such as photo processing materials, paints, or glues. It may be necessary to add portable fans or extra air conditioning.

SAFETY GEAR: Get into the habit of wearing a surgical mask, particularly important for those with any kind of respiratory problem. You may also need to wear rubber gloves and ear or eye protection.

Fresh air, a telephone, and a flashlight are musts.

Chapter Ten

GARDENS AND OUTDOOR LIVING
Smelling (and Planting) the Roses

A garden is a lovesome thing . . .

—THOMAS EDWARD BROWN

THERE'S SOMETHING ABOUT loving Mother Nature and sensing the ways she returns that love. That's what gardens are all about, whether for supplying your table, filling your vases, or feeding your soul. Size doesn't matter—gardens can range from herbs or bonsai on your windowsill to a charming window greenhouse, to a big back yard. Gardening is an endless pleasure, a celebration that does not diminish with age. Most avid gardeners want to continue energetic gardening activity into their elder years, when they have the time to indulge their passion, to experiment, even as they stretch their limbs. But herein may lie a problem: Some folks find that gardening is too strenuous.

Not necessarily.

There are ways to feast your eyes and nourish your soul without stressing your body. One trick is to be lazy. You're entitled. If you can afford to hire a gardening company to do the big chores while you continue to tend to the small plants, that's great. If not, find the easiest way to tackle a gardening chore, or don't do it at all. Some tasks you might delegate or eliminate are mowing the lawn, clipping hedges, or replacing annuals every season. They're energy-snatchers and, often, accident-makers. Try these instead.

LOW-MAINTENANCE STRATEGIES

LAWNS: Avoid them. Grass is high-maintenance. Try ground covers such as periwinkle, pachysandra, philodendron (in the tropics), and other creepers, or use spreading juniper, ferns, and other low-growing plants. Remember, small plants for small areas, larger plants for bigger spaces; scale is important. Check with your local nursery or state- or county-run agency and plant reference books for low-maintenance plantings suitable to your climate.

HEDGES: If they are there for privacy, you may wish to replace them with fences that can be covered by vines, or low trees and shrubbery that require little maintenance, or just let them go wild. If the hedges are there to ward off intruders, consider action- or light-activated lights instead. Remember that hedges also can *conceal* intruders.

PLANTS: Beautiful as annuals are, replace them with perennials, those equally lovely plants that almost take care of themselves each season. Lots of mulch will hold down the weeds. Gradually replace high-maintenance plants with lower-maintenance ones.

Choice is important. Plant what pleases you: Flowers you love to look at and touch, including those to cut and bring indoors; fresh vegetables for table treats; plants for sensory stimuli, including herbs; rocks and trees for contemplating their textures, color, and mysterious forms. A rewarding garden is rich in sensuous delights. If it can be viewed from indoors, all the better.

> **ELDER-AID:**
> To prevent extra work and disappointment, plan your garden first on paper, in colors that represent the plants you want to use. Be sure to take mature plant size, blooming or harvesting time, and low maintenance into consideration.

NATIVE PLANTS: These are good choices for reducing garden maintenance. If you plant wild indigenous things, you can let nature take care of them. Be sure your plot is well planned, not just an unruly bed of weeds, or you might justifiably hear from the neighbors and the health department—although the small critters who live there will love you for it!

XERISCAPING: In arid climates or where rainfall is unreliable, you should choose drought-hardy plants and garden designs. Xeriscaping involves native drought-resistant plants, rock gardening, and other water-saving techniques.

PERMACULTURE: This is another sensible and rewarding backyard option where nature does most of the work. A contraction of both "permanent culture" and "permanent agriculture," this is a gardening system that combines the best features of a natural wildlife habitat; "edible landscapes," where food plants mix with ornamentals; conventional vegetable and flower gardens, feeding both humans and wildlife friends. This is a fascinating concept worth looking into, to keep you busy and in shape, and feeling good about helping nature as she helps you. (Please refer to the bibliography for additional material on permaculture.)

WATERING: Don't do it yourself. Simple-to-operate automatic or sensor watering systems are available. Trickle hoses may be connected to electronic water timers for places that require frequent soakings. Be sure you have easy and adequate water access. Select manageable watering cans; water is heavy. If you must have a hose, select one that is made of rubber and vinyl, about 50 percent lighter than standard hoses. Watering wands with targeted sprays extend the reach of a hose. Beware of puddles, they can be slippery and provide good breeding places for mosquitoes.

GRAYWATER: Consider installing a "graywater" system to deliver wastewater from washers, showers, tubs, and sinks (not kitchen sink or toilet effluent, which is called blackwater). Graywater recycles valuable nutrients to plants and trees. Remember to use biodegradable or special biocompatible detergents or tablets. Some advantages of using graywater include reducing demand for fresh water (lowering water bills), promoting better plant growth, and reducing chlorine use.

BIRDBATHS: Remember to include a source of water for wildlife neighbors—birds, squirrels, and other creatures who share your world—with a decorative birdbath (change the water frequently), small pool, or pond.

TOOLS, STOOLS, AND SUCH

TOOLS: Ergonomic gardening tools have been designed to limit bending and reaching, as well as small hand tools that are easier to hold than popular models, even for arthritic hands. Ask for them at garden centers and hardware stores.

STOOLS: Necessary to avoid kneeling, they should be lightweight and portable, preferably with wheels or casters. Also investigate a padded kneeler-seat with handles to help seat yourself or rise.

CLOTHING: Gloves are a must, not only to keep your hands smooth and clean, but also to avoid cuts, bruises, stings, and sunburn. Hats provide essential sun protection. Use citronella or other "green" insect repellents that will not harm the environment or your own skin and respiratory tract.

GARDEN SITE

If you have not enjoyed the pleasure of a garden for a while, it might be wise to consider starting with a very small garden, expanding it after you've tested your own physical capabilities.

LOCATION: If you have a choice (and many folks do not), first consider the safety of the site and, second, pleasing your senses. Your garden should be level, partly shaded by either trees or a covered trellis. Slopes should be gradual; a sloping pathway should have handrails installed at appropriate intervals. There are many beautifully decorative handrails in garden and hardware stores.

ACCESSIBILITY: Provide an accessible route connecting areas of activity, such as flower and vegetable gardens, deck, mud room, trash/recycling receptacles, garage, as examples. The route should be barrier-free and 3 to 5 feet wide and, if covered, with overhead clearance of at least 6 feet, 8 inches.

AESTHETICS: Set your sights on texture, color, and form. Contrast foliage to play off each other, rough against smooth, dark against light, bold forms against the simple and graceful, vibrant colors against gentle pastels. Variation also lends direction by moving the eye from one place to the next, an excellent safety consideration. Avail yourself of fragrances. Each casts its special spell in a garden, in its own time of the year. Certain scents and colors attract birds and butterflies; others ward off garden pests. If possible, treat yourself to a private, quiet, partially shaded spot to enjoy the wildlife and to contemplate nature's bounties and your own good work. Try to include running water. A koi pond? A fountain? The sound helps you to close out the world, relax, and enjoy your life today. A wise Asian philosopher has stated that the past is dead, and tomorrow is far away; the present is all we can be certain of. Enjoy the now.

> **ELDER-AID:**
> Check out a child's "little red wagon" for transporting things around the garden—house too. (Used ones often can be found at yard sales.)

CONTAINER GARDENING

When you have no garden area, create a garden in pots, plant boxes, tubs, or other containers. Especially suited to porches, patios, and balconies, well-chosen window boxes and containers can create great visual impact, both from looking out from the dwelling and up from the ground.

CONTAINERS: Stone, ceramic, and terra-cotta containers are very attractive and do not trap moisture and mold, but they usually cost more than plastic, composite or wood ones, and are difficult to move once filled with heavy soil and pebbles. Less-conventional containers include copper or galvanized-steel pails, well-cleaned paint cans sprayed in gay colors, large mixing bowls, salt fish barrels (deodorized), tubs, or anything from a flea market that can be recycled into an interesting plant holder, such as an old baby buggy, rubber boots, a sled, whatever tickles your fancy. Gardens are for fun, too!

WATERING AND DRAINAGE: Some garden centers sell very thin, coiled hoses long enough to reach from an indoor sink to a balcony. Sensor water systems also eliminate the need to carry water. Create adequate drainage by including a 2- to 4-inch layer of stones or shards on the bottom, depending on container and plant size.

VERTICAL AND HANGING GARDENS: Rust-proof wire baskets and trellises conserve space while creating dramatic backdrops for potted specimens, and don't require bending They can hold herbs and vegetables such as cherry tomatoes, cucumbers, and squash, as well as flowers. Be sure to line baskets first with sphagnum, sheet moss, or coco-fiber mats, available at garden centers.

TABLETOP GARDENING: This is popular among those who prefer to work sitting down. Select a simple table that does not detract from the beauty of your "crops." Think of a folding aluminum table or a wooden trestle table, particularly suitable for balconies and patios. Tabletop gardening container sizes vary, but should be about 24 inches by 36 inches by 8 inches deep, with good drainage, for growing onions, beets, zucchini, and other veggies, or decorative plants with shallow root systems. Low library stairs or stepstools and plant stands also might be used.

RAISED BEDS: For flower, herb, and vegetable growing, these are easier to access and require less physical strain, such as bending and stooping. A raised outdoor bed is simply a bottomless box set on the ground and filled with loose fertile soil, and should be about 24 inches high and no deeper than 22 inches. They also are available ready-made for balconies in many materials from plywood to concrete, and in kits. If you're handy, they're easy to build, or can be custom-made in special configurations, such as following the perimeters of a porch or balcony railing.

ORCHIDS: Orchids are air-plants and, as such, do not grow in soil, but prefer fir bark, lava rock, and commercial potting mixes, and they thrive in humid surroundings. With 35,000 known species in the world, orchid growing can be a fascinating (and expensive) hobby that demands little physical exertion. And what nice gifts they make for orchid aficionados! Or just to pin one on somebody special.

> **⌇ ELDER-AID:** Avoid using freshly pressure-treated wood for garden uses because the chemicals are known to be absorbed by plants and can harm them, and possibly your skin.

OUTDOOR LIVING

Outdoor living areas are as important as indoor family rooms to many people, for barbecues, socializing, or simply relaxing. Any outdoor space, from a large patio, terrace, deck, or balcony, to a small porch for a breath of fresh air, provides a perspective of the world beyond the interior environment, and are sought by many as their "secret gardens." However, certain precautions should be taken, as in any other part of your home.

SUN AND SHADE: Choose a spot to catch some sun, or, if you prefer, to be shaded by plantings, umbrellas, or eaves, to cut glare and offer protection from the sun, screened in, if possible, away from noise and unpleasant odors.

ACCESS: Clear access to your home is important, particularly to the bathroom and kitchen, as well as an emergency exit from the property.

FLOOR LEVELS: Level changes such as those between the kitchen and patio, or the patio and a ramp, or the patio and a garden path should connect smoothly to reduce tripping, with no more than $1/4$- to $1/2$-inch difference between levels. Raised edges are good safety details on ramps, pathways, and floor surfaces where drop-offs occur. They also act as guides for the visually impaired.

FLOORING: Floors should have a firm, non-skid surface of a continuous texture, free of bumps, large holes, or cracks. Suitable materials include textured concrete, tightly laid brick, and wood decking with boards spaced

½-inch apart, maximum. Contrasting color values and textures between areas are helpful.

GRAB POINTS: Grab bars, railings, or sturdy furniture provide additional safety in movement.

OUTLETS: Electrical outlets need to be weatherproofed and located at least 15 inches above floor level.

OUTDOOR FURNITURE: Regardless of furniture type, edges must be smooth and easy to grip. Braking features are necessary on items with wheels or casters. A combination of permanent and moveable seating often works best. Choose from a large variety of outdoor furniture: Attractive wood and wrought-iron furniture is usually quite expensive, requires padding, and is heavy to move. The advantage of these materials is that they generally are stable and sturdy to support the weight of most folks. Aluminum and plastic pieces are relatively inexpensive, will withstand the elements, and are easy to move, but tip easily and may cause accidents. Cast aluminum often is more sturdy yet moveable. Weatherproofed built-in furnishings such as benches and storage cabinets are strong with low maintenance.

GARDEN BENCHES: Iron, stone, or concrete garden seats and benches, permanently placed, invite us to sit down, relax, shed our outer layers, and meditate. They offer comfort, like a kind of mental "upholstery." They also organize views: where there's a bench, there usually is something nice to pause and look at, such as a special planting or view down a path. As landmarks, they also help to control movement and define space, and usually can stand on their own as works of art. Be sure the bench you choose is weatherproof and safe. Set it in a level place or on a pad of brick, pebbles, or flagstone sunk into the ground.

> **⌒ ELDER-AID:**
> Place a stone sculpture at one end of a stone bench for "company" as you relax, a little garden child, for example, or a fat, friendly frog.

MUD ROOMS

A place to clean up is convenient when coming in from the garden—but it might also be a place for accidents to happen. Leaves cling and mud is slippery. Maybe this is why such a place often is called a "mud room," built especially for a smooth transition between the outside and indoors.

A mud room can be a porch, vestibule, or any convenient place to sit down to remove slippery shoes and soiled gloves, or simply to catch your breath before entering the house. Space permitting, add a bench with room underneath for muddy shoes, boots, or garden clogs, and slippers to change into to keep interior floors clean, Japanese style. The clean-up room might also contain hooks or pegs for hanging outdoor paraphernalia, wire or wicker baskets on a shelf (to avoid stooping) for hand tools and gloves, a place for bug repellents and first-aid supplies such as bandages, adhesive tapes, cotton balls, antiseptic wipes, activated charcoal solution for absorbing caustic poisons—just in case there's a garden accident. As always, a telephone programmed with emergency numbers should be nearby. Your clean-up room might even be a powder or shower room with outdoor access, or even outdoor hot and cold spigots or shower.

A place to clean up.

FLOORING: Floors should be easy to clean and fairly rough to prevent slipping. Textured stone, cement, or tile are good choices. Avoid smooth slate, marble, shiny linoleum, and vinyl; they are very slippery when wet, treacherous with slime. Resist the temptation to use floor mats, including rough sisal mats at thresholds; they're conducive to tripping and injury.

GRAB BAR: Install in the mud room for extra security.

WALLS: Walls also should be easy to clean. Use tile, vinyl, or water-resistant latex paint.

INDOOR GARDENS

Houseplants not only add a touch of the outdoors and beauty to your home, they also are highly effective at keeping air clean and pure. Acting as living filters, through both their leaves and their roots, plants help purge the air of dangerous substances created by manufactured items such as carpets, synthetics, building materials, electronic

> **ELDER-AID:**
> Your clean-up room is great for keeping umbrellas, golf clubs, dog's leash, tagged key rack, and other items to grab on your way out, saving time and last-minute, accident-causing, blood pressure-raising, scurrying about.

A table-top garden.

equipment, paints, and solvents. Some plants absorb certain odors, as well. As an added benefit, they emit moisture into the air, which is good for allergy sufferers, and particularly welcome during the winter months when the dry air makes us more susceptible to upper respiratory ailments. However, it should be stated that some folks don't like any kind of gardening, even caring for indoor plants, and dislike the increased humidity that plants generate.

Check with your local nursery, library, or Web sites for additional information about using indoor plants.

SPACING: The rule of thumb is at least two plants per every 100 square feet of space. Add a small fan to help circulate the moisture.

PLANTS: Choose easy-to-grow, insect-resistant varieties. The snake plant, English ivy, rubber plant, lady palm, begonias, peace lily, and chrysanthemums are especially effective air purifiers and moisture transpirators. Allergy sufferers should cover potting soil with an inch or so of gravel to hold down possible mold, and should stay away from flowering varieties. However, other folks may appreciate their fragrances.

ARRANGEMENT: Place plants carefully for maximum decorative effect and easy care in places where they will grow well and offer the most benefit. Although plants are beautiful and beneficial, be careful of plant-clutter. Co-existing with too many plants is like living in a greenhouse. (One avid indoor gardener's husband swears that his wife's Venus flytrap attacked his escargots!)

Miz Jorie, Tim, and the Little Red Wagon

Marjorie, who was new in the neighborhood, set out to plant some seedlings. This was a happy time. The snow had melted and the newly turned earth permeated the air with the pungent smell of spring. She whistled as she plopped her new straw hat with bright phony daisies atop her head, and put on her new green-thumb gardening gloves, and got to work.

Soon, she became aware that a neighbor's small son was watching her. "Well, hello," she said. The boy ran away.

Several days later, he reappeared as she was working in her garden. "Hello again," she said.

"Hi," he mumbled, and watched her move a pot almost as big as he was.

"Heavy?" he asked.

"Sure is. Wanna help?"

"Naw." He ran away again, only to return a few minutes later with his little red wagon. "This'll help," he offered. And it did.

The little boy became a frequent visitor, "helping" Marjorie (and also helping to empty her cookie jar and listen to her stories), and they became fast friends. His name was Tim, and he called her "Miz Jorie." However, by the following spring, the family moved away to another part of the country. The little boy said he wanted Marjorie to keep the wagon as his "moving-away present," and promised to write. Like so many good intentions, that never came to be. As the years sped by, Marjorie always thought about Tim in the spring when she planted her garden.

One day, Marjorie was positioning seedlings in her flowerbed, as she did every year, and moving pots here and there. "Heavy, Miz Jorie?" asked a nice, deep voice.

"Sure is." She looked up from under her battered straw hat with the drooping daisies at the tall young man standing above her. She turned happy inside, with a smile as warm and welcome as the sunny day. "Wanna help?"

"Yeah." He grinned back. "I'll fetch the wagon . . ."

Chapter Eleven

ALL THROUGH THE HOUSE
Additional Safety Tips

Growing old is a precious gift given to some lucky human beings
. . . not an award of merit.

—DICK VAN DYKE

THERE IS NO NEED for safety-oriented homes to look or operate much differently than any others, for people of all ages, including younger folks. Indeed, one of the points of this book is to demonstrate that a house can be designed to serve its residents' needs for their lifetimes, from youthful adulthood to dignified elderhood. Smooth navigation will depend a great deal on your own creativity in removing potential trouble spots and adding safety details that "invisibly" blend into the rest of your home.

Nor will making home adjustments necessarily be expensive. For example, substituting items that are elder friendly doesn't cost any more than using those that are not—from door knobs to light bulbs to carpeting. Major renovations, such as installing totally accessible bathrooms and some kitchen adjustments, are costly, of course, but home adaptations for health purposes often are covered by insurance. Check your policies.

So the message here is to think safety, comfort, and ease of handling—independence! If things do not feel good, look good, and work for you now, they never will, and may, indeed, work *against* you. Many injuries result from hazards in the home that are easily overlooked, but also easy to correct. Take the time to do so. Little changes can make a big difference in your life.

Often we need someone else to examine our homes for safety because it's easy to become too accustomed to them for realistic evaluations, and you may not be familiar with the amenities and equipment now available. A fresh eye is valuable—a knowledgeable friend or relative, or people who perform this service for a fee. They include professional interior designers and architects, some home remodelers, occupational therapists, and some social workers attached to state and national home modification/repair agencies. Fees usually are reasonable and, in the case of public services, are free (if you pay your utility bills).

The following section covers safety hints for items found all through the house, such as lighting and electrical elements, flooring, and windows. As noted in the sections dealing with specific areas, evaluate the innovations listed, and *adapt only what applies*. Don't forget to mark your plans or lists with two pens, such as red and black, where red stands for "urgent." Another color, purple or green, might also be useful to note follow-ups at a later date.

LIGHTING AND ELECTRICAL EQUIPMENT

Lighting is a science in itself, and a lighting professional or electrician should be consulted, if possible, when planning or retrofitting your home. Poor lighting causes accidents. *Without light, there is no perception, no color, no style to guide you.* Chapter 21, "Lighting," discusses this subject in greater detail, but here are some special safety suggestions:

WATTAGE: Wherever possible, increase wattage, *but not glare*, in hallways, stairs (watch landings), bathrooms, kitchens, and workrooms, with indirect or recessed lighting fixtures. Glare is difficult, even painful, to aging eyes. Torchiere-type floor lamps with reflective light are excellent to avoid glare. Be sure to keep the light level uniform in individual rooms, the living room, for example, to eliminate accident-causing "dark spots."

LIGHTS: Experts believe it is best to avoid fluorescent lights. They emit a blue-green light that can cause vision fogginess often experienced by older people. Their almost imperceptible flicker can possibly trigger headaches. Incandescent lighting is better, and best used indirectly to reduce glare. Also screen daylight with blinds, film, etc., and if possible, opt for overhangs that do not trap heat, and north-facing skylights, also to cut glare, even though they are less energy efficient.

SWITCHES: A master switch for emergencies will activate all lights throughout the home. Also install electronic sensors for fire, intruders, and health alerts, and a gas sensor for possible leakage. Light switches, electrical outlets, and phone jacks should be installed higher than normal, about 15 inches minimum to 30 inches maximum from the floor; place large-dial thermostats lower than usual. Opt for touch, toggle or rocker switches; push-button switches can be difficult to operate. Be sure switches for overhead lights are available at all room entrances. Switches that glow in the dark are excellent for hallways, emergency appliances, and, especially, bathrooms. To locate the bathroom easily at night, plug in a small night light inside the bathroom, then leave the door ajar about 1 inch to outline the bathroom door.

> ✑ **ELDER-AID:**
> For easy way-finding, install dimmer switches in all frequently used rooms, and leave lights turned low when the room is not in use.

CORDS: Check the condition of all cords, and replace those that are frayed or cracked. Be sure they are placed out of the way of traffic and are not under furniture or rugs to cause extra wear resulting in shocks. Use tape to attach cords to walls and baseboards, not nails or staples, which invite fire and are shock hazards. Remove all trailing and dangling cords from lamps and appliances. Move cords and appliances away from hot surfaces and sink areas.

EXTENSION CORDS: Extension cords should not carry more than their proper load, as noted by the ratings label on the cord or appliance. For example, standard 18-gauge cords can carry 1,250 watts. Overloaded extension cords cause fire. If overloaded, change the cord to one higher rated or unplug appliances connected to it. Plug heavy-duty appliances, such as washers and air conditioners, directly into wall sockets. Also consider powerstrips, with outlets placed every 10 or 12 inches, or to order, for multiple plugs. Circuit breakers are another safety feature. New outlets may be in order to avoid extension cords. Those equipped with ground fault circuit interrupters (GFIs) are considered safest, particularly near water.

> ✑ **ELDER-AID:**
> To eliminate the risk of overloading the circuit and starting a fire, never put more than two plugs into any extension cord. The fact that it can receive three, four, or six plugs doesn't mean it's safe. The exception is a powerstrip, specifically designed for multiple plugs and incorporating a circuit breaker.

PORTABLE LAMPS: To solve the find-the-switch problem and avoid burns, consider lamps with touch-lights, those that work by auditory signals such as a clap, and light-sensitive lamps that turn on automatically when darkness falls. Another way is to have switches placed on the cord about 6 inches from the lamp base.

LAMPSHADES: Light-colored shades on lamps, little shades on dining room fixtures, indirect globes, and frosted bulbs cut glare to aging eyes. Keep in mind that opaque shades create down-light on specific objects and surfaces, while transparent shades provide overall area illumination.

LIGHT BULBS: Take time to determine that bulbs are the appropriate size and type for the lamp or lighting fixture. Wattage that is too high may lead to fire through overheating, especially on ceiling fixtures, recessed lights, and hooded lamps, which trap heat. When you are not sure, do not use bulbs higher than 60 watts. In closets, bulbs should be at least 12 inches from clothing and other combustibles.

LARGE PRINT: Large numerals on thermostats, temperature dials, telephones, clocks, scales, books, and measuring tools, will increase visibility, possibly without additional illumination.

DOORBELL: Can you hear it from all parts of your home? If not, install a blinker, flashing light, or additional ringers.

COLOR, PATTERN, AND FINISHES

Because it is considered normal to lose some ability to perceive color, light, and depth as we age, it is important to choose colors, patterns, and finishes that provide distinct separation between planes—that is, that separate furniture from background, such as upholstery that contrasts strongly with the color on the floor and walls, making seating easier to recognize. Color, pattern, and texture also add identification. See part 2 for more detail.

COLOR LOSS: Remember that most older eyes suffer some color loss, particularly in the blue to green area of the color spectrum, causing these colors to appear muddy or dark, so select colors accordingly.

LIGHT-COLORED SURFACES: These reflect light and make the most of available light. Be sure, though, that they're easy to clean.

PATTERNS: Should be clear, not fuzzy or confusing. Pleasant textures add to tactile enjoyment and identification.

FABRICS: Wall coverings, carpets, and all fabrics in the home must be fire-retardant. Also check for toxic fume emission even though the materials may not burn.

COLORS: Avoid low-contrast colors that could inhibit the ability to distinguish boundaries. As a case in point, a black border on a dark-gray carpet might be perceived as a void or a step instead of a continuation of the carpet. Also avoid color combinations that are close in wavelength, such as yellow and white or red and orange. They will appear to bleed into each other and hamper visibility. Remember, *contrast for clarity.*

The primary colors (red, yellow, and blue) or secondary colors (shades of greens, blue-green, oranges and yellow/orange, violets and rose) usually are good choices if held to medium tones. Medium blue is said to be restful because it facilitates the secretion of tranquilizing hormones. Mauve, violet, and gray tend to be blend into shadows and, in some cases, can be depressing. Green is considered restful and uplifting as it suggests plants and life.

Choose bright colors for drinking glasses, toothbrushes, and other items that may be difficult to distinguish. Bright colors also are best for color-coding corridor doors, labels, boxes, and the like. For easy visibility, switch plates, outlets, push plates on doors, as well as the doors themselves, should contrast with the walls.

Following fashionable colors—in one year and out the other—is not a good idea. Unless fashion is your passion, and you can afford it, always base your color and pattern choices on clarity for safety and personal preference. If not in your own home, where?

Happy colors don't cost any more than dull ones. Use them throughout your home. Happy harmonious rooms encourage happy harmonious living.

> **ELDER-AID:** Remember that fashion is all about perception. If your home is attractive to you, regardless of style, period, or what the "experts" say—then it is attractive! Period.

WINDOWS

DOUBLE-HUNG AND SASH WINDOWS: The most common type in this country, they often are difficult to open. If possible, select sliding windows on rollers, casement windows, or central pivoting windows. Ideally (but it doesn't happen very often), all glass should be tempered and double-paned to prevent heat loss and heat penetration, and to block out unwanted sound. Low-e (emissivity) windows are especially energy efficient. Weatherstripping also blocks out drafts.

CASEMENT WINDOWS: These can be made easier to operate when window crank openers are mounted low. However, although they are good for wheelchair users, eliminating stretching, they may be dangerous for small children.

WINDOW PLACEMENT: If you have a choice, place them for easy viewing and cross-ventilation, even though you may have air conditioning. A nice breeze is very pleasing to the senses, and a pleasant scene goes a long way. Further, choose your exposures, if you can: east-facing windows capture early morning light and sunrises; west-facing windows are best for afternoon light and sunsets; south-facing windows are necessary for passive solar gain (heat absorption by masonry and tile by day, which is released at night); and north-facing windows are easiest on the eyes, but not so energy efficient.

EMERGENCY EXIT: In case of fire, a window at least 24 inches by 36 inches, 2 to 4 feet from the floor, at the rear of the house, or remote from the front entrance, should be provided. Be sure screens and storm windows are operable at all times.

WINDOW TREATMENTS

How we treat our windows is important, not only for heat and cold insulation and decoration, but also to block harmful UVA and UVB rays of the sun and, most importantly, to cut glare. High levels of illumination do not compensate for fading vision; glare merely adds discomfort. Think of window coverings as proper "sunglasses" for your home and choose them carefully.

BLINDS: Vertical blinds that clear the doors are good drapery replacements. They're easier to handle and light is adjustable. If you feel blinds are "cold" and undecorative, soften them with upholstered valances or softly pleated swags and side panels, preferably made of a fabric or color that appears elsewhere in the room. Horizontally slatted Venetian blinds offer excellent light control, but require more maintenance than vertical blinds.

SHUTTERS: Indoor shutters are mostly decorative and can be expensive. Be certain the louvers are adjustable for good light control. Some designs provide weather-proofing and insulation.

WINDOW FILM: Protective film applied to the inside of glass cuts glare, reduces costs of heat/air conditioning, and might eliminate the

Good natural light.

ELEVATION   Scale: ½"=1'-0"

How will you dress your windows?

need for blinds or draperies altogether, depending on your climate and exposure. Film also provides a degree of privacy.

SHADES: Finely perforated shades also cut glare while admitting light. Mylar pull-down shades cut glare. Insulated shades and draperies block out drafts and conserve energy in colder climates. Roller, theater-type (Austrian), and Roman shades should have reachable pull cords and easy adjustments.

DRAPERIES: *Important!* Always check drapery fabrics for fiber content, chemical treatment, and performance. All fabrics should be fire-resistant. It's best to stick to familiar fabrics such as natural cotton, linen, light-weight wool, even rayon. Most synthetics are unpredictable: some will flash-burn, giving you no time to back away; others seem to wear well, particularly when blended with natural fibers.

Be aware that, to date, there is no such thing as a perfect fabric. Some materials melt rather than burn and emit harmful fumes. Fiberglass will fall apart from a great deal of vibration, so if you live near a railroad or airport, this would not be a good choice. Silk will disintegrate from direct sun, not good in the tropics. All fabrics will oxidize or fade. Read fabric labels and specifications (mandatory on fabrics designed for public and commercial installations) and choose what seems best for you.

WINDOW QUILTS: Insulated shades that seal on all four sides, window quilts improve energy efficiency in both summer and winter.

Puddle, Piddle, Poodle

Dennis and Rosie seemed to thrive on disagreements. Differences of opinion about window treatments for their retrofitted house were no exception. Rosie wanted draperies; Dennis preferred vertical blinds. Dennis gave in and Rosie was jubilant—until the draperies were being hung. She watched like a sentry during the entire procedure. When the hangings were finally up, she was unhappy.

"They don't puddle," she said.

"Don't piddle?" asked her husband.

"No, *puddle*. Not enough fabric on the bottom."

"Who needs more fabric? I wanted *no* fabric to tangle with and replace in a few years. Whattyamean piddle?"

"Not piddle, Dennis, puddle. The material should sit on the floor and make like little puddles at the bottom. These only touch the floor."

"Piddle on the floor? Drapes don't piddle, poodles piddle."

"Not piddle, Dennis—puddle!"

The designer couldn't keep a straight face any longer. Laughingly, she explained to him that puddling was a popular preference; that is, the draperies ended in soft swirls on the floor, and Rosie was right, these draperies didn't puddle.

Dennis grew silent, then stated in crisp no-nonsense sentences, his voice rising like a dust storm, that piddles, puddles, poodles, whatever they were, would be hard to move, would be dust collectors, would get tangled in the vacuum cleaner—which was his domain—and if Rosie persisted in this foolishness, he'd throw out the whole piddlin' puddlin' mess!

He won that argument.

FLOORING

HARD AND/OR RESILIENT MATERIAL: Hard surfaces should be nonskid and unpolished, with significant texture. Textured clay, including quarry tile, rough terrazzo, PVC, and resilient vinyl and rubber are said to be good choices. Tile is preferred to sheet material because tile joints provide additional friction, helpful to avoid slipping. Beware of "non-skid" ceramic tile and vinyl; many are slippery when wet. Replace floors in bathrooms, outdoor hose areas, and patios, where water can collect.

LARGE EXPANSES: Be careful of bright, total illumination in areas with large expanses of hard surface flooring; it can create "hot spots" that are visually confusing.

WAX: Avoid waxing all floors.

CARPETING: Carpeting often is preferred over hard or resilient flooring for feelings of warmth and luxury, and to lessen risk of injury from falls. It must be well fitted and secured; exposed edges need to be fastened and trimmed along the entire length. Tight weave and low pile (½-inch maximum) help to avoid tripping, and are more easily navigated with walking aids. Avoid long loop pile or shag carpeting.

🙠 **ELDER-AID:**
Add 8- to 12-inch baseboards made of carpeting to walls to reduce walking-aid damage. It also looks good and tends to "stretch" the space visually. Plexiglas or plastic laminate "skirts" placed on bottoms of doors helps to protect them from scuffing.

FIRE RESISTANCE: Fire resistance or retardation are essential qualities of carpets. Noted on the back of carpet samples is information about chemical changes that take place when synthetic carpet is subjected to extreme heat or flame. There are many recorded deaths of people, especially the elderly, who inhaled lethal fumes even though the carpeting itself did not burn.

PADDING: Avoid thick padding. Firm padding, or no padding, is preferred for safe mobility on carpeted floors.

AREA RUGS: Avoid them, even when fastened to the floor. They are higher than the floor they cover, and can cause tripping, as can uneven floor levels anywhere. To incorporate the decorative qualities of area rugs, insert same thickness tile patterns into tile flooring, or insert patterned carpets of the same pile height into the field carpet. Inserts such as these may be expensive, depending on quality.

COLOR: Choose happy colors, or neutrals that are good backgrounds for upbeat furnishings and art. Cheerful colors don't cost any more than dull ones. Avoid very dark tones. They can be difficult to identify visually, and will show as much soil as very light tones. Contrast patterns and colors from area to area throughout the house for easy visibility and definition. For example, steps and the floors surrounding them should not be the same color, or should be defined with a border around the carpet. If flooring is somewhat dark, baseboards should be light. Carpeting with some pattern or texture is preferred to define areas more easily, but be aware that too much pattern can cause dizziness and confusion to those with limited sight. The world is filled with beautiful colors; choose the ones you like best. It's your house!

🙠 **ELDER-AID:**
Sometimes those labeled "Kitchen Karpet" are more costly than a good grade of low-pile commercial carpet. Check both for price and quality.

KITCHEN AND BATHROOM FLOORING: Flooring materials in these much-used rooms should be safe and easy to wash and maintain. Many people prefer to carpet these areas. If you do, be sure the carpet is easily shampooed to remove stains, odors, and bacteria. Be prepared to change it every couple of years or so, depending on quality of the carpet, and the wear you give it.

Chapter Twelve

SOUND
Hear Ye! Hear Ye!

Music repeats the entire world of sense . . .

—SCHOPENHAUER

THE POWER OF SOUND, which includes music of all types, is recognized throughout history by all the cultures of the world. Physicians of ancient Egypt used incantations to minister to the sick. Africa is well known for its use of drums, not only as a means of communication, but also for sexual stimulation, excitement, and exorcising spirits. Sound and music have been used to incite men to battle, to calm the savage beast, and to create moods and stimulation of every order.

We respond strongly to sound because of a process professionals in acoustics call *entrainment,* which affects brainwaves, respiration, heart rate, and so forth, by synchronizing our physical responses with the frequencies of what we hear. For example, loud rock music, noise on the street, and sometimes thunder make our hearts pound, and may give us headaches, while a relaxing walk on the beach entrains our physiological responses to the calming sound of the surf: our respiration slows down, we breathe more deeply, and, generally, feel at peace with the world. The examples are endless. In fact, a science called psychoacoustics, a study of the effects of sound (including music) on our nervous systems, shows that what falls upon our ears affects our lives significantly.

Yet sound, which constitutes an important dimension of any interior, is the most neglected design element, probably because it cannot be seen or touched. Unwanted noise (or music) can cause a sense of unrest, even physical discomfort, and, in our rush to get away from it—accidents! While some of us can tolerate more noise than others, the truth is, like odors, the only noise most of us can stand is our own.

There is a fine, very personal, difference between noise and sound. What is noise to one person is joy to another; what may constitute distracting background noise to the hearing-impaired may to normal ears be music or a waterfall or an interesting conversation at the next table. But if it's noise to you, then it's noise. Remember: *No one enjoys another person's noise.* This chapter contains some tips for controlling and using sound in your house.

INTERIOR MATERIALS

Be aware that stone, tile, and painted or textured walls, tile and aggregate flooring, large expanses of glass, and high and uninsulated ceilings, especially those with exposed pipes, bounce sound back and forth as though in an echo chamber with no place to go. These are popular design choices in warm climates where quiet surroundings often are sacrificed to the feeling of coolness.

SOUND-ABSORBING MATERIALS: To offset noise, use fully upholstered seating, fabric window coverings, carpeting, and felt or woven-fabric wall coverings, as opposed to the above-listed hard surfaces. In severe situations, you can install special synthetic sound-absorbing materials used in places like concert halls.

HOUSEPLANTS: Divide rooms or sections of rooms with plants to absorb sound, odors, and chemicals, and provide a sense of privacy and beauty. Reverberation problems, common in homes with high ceilings, can be helped by strategic placement of plants to reduce echoes by absorbing sound. Traffic noise can be reduced by growing a thicket of trees and bushes between your property and the street.

INTERIOR NOISE CONTROL

Most people hear, few people listen, and even fewer understand. Such is the state of humankind. This usually is caused partly by lack of attention, partly because of noise interference. It seems that our heads are discombobulated by noise, the world contaminated by it!

Hearing, next to sight, is our most valuable, and least appreciated, gift. Just ask anyone who is hearing-impaired. Most of us take hearing for granted and assume that sounds we acclaim pleasurable are accepted as such by everyone. This is simply not so.

We can take control of noise within our own homes. Below are some ideas for blocking out noisy neighbors and containing outdoor sounds.

- Insulate walls with layers of cork, felt, carpeting, or fabric that is quilted or stretched over cotton or Dacron batting.
- Spray insulation into the walls. This requires drilling three- to five-inch holes, then closing them.
- Install special sound proofing sheets from your lumberyard between party walls (those between apartments or joined houses or offices).
- Where there are dropped ceilings, add insulation on top of the party walls, extending it two to three inches on either side of the walls.
- Insulate party walls with closets of clothes, armoires, or filled shelves and bookcases.
- Insulate pipes, enclose ducts, and fill in other places that could carry noise from one apartment to the next or from common areas.
- Build buffer walls in extreme circumstances. They should be an inch or so from party walls. The air space between the walls becomes the noise barrier.

OUTSIDE NOISE CONTROL

In severe cases, such as living within airport flight patterns, install windows and sliding doors that have been soundproofed with a secondary layer of glass, and a gap of 150 to 200 millimeters between the layers. This method is expensive but effective. However, it's best to consult a professional sound expert for alternatives.

In moderate situations, such as traffic noise, install insulated shades, or sew acoustic linings into draperies, extending them 4 to 6 inches beyond the window edges, or cover the entire wall.

> **ELDER-AID:**
> Noise from a washing machine or other appliances can be reduced by adding rubber feet.

PLEASURABLE SOUNDS

Pleasant sounds can produce feelings of tranquillity and well-being that often are amazing, just as unpleasant ones can make you want to scream. In the natural world, we enjoy bird songs, bubbling water, rustling leaves, the rolling sea. In a human environment, you can make your own pleasant sounds with a fountain, a small waterfall in a fish pond, soft and gentle background music, or a tape recording of natural sounds. Even the hum of an air-conditioner lulls some folks to tranquillity. Sometimes *silence* is the most welcome "sound" of all.

For the Hearing-Impaired

Not being able to follow the sounds of the world about you is a frustrating (to put it mildly) deprivation, and sometimes an inconvenience to the other humans in your life. Unfortunately, hearing aids, which can enhance volume but usually not clarity, are only part of the solution to a widespread problem, particularly among elders. While progress is slowly being made by hearing specialists, including surgical ear implants, here are some things you can do to help those who do not hear very well.

- Speak in slower, deeper tones rather than louder and more shrill tones because, typically, elders have lost sensitivity to higher ranges. Enunciate clearly, and face the person. This may involve rearranging chairs to face each other.
- Consider keeping cellular or cordless telephones nearby for safety and convenience. A volume control is useful, along with devices for blinking lights and bed-shakers that are activated by the ringing of the telephone. A TDD, the phone attachment that prints words, is valuable. Contact your local telephone company.
- If possible, eliminate background noise, such as radio or TV, buzzing electrical appliances, other people's conversations—until such time as hearing aids are made to block out background irritations.
- And, please, have patience. Hearing loss is a burden to everyone.

"Do You Like My Nose?"

Leslie, who was hearing-impaired, was taking her morning constitutional when she came across some beautiful pink blossoms on the ground, obviously having fallen from a nearby tree. Envisioning them floating in a crystal bowl, she stopped to gather them. With her nose to the ground, she suddenly saw two sandal-clad feet, and looming above them, a tall, handsome woman, whom Leslie took to be the owner of the tree.

"I hope you don't mind my taking these blossoms," she said to the woman. "They were on the ground." And she stood up.

The woman replied, "Do you like my nose?"

Leslie was taken aback, but quickly answered, "Yes, I think it's a fine nose."

"No . . . no!" said the woman. "Do you like mangoes?" She offered Leslie a bag of her favorite fruit.

Chapter Thirteen

SECURITY AT HOME
Rest Easy

I will never be an old man. To me, old age is always fifteen years older than I am.

—BERNARD BARUCH

SAD TO SAY, in many places, a professionally installed and manned security system, or, at the very least, an electronically operated home system is a practical necessity these days, especially in single-family dwellings. Most apartment residents feel more secure with extra locks and precautions and twenty-four-hour guards at the front desk. Gated communities also are somewhat helpful in fending off unwanted visitors, but certainly not foolproof; an agile burglar can easily hop over a hedge. It is estimated that 38 percent of all assaults, particularly on elders, result from home intrusions.

Some measures you can take against break-ins are bright lighting, good locks, trimmed shrubbery, and a big dog (or a recording of a guard dog at work). This chapter presents suggestions for being safe at home.

ALARM SYSTEMS

COMPANY-MONITORED ALARM SYSTEMS: These generally summon the police or fire department when the signal goes off. You are given code numbers to use should you accidentally set it off. Typically, you also receive a "hostage code" to secretly alert police that you're being held.

AUDIO/VIDEO ALARM SYSTEMS: Dual systems are important, especially for those who are hearing-impaired.

PORTABLE ALARM UNITS: These are hung on the outside door and will go off when someone tries to enter. Security alarms also can be hung on the inside doorknobs of exterior doors.

PERSONAL DEVICES: A special device with a button worn around the neck or wrist is available to signal for help through a twenty-four-hour emergency response center.

INTERCOM SYSTEMS: Placed at your doors, intercoms help to identify callers. Portable models that work anywhere in the house are available.

PEEP-HOLES: One-way peep-holes and view panels in the door also are helpful.

CLOSED-CIRCUIT SYSTEMS: A closed-circuit TV monitoring, security, and intercom system is an expensive miracle, but if you can afford it, why not? It will:

~ monitor front door and other security areas with automatic visual contact, two-way communication, remote locking or unlocking of doors and windows, draperies or blinds;
~ automatically change heating and cooling temperatures, turn lights on or off, monitor all systems for malfunction, fire, smoke, and sound an alarm and send a signal to the police or appropriate municipal service,or medical support;
~ control electrical aids such as automatic beds;
~ Provide phone and intercom connection with all rooms of the house, a message center, or with places or people outside the house.

LIGHTING FOR SAFETY

ENTRANCES: All entrance doors should be illuminated. For greater protection, install motion-activated lights and those that go on automatically when night falls. Self-lighting automatic garage doors provide safety when leaving your car.

YARD LIGHTS: Here is a word of warning from the International Dark-Sky Association: Glary "security" lights actually can *help* intruders to see better while they hide in shadows created by the glare. It's better to have several shielded lights directed downward on shrubbery and the walls, where intruders tend to hide. To reduce glare (and save money),

Security lights for safety.

use high- and low-pressure sodium lamps, which work better than traditional mercury-vapor lights.

LOCKS AND DOORS

DEAD-BOLT LOCKS: Add dead-bolts to exterior doors, front and back, and to the entry door between the garage and house. (Slide bolts provide almost the same security as dead bolts.) Never rely on overhead garage doors for total security; the opening mechanism can easily be stolen from your car parked temporarily on the street or in the driveway. Always remove the automatic garage door opener from your car at such times.

OTHER LOCKS: Remote control locks, magnetic card readers, and combination locks that are push-button activated also work. Not as common are voice-activated locks and those that are programmed to recognize fingerprints.

WINDOW LOCKS: Window locks should work easily from the inside. Add window bars if necessary and be sure they also work easily from the inside, for fire safety.

SECURITY DOORS: Metal burglar-proof doors hung in place of, or in front of, ordinary doors are usually too heavy to handle for normal use.

ELECTRICALLY RIGGED DOORS: These are usually, but not always, part of a total residential alarm system.

METAL DECORATIVE GRILLE DOORS OR GATES: Added in front of doors for security, especially on ground level, they do not have to look like "jail bars" and can add architectural interest to entryways.

COMMON-SENSE PROTECTIONS

NEIGHBORS: Trust a close neighbor with the key to your house for emergencies. Many people exchange keys. Use a signal system: for instance, a particular window shade halfway up means all is well; down means help is needed. Create your own signal. Some communities provide phone assurance programs. Participants are assigned phone numbers of the elderly and ill, and call daily.

COMING HOME: If you see a suspicious-looking person loitering about when you come home, don't enter. Instead, go to a neighbor's and call the police. If you're being dropped off at your door, ask the driver to wait until you're safely inside. Always have your house key ready.

INSIDE YOUR HOME: Never, never open the door for strangers, including delivery people with unexpected packages (flowers are a favorite ploy for entry), uncalled service people, salesmen, and those who claim accidents or seek directions. Use the peep-hole and speak through the door or intercom. Do not rely on the chain guard. If the person is persistent, offer to make a telephone call to help out, or call the police. Never mind good manners, or a desire to help, particularly if you are a woman.

SERVICE AREAS: Beware of unoccupied apartment house areas such as laundry rooms, garages, basement storage areas; take a companion with you. It's a good idea to establish a buddy system with someone nearby. Elevators can also be dangerous. Don't stay on them with strangers; get off at the next floor and take a different elevator. Also avoid little-used staircases. If you are attacked, make all the noise possible to scare the attacker away and to attract help. Or carry a lightweight alarm and engage it. Remember that mace, acid, and weaponry can be used against you.

IF YOU LIVE ALONE: Carry a personal emergency response device for help when leaving the house. List only your last name and first initial in the telephone directory and mailbox. Know whom to call in an emergency

---

Some Good Advice

Writers to "Dear Abby," the advice column, didn't know what to do about their neighbors' security light. It had been installed after a break-in, and now glared into their home, disrupting their life. "We want our neighbors to feel secure, but we want our lifestyle back. What can we do about their light pollution?" they asked.

Abby suggested alternatives such as "shifting the light's position, using motion detector lights, or adding shields that redirect the light from your house and yard back to theirs."

Abby added another suggestion: The neighbors might be more considerate if they knew security lights could very well help, not expose, intruders (see page 107). The neighbors should be spoken to on a positive note, offering full cooperation. "After all, it's for your security, too!"

FIRE PROTECTION

SMOKE DETECTORS: Mandated by law in public places, smoke detectors provide an additional safety measure should someone set a fire. Many injuries, even deaths, are caused by smoke and toxic gases, as well as by fire in your house. Smoke detectors provide early warning. Some fire departments and/or local governments will provide free assistance in obtaining and installing them.

At least one smoke detector should be placed on each floor of your home, preferably one in each room, particularly bedrooms, especially if you are hearing impaired. Install it on the ceiling or on the wall 6 to 12 inches below the ceiling line, away from air vents.

Batteries and bulbs should be changed when the units signal to do so, or according to the manufacturer's instructions. Also vacuum the grillwork periodically.

SMOKE-PENETRATING FLASHLIGHTS: These go off with the smoke detector alarm, and should be wall

> **⌒ ELDER-AID:**
> For extra safety, test smoke detectors every month, change batteries every six months, or according to instructions. Many people change batteries when they change their clocks to and from Daylight Savings Time.

mounted. Another handy gadget is "Light-A-Way," a light fitted to floor level that begins flashing when electrical power is lost, or when the fire alarm is signaled, and penetrates dark and smoke-filled areas. A necessity in apartment buildings.

FLASHERS: A flashing light on the fire alarm is an additional alert signal.

EMERGENCY PLANS: An emergency exit plan should be posted or memorized. Everyone in your household should know what to do, including where to meet outside your home to be sure all have escaped. Post it on a wall accessible to everyone.

DOORS: It is sometimes recommended to sleep with bedroom door closed to keep out toxic gases in case of fire. But remember that this also will close out the sounds of the house and other family members, and this may not be such a good idea. It's a judgment call either way.

TELEPHONE ASSISTANCE: Dial 911 at the first sound of an intruder. A cellular or cordless phone—easy to grasp, easy to dial, easy to see—kept near your bed makes calling for help possible when phone lines have been cut. Look for a model with easy-to-read or illuminated numbers. Automatic programmed phone numbers should include 911 as well as your neighbor's and children's, for example. Other important numbers should be taped to or placed near every phone. They must be easy to reach.

> **⌇ ELDER-AID:**
> Do not wear long, loose sleeves in the stove area. They tend to catch on pot handles, causing spills and scalding. Also avoid wearing highly flammable synthetic fabrics when cooking. They're known for instant flare-ups.

KITCHEN DANGERS

RANGE FIRES: Never remove a flaming object from an oven or cooktop. Instead, immediately turn off the heat and cover the pot with a lid. For oven fires, turn off the oven and keep the door shut. Do not use water to extinguish an electrical or oil fire; the fire will flare up. Instead, use a dry chemical extinguisher.

MICROWAVE OVENS, ELECTRIC APPLIANCES: Be sure you understand manufacturers' instructions for use, and have all equipment checked from time to time for safety.

ELECTRICAL CORDS: Cords should be located away from water, which can cause shock or electrocution if contacted, and away from hot surfaces, which damage them.

GAS VERSUS ELECTRIC RANGES: Live flames can be dangerous, especially if you're wearing clothing made of flash-burning synthetic material. In addition, it is possible for indoor air pollutants to accumulate to risky levels where gas- or kerosene-fired equipment is used. Check kitchen ventilation systems and range exhausts. On the other hand, sometimes it's difficult to tell when an electric burner is on. Also, if you are concerned with energy consumption, and with global warming, as so many people are, you may not want to install an electric stove in your home. Compared to other means of cooking, these appliances are the least energy efficient.

OTHER HOME SAFETY MEASURES

RADON: Check for radon, a radioactive gas that cannot be smelled, seen, or tasted, which can infiltrate homes from the ground. Radon exposure is more likely in certain parts of the country. Test kits are available at hardware stores, or you can hire a professional consultant. Or ask your local power or fuel company or, possibly, a building contractor for assistance.

SPACE HEATERS: Avoid shock from a space heater by using a three-prong plug in a three-hole outlet or a properly attached adapter; that is, the adapter ground wire or tab must be properly in place. Space heaters and small stoves should be placed away from traffic lanes, furnishings, and flammable materials such as curtains.

WOOD FIRES: Wood-burning stoves and fireplaces must be installed in accordance with the local building codes, provided by the fire marshal or building-code inspector. Insurance companies may not honor claims for wood-burning equipment improperly installed.

Chapter Fourteen

RETROFITTING APPLIED
Flo and Henry's Retrofitted Home

A house is a machine for living in.

—CHARLES LE CORBUSIER

IF, AS THE CELEBRATED ARCHITECT Le Corbusier saw it, a house is a machine, then its parts should mesh smoothly in order to do its job: to provide shelter, safety, comfort, and joy. But should that house become the scene of obstacle courses and booby traps, stress, frustration, and physical injury, then it's time to move—or to retrofit your home, as outlined in previous pages. An actual success story better demonstrates how places can be adapted to fit people, in this case, Flo and Henry. Their story and plans of their home follow.

First, some background.

Henry wanted to take an early retirement because of his failing eyesight, and also because he was tired of the "same old, same old." An environmentalist at heart, he planned to spend the rest of his life helping to "put things back," as he phrased it. When Flo suffered serious injury from a fall in her kitchen, and could no longer care for the house or tend her garden, Henry decided that that was the time for retirement. Flo had reservations. What would he do all day? His plans sounded good, but, still, she had heard dour stories of retirement from friends. So they persevered, Flo exhorting that this was where they had built their life and raised their family. This was home. But it grew increasingly difficult to manage.

Their son, whose work had taken him and his family to another part of the country, announced one day that they were returning. Flo and

Henry were overjoyed, and before long decided to sell their beloved home to him at a price he could afford. "Keep it in the family," Henry said.

They purchased for themselves a much smaller condominium unit in a new building nearby. Flo was very unhappy about giving up the large house. She missed some of the household chores, her garden, and the other activities that had constituted her care-giving life. The condo presented a different, unfamiliar lifestyle, and it took a long while for her to call the condo "home." She found daily reasons for visiting her son, only to complain later to Henry about what *they* were doing to *her* house. At these times, Henry buried his face in a book. "Umm," he would mutter.

Prior to moving out, Flo had new carpeting and draperies installed in the big house, along with fresh wallpaper and paint, and had some furniture they could not fit into the condo reupholstered. It was a special surprise to their kids, but an unappreciated one. Their son and daughter-in-law soon redecorated her cherished home to their own taste and, of all things! disposed of some of Flo's favorite furniture. Flo's feelings were deeply hurt—insult added to her dislike of the condo.

Henry saw it differently. After all, the kids were the rightful owners, he said, and Flo should accept as a tribute their choosing the old homestead for their own. But all Flo could see was that her good intentions and taste had been rejected.

For awhile, working with a designer on the condo distracted Flo from her gripes and malcontent. She was beginning to change her lifestyle concepts, and enjoyed shopping for new things. The new home was adapted to Flo's and Henry's physical needs, and was secure and comfortable, she had to admit. Despite not having a separate den, music room, or formal dining room, it did provide for entertaining, TV viewing, reading, and music. The plan of the furnished unit is shown on page 116. Changes are explained in a "walk-through," below.

THE FOYER ENTRANCE

~ Ceiling-to-floor walls to divide the entranceway from the living room were replaced with built-in shelf units. The left side houses books and family mementos; the right side, china and decorative serving pieces.

~ A closet was added near the entrance door for outdoor clothing and some storage.

~ A decorative chest and mirror provide elegant welcome notes and additional storage space for table linens. (A tiny but glamorous powder room is on the other side of that wall.)

~ An unusual specimen plant is placed on a decorative pedestal.

THE LIVING AREA

~ An L-shaped sofa arrangement, with a concealed sofa bed, turns its back on, and thereby delineates, the dining area. One end of the sofa forms a comfortable chaise longue where Flo views TV.

~ A comfortable lounge chair and ottoman provide a cozy reading area for Henry. Seats of the upholstered furniture are firm to afford easier rising. All have arms to the ends of the seats. The fabrics are cheerful, durable, and spongeable.

~ Twin round tables, as opposed to one heavy large one, are easily moved to free the sofa bed when needed.

~ All tables have rounded corners to prevent bruising, and lips around the edges to prevent items from slipping off and spills from going farther. They are the same height as sofa and chair arms to make it easy for Henry to place or retrieve articles.

~ Built-in units flank the fireplace and contain stereo, VCR, tapes, and other equipment. They are topped by additional shelves for books and a collection of antique glass.

~ Flo's small grand piano (which Henry was positive would never fit) completes the room, along with carefully placed, low-maintenance plants to add humidity to the dry atmosphere and absorb cooking odors.

~ Carpeting throughout is a firm, low, and tight pile easily navigated in a walker or wheelchair, if ever needed, and easily cleaned. There are no throw rugs. Thresholds to the kitchen (Flo would not hear of a kitchen carpet!), powder, and bathrooms have been wedged to carpet level to avoid tripping.

LIGHTING

Henry's vision problem was accorded special attention, as follows:

~ Vertical blinds were used on the windows (tinted to cut glare), for natural light in the morning hours, easily closed to block out the

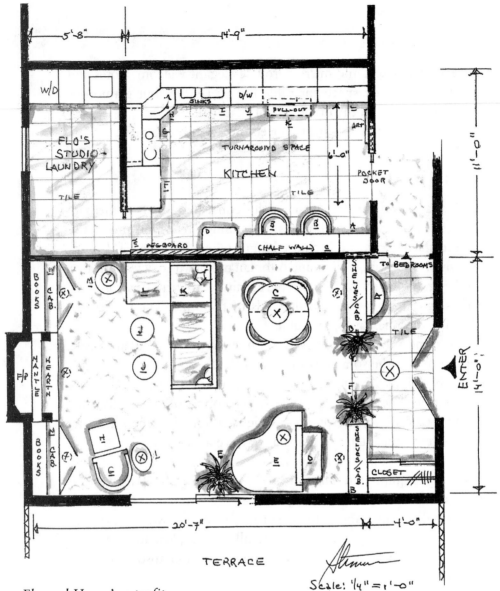

Flo and Henry's retrofit.

Living/dining areas
A   bombe chest and mirror
B   shelves, cabinet dividers
C   extension dining table, chairs
D   piano bench
E   piano
F   plants on pedestals
G   lounge chair
H   ottoman
I   table and lamp
J   small cocktail tables
K   sofa
L   ottoman
M   table and lamp
N   built-in cabinetry

Kitchen
A   open shelves
B   swivel chairs
C   counter
D   cart
E   pegboard
F   oven/microwave/drawer
G   cooktop, cabinets
H   easy-reach upper cabinet, turntables
      lower cabinet
I   sinks; open under, upper cabinets
      adjustable
J   dishwasher, open cabinets
K   drawers, trash, open cabinet
L   built-in refrigerator

X=plants

afternoon sun, and adjusted again, if desired, to enjoy the sunsets. Light sources include floor lamps (no table lamps to knock over) and perimeter cove lighting; decorative chandeliers in the foyer and above the dining table, with small shades to eliminate glare; and recessed non-glare swivel lights focused on the divider shelves and on the built-in units and fireplace wall.

~ "Light trails," small lights left burning, help Henry move from room to room.

~ Decals clearly identify glass doors.

COLORS

~ Colors are clear and easy to define, optimistic, in light yet non-reflective tones, including one accent wall of "pacifying pink," said to create a restful mood. Dollops of this color are repeated in toss pillows and elsewhere for color rhythm. Flo loves it. Henry is not so sure.

~ Carpeting and upholstery are soft aqua, also said to be restful and cool, blended with jewel-tone teal for accent and a little stimulation.

~ Wood tones in the eclectic condo vary from the rich teak and traditional dark mahogany antiques to bleached finishes and metal accents. The mix is interesting, happily blending old things with the new.

ENTERTAINING FACILITIES

~ Half a kitchen wall behind the dining area was removed to let in natural light and create a lovely view for the cook.

~ A serving counter was added to the dining room side, which doubles daily as a breakfast bar and is used for drinks and hors d'oeuvres, desserts and coffee for entertaining.

~ Dinners for more than six are served buffet style from the extension dining table (additional folding chairs are kept in a storage room down the hall).

KITCHEN

The new kitchen is compact, sleek, cheerful, and well-equipped, and designed to accommodate physical limitations, should they occur.

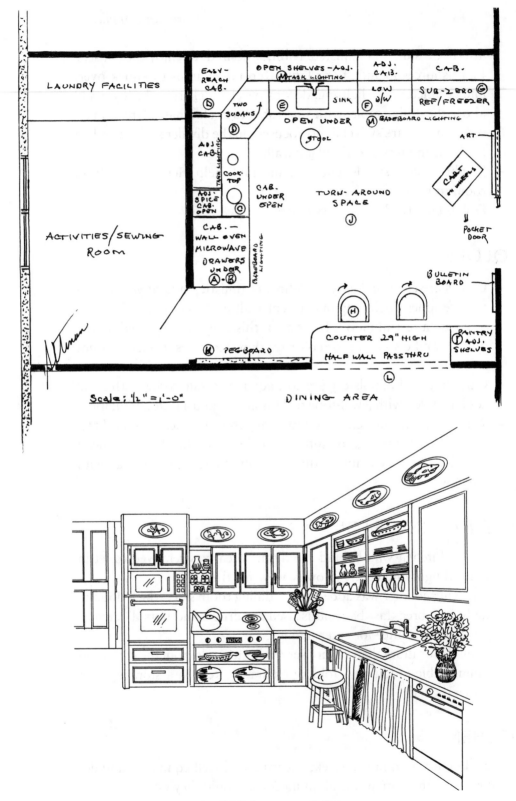

An "A" for accessibility.

Flo's Accessible Kitchen

A-B. Microwave oven can be placed on countertop for wheelchair user, and the original space utilized for extra storage. Wall oven is installed lower than usual, more easily reached to avoid burns.

C. Cooktop is built-in ceramic for easy care, with automatic cooling device to avoid burns, front controls to avoid reaching across hot surfaces. Some base cabinets have no doors for easy access. (Doors can be eliminated on any or all cabinets, if desired.)

D. Corner cabinets have fold-back doors for easy-view, easy-reach, with portable Lazy Susans (turntables) on the shelves.

E. Sink with stool are designed for working at the sink while seated. Curtain could be replaced by fold-back or retractable doors. Pipes are insulated to prevent burns. Cabinets above are open.

F. Dishwasher is installed lower than usual.

G. Side-by-side refrigerator is the same 24-inch depth as the base cabinets for easy reach, instead of the usual 33-inch depth.

H. Swivel chairs with firm seat and back and sturdy arms to help rising are placed at a 29-inch-high counter for either working or dining.

I. The pantry is 15 inches deep for easy reach, and has adjustable shelves, some fitted with Lazy Susans.

J. Turnaround space is left open to accommodate wheelchair, if necessary.

K. Pegboard is for easy access storage.

L. Half-wall pass-through is to let in the view and daylight, and for easy serving, table clearing.

M. Baseboard lighting is for soft lighting and wayfinding.

~ Cabinets are bleached maple, with major appliances faced in the same material for a built-in appearance without the built-in cost. Cabinet shelving is adjustable.

~ Lighting consists of an incandescent ceiling fixture, along with under-counter task lighting and lighting in the kick-space under the cabinets. A night light in the refrigerator remains on all night for kitchen raiding.

~ Countertops are two-level, for working standing up or sitting down, made of speckled aqua-colored Corian, the edges banded in ivory for delineation.

~ Flooring is a patterned aqua/rose/ivory vinyl tile. (Flo says she can't find the dirt!)

~ Special accommodations include easily reached storage, a mobile cart, and corner sink (please refer to the plan).

MASTER BEDROOM

~ The entrance is 42 inches wide with a pocket door, to accommodate walking aids.

~ Furniture consists of twin beds with individual mattresses and springs, pushed together and flanked by a small chest on one side, a writing table and chair on the other, often used by Flo as a dressing table. All furniture is fitted with easy-to-grasp handles instead of knobs.

~ Closets are fitted with dual-level hanging space and special storage accommodations, as is the walk-in closet in the dressing area. Bi-fold closet doors were used to clear and reveal the interior at a glance, as opposed to sliding doors (especially mirrored ones) that often are difficult to maneuver. Careful closet design has made bulky storage pieces unnecessary in the bedroom, leaving sufficient space for walking aids and wheel-chair turn-around space, if they're ever needed.

~ The general ambiance of the room is spacious, open, and cheerful. Its light, gay colors and soft, leafy pattern on the walls allude to Flo's small garden on the balcony, where she grows plants and flowers for the house, and fulfills her need to garden.

~ The adjoining bath is totally accessible and contains many of the safety components referred to in chapter 8. Colors continue the outdoor feeling in green marble ceramic tile, which is less expensive than the real thing. The whirlpool tub also faces the tranquil outdoors.

~ A small room facing Flo's balcony garden is reserved as Henry's computerized office, and for an occasional sleep-over guest. Henry will plan this room himself, when his retirement plans are more firmly set.

One day Henry phoned the designer's office to report a loose table leg. But that wasn't the real reason for his call. He seemed really upset, and confided that he had just told Flo to go out and get a job . . . or something . . . and to stop picking on the kids and the new decor of their old house. Now they weren't talking. Perhaps Flo could be a design assistant? She'd had an art education. "Umm . . . she really needs to be busy," he said.

At that point, Flo bounced into the room. She had been approved as an art teacher's assistant two afternoons a week in a nearby public school, she announced.

"Huh? Did I hear you right? Teacher?" Henry asked.

"Assistant teacher," she said, obviously quite pleased with herself. "I'll be working with kids again. It's been a long time since I taught school. You know . . . I just might go back for a refresher course."

"Ummmm," said Henry, grinning.

PART II

SMALL GEMS ARE BETTER THAN WHITE ELEPHANTS

Chapter Fifteen

Perspectives and Priorities
Bye-bye, Big

The first prerequisite of effect is impression.

—George Santayana

Once we believed that, with age, the golden cloth of wisdom would enfold us. But as we wait for this elusive miracle, we learn, instead, that wisdom doesn't always accompany age. Age usually travels alone. Wisdom, often regarded as an accumulation of knowledge, turns out to be a gradual erosion of preconceived mores and morals and previously unquestioned acceptance of intellectual ideas. With experience, it is perception that changes, not necessarily intellect, and that may be the true warp and woof of wisdom's golden cloth, after all.

New perception begets new priorities, new frontiers. As our views of life and its multi-faceted panorama change, our values and choices keep pace. We've had time to rethink initial approaches, and possibly abandon them in favor of what is appropriate to our lives today.

Indeed, many of you recognized the wisdom and sanity of small homes and fewer possessions long ago, and may already have embraced the opportunity to create homes of appropriate scale designed to serve you well for a lifetime—from youth, through middle-age, to elderhood. And perhaps you're chanting a new mantra about your house: not "big is beautiful," but small is safe, comfortable, and ecologically in sync.

Increasingly, fear of the upheaval of the world and of Earth's ecology has assumed great importance in the minds of many people of all ages. The size of a house is perhaps the most important factor in lessening its overall environmental impact—its "footprint," as it is called. A small house will use less land, less fuel, fewer materials and natural resources, and cause less pollution, now and in the future. And, ironically, a large house does not always provide more living space. Do we really need large hallways, lofty ceilings, living rooms that are not lived in, libraries where nobody reads, kitchens that can cater to a crowd, and four or five places in the house to eat? As Daniel D. Chiras says in his book, *The Natural House,* "You won't find a robin with two nests, one for the chicks and the other to hold all the stuff."

Many of us have come to see that this observation is true. When once you may have lusted after the Big House with rambling roses (or bougainvilleas) in its gardens, you may now prefer a scaled-down home, with parsley and chives on the windowsills. Rather than spending your money, energy, and time maintaining a large house, you may prefer to devote your resources to your kids and their kids, to teaching, perhaps, or to lifelong learning, to traveling to those vistas you've ached to see. You do not want to use—and lose—the time and energy large residences demand, nor pay their financial and ecological price. Life holds different promise now.

In recent decades, our lives have been influenced by mega-macro-super-everything, mergers, conglomerates, and multinational corporations stretching their tentacles like monstrous octopi. The world shrinks as we massage egos with acquisitions, and build "McMansions," now claiming the ubiquity of a fast food chain—to house more things we do not need, and flaunt more space we can afford not to use. This is the Age of Big. Big is in. Big means better.

But not to everyone. Bigger and better are not always on the same page.

Many of you may now be asking, where do you go from up? You may have visited these ports before, and choose not to sail again with the prevailing tides. And millions of you never bought into it at all. In fact, a recent study has shown that while higher average incomes, bigger houses, and new opportunities have increased in this Age of Big—happiness has not. Often, results are quite to the contrary. We've acquired more possessions but less time to enjoy them; two incomes, and more divorce; deep pockets, and shallow values. It is no wonder that simple pleasures beckon once more, and uncomplicated downsized homes are making more sense than ever. You've come to realize that a simpler lifestyle is, or surely will become, more appropriate. Even if you've never had a large house, maturing encourages living light, sharing love and fun and laughter, instead of burdensome responsibilities. It's been said that you don't stop laughing because you're growing old—you grow old because you stop laughing!

Psychologists explain another reason for choosing small homes. Often having little to do with the space you can afford, compact homes satisfy a need for secure, non-threatening, cocoon-like environments. A small safe home is, in a way, returning to your most comfortable psychological space, usually established in your early years. As it is with most things, patterns are repeated, shrinks say.

Retrofitting present homes to fit present needs, as explained in part 1, is one option for safe and comfortable living, and there are many, perhaps too many, other choices. Our newfound longevity has produced a very lucrative elder housing industry, from acres of modest Eldervilles and Leisureboroughs to those with amenities befitting luxury cruise ships. Whatever your choice, smaller living spaces are, or probably will become, a fact of your life.

Yet despite valid reasons for choosing small homes, many people have a hard time giving up the Age of Big. They allow long-time habits and negative feelings, generally rooted in the past, to persist and rob them of suitable and happy new lifestyles. In this regard, many of us refuse to develop our "mind muscle," which, like any other muscle, can be stretched and strengthened. Surprisingly, science has proven this to be easier to do as we grow older. Aging lessens your level of stress and increases your ability to cope, your sense of humor, and your capacity for love, altruism, and curiosity. Intellectual curiosity is not only a powerful motivator; it also keeps you young. Whoever said you can't teach an old dog new tricks was mistaken.

So go ahead, let new ideas take root, reach beyond what you know, and discover the joy, the excitement, the surprises, of what you don't know. As you change your perspectives, your emotional responses also change, and new lights enter your life. If you let them.

So it is with compact homes. If you formulate upbeat, creative thoughts about your small home, believing that it will be your own very special place—independent, safe, accessible, aesthetically appealing, and ecologically friendly—so it will be. Tell yourself you can't do it, and you won't. As Norman Vincent Peale once said, "Change your thoughts and you change your world." *Thoughts are things.*

And time is too precious for looking back. Antonia (née Annie) learned this the hard way. . .

Antonia's Little Castle

Antonia had grown up poor. Very poor. She had been a difficult middle child of a large family, rejected, shuttled back and forth among relatives who tried to "handle" her. She had no sense of home.

A Cinderella story followed: She became a bright student, won a scholarship, earned a good job, made a promising (meaning lots of money) marriage, raised three children, and lived in a big house on a rolling 5-acre tract, furnished with things impossible for her even to have imagined as a rootless child. Retired now, her husband one day announced he wanted to put Antonia's dream house up for sale. Zap! His words caused an instant replay of her childhood: No home.

"Give up my home? Ask me first to cut off my right arm. Or let my hair go natural. Never! You'll have to carry me out of here feet-first!"

He reminded her that their children now lived in other states, that the house was too large for the two of them, that it was too expensive, and on and on. But logic could not penetrate. Antonia slipped into a deep funk, which her doctor diagnosed as mild depression. He suggested that she find a pleasant activity to occupy her mind. A good idea, she agreed—and decided to redecorate the house!

Following several false starts, many indecisions, and much procrastination, it became apparent that Antonia really didn't want to "redecorate" at all, although she claimed otherwise. Every piece of the house was a page in her memory book. Even the nursery and children's rooms remained intact—for the grandchildren (not yet born), she said. And just the thought of righting obvious mistakes made long ago turned her misty. She did nothing except have some faded draperies replaced and some furniture reupholstered in new fabrics much like the old.

After about a year of miseries, including broken bones from a fall and a strange skin condition that was driving her mad, Antonia and her husband settled on an agreeable compromise. They would move—but not into any ordinary house, she was quick to add. Her son had been transferred back to the area, and he and his family were going to occupy Antonia's "castle," as the son called it, and build a small home for his parents on their grounds close by.

This is a lived-happily-ever-after tale. It's a shame, though, that Antonia had first to become ill in order to resolve the problem. She had to learn that there was no threat fromf days long dead, only joy of those still to be lived. By the following year, she was settled in her "little castle," her family was close by, the bones had healed—and the skin problem had disappeared. In her own complaining way, she was happy.

Change often is an unwelcome guest, as it was for Antonia. While the past is known and so feels comfortable (although it may not really have been so), future unknowns tend to be scary. Yet it need not be that way. Assume, instead, that the years ahead will be the best time of your life and meet them in an easy-care, small home. This new way of life is especially appropriate, indeed direly necessary, in this new millennium.

If you are afraid of feeling squished, just look about you. Examples of space-stretching abound. Friends' homes, compact model apartments, and townhomes epitomize methods of using space economically while creating the *feeling* of more space than actually exists. Clever interior design, decoration, architecture, and attractive amenities are used to camouflage the actual lean square footage. The senses can be fooled. You can learn how to achieve the same results for yourself if you carefully assess your material needs and do not overload your home with "stuff" that no longer serves any purpose (see chapter 16).

Interior design is not science. Although many states now issue licenses to qualified practitioners or sanction those who practice without a license, and it is possible to earn a Ph.D. in design, no reliable formulae exist for creating perfect environments for everyone. Continually changing variables dictated by human need, physical properties, technologies, finances, and other contingencies always must be taken into consideration, and plans will change accordingly. Even in this computer age, when most interior design and architectural firms use CAD (computer aided design) equipment that allows data to be fed in and mass designs to be spat out, allowances must be made for individuals, if the designs are to work.

How you design your compact home is up to you. It can feel as inviting as the most cleverly staged model homes and designers' dreams. In a sense, interior design involves a certain amount of showmanship. Yet showmanship doesn't mean showy, it means presenting yourself in the best light. One of the attractions of the stage is the way a well-designed set enhances and reflects the players, yet never overpowers them. So bring on your own players! A room without people is only a background for living, like the empty set when the curtain rises. Your presence, your family and friends, your own sense of beauty and purpose, call rooms to life. Only you can make it happen. Only you can make a house a *home*.

There's help ahead. The following pages will assist you in making the transition from the big white elephant of your past to the small gem of your present and future years, or to rethinking the possibilities of your present home. We will discuss the elements of design, those decisions that go into the planning of a home, from clearing out the clutter, to architectural boundaries, to the sensual approach to design, to its ecological impact. In other words, here are the basics for making the very most of the best small house of all—your own.

Perspective is everything!

Chapter Sixteen

CLUTTER AND COLLECTIBLES
How Much Is Too Much?

We desire nothing because it is good, but it is good only because we desire it.

—SPINOZA

To GREATER OR LESSER DEGREES, acquisitions—or the lack thereof!—have created most of the problems of humankind, from nations that covet their neighbors' land and power, to individuals who covet everything they see as greener pastures. Assuming that the overwhelming majority of us were not to the manor born, we work most of our lives to meet peer standards, and once attained, will not part with our hard-won rewards. Why should we give up what we have? Never mind efficiency. Forget cost. Waste be damned. Let's keep it all! We earned it . . . didn't we? This is who we *are*!

Witness Jack and Susan . . .

Things

When Jack announced to his wife Susan that he felt it was time for them to retire in a warm climate, she was delighted, and envisioned a tropical version of their spacious suburban Chicago residence. Jack, ever the realist, disagreed, stating he wanted a comfortable condo with minimal square footage to fill with her "things."

"We live in a world of *things*," he boomed. "Some *nice things* to live with today—that's okay—but why must we have *things* from yesterday we don't use, your mother's things that she didn't use, *things* for tomorrow in case the world runs out of *things*? I'm tired of possessions owning me!"

Susan was a packrat and a sentimentalist; Jack wanted to dispose of everything and start fresh. She was conservative with money; he was generous, even extravagant. She looked back; he looked forward. When she refused to change her mind about wanting to recreate their present home, he threatened to join the Peace Corps.

"So I won't have to sit on your mother's old chairs," he exploded again. "And I won't be eating from dishes you got with boxtops during the Depression!"

In the months that followed, Susan held her ground. She would not part with her possessions. *My things are who I am,* she insisted, "my lifetime treasures." Jack would not move with them. Each was unable to convince the other. She stopped cooking. He stopped talking. They seemed to be headed for the divorce court instead of California.

Susan complained to their son, "After all these years, he wants me to live without my lifetime treasures in a condo, under other people's rules, other people's noise, other people's garbage. At my age. No thanks!"

Jack complained to their daughter, "After all these years, she wants me to live like a caretaker of another white elephant, with stuff we don't need in rooms we don't live in. And help to worry about—cleaners, gardeners, handy-men, pool people. At my age. No thanks!"

They were at an impasse. The move was abandoned, temporarily.

Then their children decided that arbitration was in order. Their son convinced his mother that a roomy, not sprawling, home in a golf-course community would hold most of her dearest treasures while freeing the couple of the chores and responsibilities of their present home. Besides, he assured her, he and his wife would be happy to "take care" of some of her possessions. Their daughter had a more difficult time persuading her father that his get-rid-of-everything attitude was not practical, and, surely, practical man that he was, he could see that, couldn't he? And besides, she assured him, she and her husband would be happy to "adopt" some of the *things.*

Provided that Jack also would agree to part with his stuffed swordfish in the den, the matter seemed settled. But not for long. What to do with the overflow, the things the kids did not want?

Susan could not bear the thought of her treasures going to strangers. Oh-oh, another impasse?

Indeed not. The family settled on a *things* auction, to which they invited all their friends and neighbors, and the relatives they were still talking to. Jack had a grand time playing auctioneer, and the proceeds were donated to charity, along with the *things* they couldn't even *give* away.

It took Susan a long time to realize that her possessions were not who she *was*, but what she *owned*. Smaller quarters forced her to acknowledge that too many *things* really did create visual clutter, the enemy of small spaces, and often, emotional unrest, as well.

WHAT IS CLUTTER?

Clutter rarely means the same thing to everyone. *How much is too much?* To the minimalist, an ash is a crowd in an ashtray; to the collector, a bare tabletop is a crime. Lots of the other folks just head for the TV, unaware of what is around them. Most of us fall somewhere in between. While we like to have beautiful and familiar objects around us, to be stroked by their presence and the memories they hold, we recognize the need for *clutter control* in small spaces. Clutter destroys negative space (see below), and often causes accidents. Clutter creates visual confusion as the eye jumps from one thing to the next, and robs your home and you of feelings of serenity and relaxation.

Clutter isn't necessarily random piles of this and that, just *too many unorganized objects in too little space*. Some folks have difficulty defining clutter because they don't see their possessions merely as objects, but as sacred memories, precious reminders of people and good times. Many people fill every available square foot and cover every flat surface of their new compact homes, thinking that this tactic "will get more out of it." Wrong. What they get is clutter and reduction of visual space.

Many folks cannot live happily without clutter—or collections, their preferred term. It's not unusual to find several sizable collections sharing space in a single small room. But this is not clutter, owners say, these are important collections, meaningful acquisitions, good investments. Then why do their homes look and feel so small? And why does a visitor tend to feel like the proverbial bull in the china shop?

Unfortunately, some folks resist moving to small homes because their present possessions will not fit, and even contemplating their disposal becomes traumatic. Yet paring down is necessary and inevitable when moving to a smaller home.

Do you really need all those *things?* In most cases, the first response is a timorous and questioning *yes,* but eventually, a breathless *no.* Paring down can be cathartic, creating a welcome sense of relief that comes with lessened housekeeping responsibilities and more time to pursue life's rich pleasures, often with extra money in your pocket. Once the deed is done, most folks feel they have chased out old ghosts and—well—even feel young again.

PARING DOWN

There's no denying that possessions are important to most of us. Materialism, to whatever degree, is part of being human, lending us comfort and pleasure, like gifts we present to ourselves to get along in a difficult world. When you think about it, the geometric progression of possessions can be amusing. Acquisition has a way of feeding on itself. If one of a thing is good, then two must be better. If we are judged by what we own, then let's own more. And so it goes, until the day you decide to move to compact quarters.

Most of us can't afford to dispose of all our possessions, nor would we find the idea particularly appealing if we could. How do you accomplish the masterful deed of paring down without becoming wedged between sentimentality and practicality? It's a tough job, at best. Read on for some suggestions.

THINK SMALL: The first step to paring down is thinking small, that is, setting your mind to deal with spatial restrictions, proper scale, and maximum performance of everything you plan to move. One major difference between thinking small and small thinking is quality. You have no space now to house mediocrity, no odd corners or upstairs rooms to tuck away yesterday's big bargains and big mistakes. In compact quarters, everything shows. What you keep should be necessary to daily living, appropriate, and of good quality. Having somewhat to do with the training of the senses, the quality of quality defies glib definition. Ineffable, it's similar to putting into words the meanings of "salty," or "love," or "beauty," so it suffices here to designate quality as *the best you can afford.*

TRUE TREASURES: Decide which possessions are "true treasures"—that is, items that fall into the following categories:

~ *Items of practical use,* the nitty-gritty indispensables of everyday living that make households work—tables, lamps, seating, bedding, kitchen tools, and the like.

~ *Items of high intrinsic or replacement value.* This means a lot to many folks; others don't care.

~ *Items of beauty.* While there is no easy definition for beauty, simply stated, it is the possessions that please your sensibilities, not the aesthetic evaluations of others.

~ *Items of true sentimental value.* We all have them—tokens of happy times, favorite people or, sometimes, our dreams. They may or may not be of practical, intrinsic, or aesthetic worth, yet they can be valuable to you.

Simplistically, things that fit three or four categories are worth keeping. However, this slide rule of values may not work for many people. Another, more accurate, way is to tune in to what your floor plans (please refer to Part 3,) show you in feet and inches. Even though many people can "eyeball" space fairly well, it's better by far to back up guesstimates with measurements. Do you really have room in your new home for your mother's old chicken soup pot or other can't-live-without items?

ORGANIZE AND EVALUATE:

~ Arrange similar items together into piles, boxes, whatever. Forget the "just-in-case" philosophy and part with the defective and/or duplicate items, those useless "indispensables" we've held onto for years. Rethink their importance. They gobble up space.

~ Weed out possessions you no longer want, or like, or have not used in the last two or three years. If the articles, particularly clothing, have been out of service that long, it's time to give them up. When this takes more self-discipline than you think you have, look to the bright side—who would be happy to receive these things as gifts? Or to which of your nearby thrift shops can you donate them for a tax write-off?

~ Dispose of an old, possibly unwanted, piece when (or if) you replace it. Why hold on to

> **ELDER-AID:**
> To weed out clutter, approach one area at a time with three bags or boxes labeled "throw-away," "give-away," "store-away" (easy on the last one)—and follow through. Don't forget to include the contents of drawers, closets, shelves, garages, and secret, perhaps forgotten, cubbyholes.

something that is no longer useful or needed? A good rule: When something new comes in, something else must go.

~ Books, who are like old friends, take up space, but are hard to part with. Consider giving some of them to your friends, local library, or thrift shop, for new good homes.

PROVIDE SUITABLE STORAGE:

~ An efficient storage system is a must-have for compact homes. Investigate the large variety of reasonably priced, ready-made systems that are relatively easy to install, ranging from simple pegboards to a wide selection of prefabricated components. Forget cellars and attics and hard-to-reach places.

~ Preplan the system. List what needs to be stored, take measurements, and choose storage components accordingly. Most stores that sell storage systems also provide planning and installation services. Also, professional "organizers" and "closet consultants" are available for hire by the hour, day, or job. Or ask your kids to help you!

~ Organize your garage to avoid accident-inducing clutter. Use sturdy pegboard or specially fitted, inexpensive storage modules, usually carried by hardware stores.

CONTROLLING COLLECTIBLES

ELDER-AID:
Recycle old base and upper kitchen cabinets for use in your garage. A worktable can be constructed with a sturdy plank of wood bridging two cabinets. Remember that base and upper cabinets often are interchangeable. Height can be added with ready-made legs from the lumber yard, or with a platform.

The first cousin of clutter, collectibles also can get out of hand and command more space than compact quarters can afford. Many folks are longtime collectors who can't bear to part with their treasures and are unable to stop collecting. It's so much fun to find treasures in antiques shops and flea markets, on the beach, and in the woods. But where do you put your finds in small quarters? Try these ways to reconcile collecting with spatial restrictions.

SPECIALIZE: Restrict yourself to one or two kinds of collectibles that complement each other when displayed together, such as old pewter and antiquarian books or blendings of antique glass and porcelain, to name but a few possibilities. Keep only the best examples of each category and sell or trade off duplicates and less desirable pieces.

MASS SMALL ART OBJECTS TOGETHER: Small (in size, not importance) treasures placed alone here and there make for spotty, busy rooms. For visual importance, arrange them in groupings in breakfronts, hutches, vitrines, curio cabinets, special shelves, and the like. When properly displayed, a collector's pride can be the focus of a room. Often, shelves can be built in unlikely places, such as between architectural jogs or in spaces between studs.

MASS SMALL PLANTS TOGETHER: Consider an indoor garden in one large plant box, or in matching or similar pots. Place plants on shelves or on objects of interest in themselves, such as bakers' racks, pie-holders, library steps, decorated ladders, or tabletops.

HIGHLIGHT LARGE PIECES: Display large objects by themselves for emphasis and to avoid crowding. Place them on pedestals (out of traffic lanes), in niches, or as focal points in wall units or breakfronts, or on furniture tops. Don't be afraid to display large treasures in small spaces. A sizable interesting box or urn on a cocktail table, for example, works better than several small pieces. Large plants can be placed strategically to add softness in a room, or to divide areas.

Group collections together.

PUT COLLECTIONS TO WORK

Using decorative items in practical ways saves space in small homes, while offering the psychological perk of being treated to the daily use of fine things. Household items, possibly of another era, other parts of the world, or beautiful contemporary things originally were made to be tools of daily living. Make them yours.

CONTAINERS: Use antique flower holders, planters, vases (with plastic or glass inserts to protect them) for arrangements of fresh, dried, or silk flowers. Bowls and trays are fine containers for potpourri, or to display other small collections such as seashells or arrowheads.

WALL HANGING: Use your walls for hanging interesting plates and platters, instead of storing them in cabinets. They're more convenient for use as distinctive tableware.

LAMP BASES AND TABLES: Convert large pieces into lamp bases, or, with glass tops, into small tables. This can be done without lessening their value. A large cocktail table can be fashioned from four high alter sticks or architectural elements such as columns and stiles. Don't overlook gifts of nature such as driftwood made into lamp bases; gnarled tree stumps, into tables; a quarried chunk of beautifully marked stone or coral into an unusual cocktail table base. Shell craft is legendary.

FRAMING: Group similar things together in single frames—old prints, coins, family diplomas, portraits. Montages such as these cast unmistakable personal imprints and circumvent the visual clutter of "spots" on the walls.

A Sword Room?

Some serious collectors are like Linda and Prescott, who use their entire homes as showcases for their collections.

Prescott, who was both an attorney and an accountant, had become disenchanted with the high cost and inferior workmanship of much of the new furniture now available. He also looked at his possessions as serious investments, and put his money into items of proven appreciation in value. This couple chose American Victorian antiques, and it was interesting to watch their collection grow in three different homes. The last, formerly of turn-of-the-century working-class genre, and now expensive urban chic, was the best.

They had selected the house for its own interior appointments, little changed from the mid-1900s when it was constructed, such as the original oak paneling in the dining room, leaded glass windows, and many typically Victorian architectural elements. They added many touches of their own, always period authentic, and held the furnishings, fabrics, and wall coverings to the moderately small scale of the house.

To enter their home was to be thrust suddenly and delightfully back in history. Of special interest was the sword room.

Sword room? In his collecting, Prescott had become intrigued with antique jewel-hilted swords, and began a collection that, today, rivals that of any museum. Instead of displaying them all over the house, he had consolidated the collection into one fascinating small room that highlights every visitor's stay.

NEGATIVE SPACE

Sometimes in your desire to include as much as possible in your compact home, you might overlook the important space that contains nothing, "does" nothing—nothing, that is, but give you and your possessions "room to breathe."

DON'T CROWD OUT BEAUTY: What the art world calls *negative space* refers to the spaces that surround subjects on the canvas; in the home, articles of furniture, closely related groupings, accessories, wall hangings, or the like. In any type of art, including interior design, the spaces and light surrounding objects give them dimension, delineation, and importance by separating them, indicating size, and serving as an eye path from one detail to another. Without negative space, the positive can become an undefined, confused blur.

—*ITWILLLOOKSOMETHINGLIKETHIS*—

ALLOW FOR NEGATIVE SPACE: When intelligently allowed for, negative space keeps small rooms feeling open, indicates function, and permits each piece to be seen and appreciated for itself. In other words, without this important, often overlooked element of design, the area would seem confused, untidy.

WHAT IT'S NOT: Don't confuse negative space with "boring" or "empty places" in your home. Minimalistic furnishing is something else, the sparse "less is more" approach.

HAPPY MEDIUM: Find a middle course, allowing sufficient space between possessions to appreciate each piece or each grouping, for its own beauty and value. Also remember that open space often can draw the eye to a background scene, beautiful color, or other point of focus, thus "enlarging" the space closest to your eye.

The New Janice

Some years ago, when planning her new studio condominium, Janice learned about negative space.

Bubbling like a mountain stream one day, Janice announced her good news. An uncle was retiring and offered Janice his city *pied-à-terre* at a price far below market value. She could afford it!

"I've dreamed a long time about a home of my own," she said. "I've always wanted pretty dishes and crystal and a silver tea service, but figured I'd get them when I got married. Then I started thinking, 'Why wait? It's time I bought nice things for my-self. This apartment will be the beginning of the new Janice.'"

A former flower child of the sixties, Janice now was an account executive for an advertising agency, and her future looked bright. Her present life bore almost no vestige of her former helter-skelter existence and a failed marriage—except her apartment. Reluc-tantly and apologetically, she permitted a visi from her designer, hoping to use some of her things in the new condo. She warned, "It's a mess."

It was. Untidy and disorganized, it contained a mixture of her "phases," ranging from sundry hand-me-downs and baskets—oh, were there baskets!—of her hippie days, to decrepit wicker of her short marriage, to some valuable antique farm furniture. It was suggested that she dispose of most of her disparate possessions, retaining the good antiques and better baskets for interesting ac-cent pieces in her new place.

Janice objected. "I'm not going get rid of any of my good old stuff. I'll have room for almost all of it, after I clean out the junk. I know. I measured. There's space."

There was sufficient linear space to have crowded it all in. Al-lowing for *negative space* and her tendency to be messy were other matters. She'd had an extra bedroom in her old apartment, formerly occupied by a housemate, to hide some of her mess, a luxury her new condo did not afford. It totaled only about 800 square feet, but despite its compact size, it was suggested that she turn the dining area into a tiny bedroom, allowing just enough room for her double bed, nightstand, and a small chair. Janice objected. "I thought closing off spaces made small places seem smaller," she said.

This is usually true. But, in her case, did Janice want to open and close a sofabed every night? It rarely would be closed, adding to the crowdedness. And where could she hide even a little mess? Floor plans showed that given the alternatives, Janice's apartment would appear as spacious as was possible and work more effi-ciently with a bedroom, tiny as it would be. The plans also showed where and which of her country antiques were to be used.

In the bedroom, 10-inch-deep bookshelves under the window and on the two narrow walls that flanked it were added to catch some clutter. Some fresh paint and wallpaper in the tiny entrance foyer, kitchen, and bath (applied by handy friends) and recondi-tioning the existing parquet floors completed the renovations. She

A, B dhurrie area rugs
C   country cupboard
D   glass-top table (new)
E   old country kitchen chairs
F   sofabed (new)
G   cobbler's bench
H   old chair (recovered)
I   antique table
J   antique paperhanger's table
K   shelves (new)
L   antique baskets
M   old floor lamp (refinished)
N   double bed
O   old table (painted)
P   sea chest
Q   country chair (recovered)

X=lighting

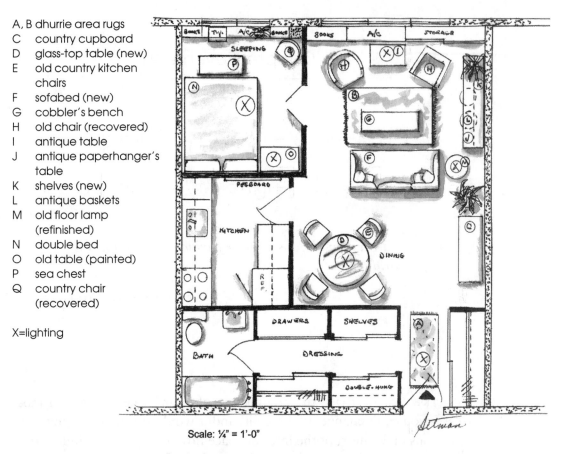

Scale: ¼" = 1'-0"

Janice's new apartment.

also could afford to have an old Navaho rug cleaned and repaired, to purchase a loveseat-sized sofabed, and to reupholster a lounge chair.

Janice moved in with light pockets—and a light heart. Ultimately, she was glad to be relieved, emotionally and physically, of baggage from yesteryear's bad scenes. Her new place was tiny, to be sure, but contained all she needed to go forward, with "room to breathe." Her experience also depicted the crucial psychological person/place link—that is, how our environments can affect our lives. The new Janice was up and running! "It's a catharsis," she noted.

The floor plan of Janice's studio apartment follows. Future projects included mirroring a dining area wall, and remodeling the kitchen and bathroom. But, as she promised herself, pretty china, crystal, and a silver tea service came first.

Chapter Seventeen

The Architecture
Don't Fight It, Join It!

I live in a very small house, but my windows look out on a very large world.

—Attributed to Confucius

Like it or not, the architecture of your home is there. In most cases you can't change it or hide it, and it won't just go away. Jogs and columns may interrupt the interior space flow, or a picture window may face a blank wall, or you may not have enough natural light, or the house may be just plain architecturally dull. The list continues. Still, your home may have many valuable advantages such as elder-friendly features, a good neighborhood, friends nearby, or adequate square footage.

What to do?

Some folks will say, "Not much. Love it or leave it." Other folks have tuned to other possibilities.

Don't fight architecture—join it!

GO WITH THE (ARCHITECTURAL) FLOW

Do not fight the architecture, join it! Work logically around existing architectural elements to make your rooms seem larger, more attractive. Always emphasize the heights in a room to draw the eye away from constrained lateral space.

~ Place your tallest piece between two tall windows, if you have them, or between structural columns, or alcoves between closets. A tall bookcase or étagère will emphasize height.

~ Heighten the appearance of low pieces, such as a sofa, bench, or long buffet, with important wall decorations arranged vertically or in a pyramid.

~ Place your longest piece of furniture against the longest wall to minimize its size, especially if it matches or blends with the wall color. But be aware that matching furniture to the walls decreases definition, bad news if you're visually impaired. It's better to err on the side of safety. Also, remember that small things on a long wall tend to chop up the space and "shrink" it.

~ Fit small pieces into small corners or unused spaces. Trying to "hide" a small space with a large, bright, or important piece of furniture usually makes it look out of place and defeats your intention.

~ If your furniture is tall and the windows are short or high on the wall, treat your windows with full-length draperies or blinds to give the appearance of height. When one window is tall, the other short, drape them as though they were both tall.

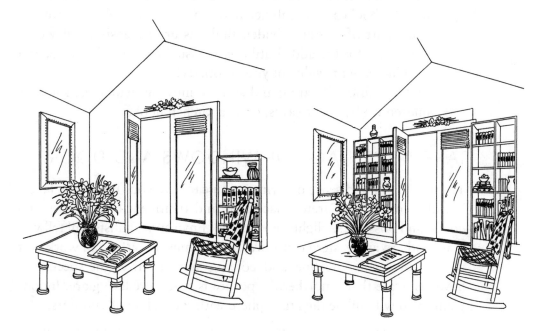

Tall bookcases help emphasize the height of a room.

~ Follow the wall space and avoid arranging furniture away from the walls, if possible, not only because this arrangement requires more space than most small rooms can afford, but also because they obstruct traffic lanes, particularly important to physically challenged folks. An exception might be using the furniture to divide a large space—a turning sectional sofa that separates the living from the dining area, for example, or a two-sided bookcase or étagère to define a special area such as a study or an entryway (see chapter 23). However, if there is no alternative, prevent walking into free-standing pieces by painting or upholstering them in colors that contrast with, not match, the room. Always place safety before aesthetics.

~ Utilize unwanted columns or jogs to define areas, for example to set off a TV or study area from the rest of the room. Columns also can be effective places to highlight art or hobbies.

~ Consider built-in cabinetry. It's interesting to note that Frank Lloyd Wright designed and built much of the furnishings into his famous buildings, for custom fit as well as individual style.

~ Camouflage pipes, radiators, jogs, columns, and other objectionable architectural elements. For example, in some cases, pipes can be hidden behind a wall of books. Jogs can be incorporated into an entertainment unit. Radiators can be enclosed and included into a built-in bookcase or cabinet under a window. Columns can become part of a room divider. Built-ins are expensive, but worth their price for the added utility and visual pleasure they give, and they increase the value of your property!

~ Build additional seating and storage into bay windows, short or uneven walls, under eaves, or as a kitchen nook.

TAKE ADVANTAGE OF WINDOWS AND DOORS

The more light and sense of airiness you can give your home, the larger it will seem to be. Careful placement and treatment of windows and doors, and possibly skylights, is essential. Environmentalists will tell you that southern and eastern exposures are the most cheerful and work best with passive solar heating and cooling systems. Eyesight specialists, however, state that a northern exposure is best to reduce glare. Indoor plants also will imbue the atmosphere with the feeling of outdoors.

SHORT OR UGLY VIEWS: If your windows face an ugly blank wall, get around the problem by

~ hanging sheer, patterned draperies to let in the light, but block out the wall;

~ covering only the lower half of the windows with curtains, blinds that roll up instead of down, or shutters, allowing light to enter from the top, above eye level;

~ angling vertical blinds to block out the wall, yet admit light, and possibly painting a pleasant scene on them.

> **ELDER-AID:**
> No garden? Paint one on the wall and place live plants in front of it.

CREATING YOUR OWN VIEW: You can make your own pleasant view with a window box or a window greenhouse. If you overlook a rooftop, perhaps some potted plants or a garden can be added, with permission of the owner. "Greening" the interior of your home always adds cheer, even to blank walls and rooftops. A window greenhouse will "enlarge" the space by encouraging the eye to go beyond the limit of the walls, while providing an attractive means to grow herbs and decorative plants. Be sure the greenhouse is easily reached without ladders or undue stretching. And don't cut off the natural light.

PLACE SIMILAR LOW PLANTINGS ON BOTH SIDES OF A LOW GLASS WALL: This makes the garden seem to be both inside and outside, and the wall "disappears" to create visual space expansion. Be sure glass walls are free of furniture to permit the eye to travel beyond the spatial limitations of the room and "borrow" space from the outdoors, the way many people, particularly the Japanese, include distant fields and mountains to add feeling of space to their own tiny homes and gardens. You could "borrow" from an attractive view, back yard, or balcony garden.

Another version is the Japanese sand garden that uses only white gravel raked into pleasant patterns, and rocks, behind which plant containers are hidden. To avoid accidents, however, be sure the glass wall is clearly marked with some recognizable symbol or decal.

> **ELDER-AID:**
> Plants help to purge the air of dangerous chemicals that may "off-gas" from carpets, building materials, or electronic equipment. Also, plants release moisture in the air that is necessary in artificially heated interiors to avoid colds and other ailments. Try English ivy, begonias, rubber plants, peace lilies, for example.

ENCLOSE A DECK, BALCONY, OR LANDING WITH A BUBBLE ROOF: This technique, expensive but effective, often is used to add a greenhouse, an area for outdoor dining, or a luxurious bath under the stars. The disadvantage is that heat can accumulate and encourage slippery and accident-causing algae, so the space requires constant maintenance. Elders should not attempt to clean the bubbles themselves. A less expensive alternative may be a small screened-in deck, space permitting.

DO FIGHT THE ARCHITECTURE—IF YOU MUST

If you have the perseverance and the resources, it usually is possible to move or remove fixed partitions such as ceiling-to-floor dividers, some non-load-bearing walls, and other barriers that create space-stealing cubicles within small spaces.

As a case in point, many turn-of-the-century townhouses and older apartments can be made to appear far more spacious by removing dark hallways and partition walls between tiny rooms, and by defining areas by color, light, and furniture placement instead. The eye should be permitted to pass beyond furnishings for the feeling of free circulation through space, an important objective in small-space design. Or put another way, *the farther the eye can travel, the larger the space will appear to be.*

Many people may argue that when most of the architectural delineation is removed, the charm of old places goes with it. This may be true to a degree—it depends on what you do with the area—but if all the little dark rooms are allowed to remain, it can be nearly impossible to create illusions of space.

Capital Decisions

A newly-elected member of the Senate and his wife had purchased a charming three-story Victorian home on Capitol Hill, an area favored by many lawmakers for its proximity to the seat of government. Most elected politicians who live in our nation's capitol do not regard their Washington homes as "home." They must be there to do a job, and when Congress adjourns and the hot sticky summer sets in, or their terms of office terminate, they retreat to their "real" homes elsewhere. But this does not deter them from feathering beautiful nests in Washington; frequent and elegant entertaining goes with the turf. Often these homes are very different from their "real" residences.

This particular home was furnished in the American Federal style, mixed with eighteenth-century mahogany, so popular in D.C., down to the traditional White House colors such as deep, saturated reds and blues. The couple's ideas of decorating fit the

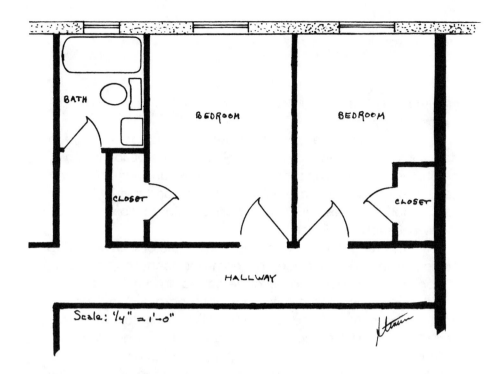

The Senator's office before (above) and after (below).

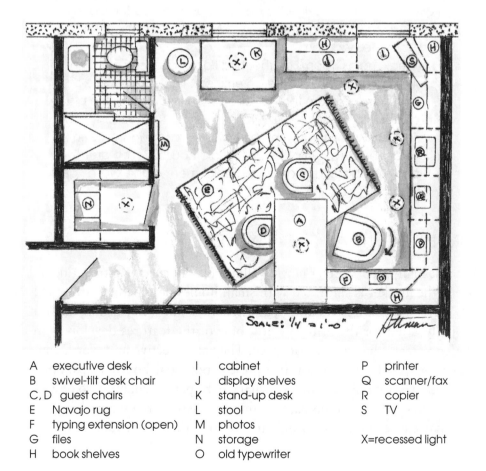

A	executive desk	I	cabinet	P	printer
B	swivel-tilt desk chair	J	display shelves	Q	scanner/fax
C, D	guest chairs	K	stand-up desk	R	copier
E	Navajo rug	L	stool	S	TV
F	typing extension (open)	M	photos		
G	files	N	storage	X=recessed light	
H	book shelves	O	old typewriter		

architecture—but were difficult to execute in the labyrinth of cubbyhole rooms.

So some rooms were joined together, often reapportioning and delineating areas with arches and columns of the period instead of solid walls, eliminating some of the hallways and lightening the color values, while still maintaining the feeling and spirit of the original house. Accessories, mostly period antiques, completed the Washington ambiance.

The master bathroom was a good example of space-stealing cubicles within a small space. The room was opened by replacing the bathroom wall with glass brick, removing an unnecessary wall and its pocket door in the bathroom that separated the toilet from the room. An unneeded, eye-blocking ceiling-to-floor closet was taken out and replaced with a bidet. A dark-paneled, old-fashioned back fire escape door was replaced with one of opaque tempered glass. Glass shelves were added over the toilet and bidet to hold bath towels and accessories. The lighting was improved. Monotone beige tile and fixtures retained the open feeling and were accented by rich russet and turquoise introduced from the bedroom.

Two small maids' rooms on the third floor, no longer needed, were joined together to create an efficient, light-filled home office, sanctum sanctorum for the senator. An equally private place was provided for the senator's wife in the small former nursery adjacent to the master bedroom. The couple was delighted with their refurbished and retrofitted "new" old house, which greatly enhanced their participation in and enjoyment of the Washington scene.

ARCHITECTURAL EYE-FOOLERS

Because many elders prefer new dwellings (as opposed to retrofitting old ones), the market is saturated with small homes designed to attract elderly buyers. They are fresh, new, and seem spacious, but usually are not properly fitted for them. Below are some of the features developers include to create the illusions of space. They are effective and worth emulating, provided they do not also present potential booby traps. Space perception is not only a matter of what can be perceived, but also of what can be *screened out*, in this case meaning attractive architectural features that may cause you unknowingly to overlook their disadvantages.

HIGH CEILINGS: High ceilings sell houses. They invite the eye to move vertically rather than horizontally over what often is constricted space. Further, spaciousness is sensed at the head and shoulder level, not below. High ceilings also tend to make you feel smal,l so the space seems large by comparison. Think of a place of worship. The founders of our faiths *intended* you to feel small and mortal in the presence of omnipotent power. Many homebuyers today prefer the churchlike ambiance because it is a fashionable, so-called status symbol that conveys the "power look" of large spaces and high ceilings. Open vertical space seems to expand room size. Again, the eye has been fooled—so buyers beware.

> ⮂ **ELDER-AID:**
> Buyers also should beware high-ceilinged spaces because they are energy-inefficient due to heat rising and accumulating at the top, setting in motion strong convection currents. Small low-wattage fans can help distribute the heat, however.

TO CREATE HIGH CEILING EFFECTS: Rooms can be made to take on a higher, slimmer look, a quality often needed when spaces are furnished with bulky things—similar to the way vertically striped clothing helps to camouflage short, plump figures. To "raise" the ceilings, try:

- ~ tall, built-in cabinetry and entertainment walls with bold vertical supports;
- ~ tall furniture such as étagères, high free-standing bookcases, breakfronts, and secretaries;
- ~ vertical wall hangings such as scrolls, tapestries, and pyramid arrangements of framed art;
- ~ vertically patterned wallpaper hung in strategic places, and vertically striped draperies. For unity and rhythm, be sure to repeat the stripe elsewhere in the room. (Please refer to chapter 19, Balance, Unity, and Harmony.)
- ~ eliminating wall/ceiling boundaries. Remove borders at the ceiling line and paint moldings a lighter shade than the walls.

BALCONIES: Many new homes with high ceilings feature balconies. These also create feelings of space because one wall of a room has been opened, and the space below seems expanded. Balconies also afford the opportunity for private nooks often lacking in small homes, or for an infrequently used guest room, a hobby room, or additional storage space. However, elders should be careful of the balcony approach; steps and landings can be dangerous, even when well lit and covered with appropriate flooring material.

OPEN SPACE ABOVE PARTITIONING WALLS: Rooms seem larger when at least the height of the soffit space (the area between tops of cabinets and the ceiling) of partitioning walls is left open—between living room/dining area and kitchen, for example—especially in homes with high ceilings. This technique will:
  ~ permit light to penetrate adjacent areas, and create interesting chiaroscuro (light and shadow) effects. Light "stretches" space and makes the areas seem larger when they may not be large at all.
  ~ allow heated or cooled air to circulate more efficiently, a technique very popular in warm climates;
  ~ accentuate the ceiling height and add to the feeling of space.
  ~ Don't trust your eye! The above architectural techniques are popular eye-foolers, particularly among new developments of small homes, so be sure to carry your tape measure along when shopping for your home or adapting your present one. *Feelings* of space will not hold that long sofa, say, or your wonderful 8-foot wall unit. And remember that steps generally accompany high ceilings. Be sure you can handle them without inviting mishap.

Sometimes it is not the architecture of our homes that presents problems, but, rather, the architecture of our dreams. Few of us have lived without some type of structure in our minds that we want to call home "one day." Sometimes folks think of their dream home as the place they'll retire to, a refuge of comfort and beauty to soothe the body and heal the soul—"one day." But sometimes "one day" never happens. Life is like that, you may say. Not necessarily. Many people are able to create homes and landscapes to fit their dreams. That's what David did.

David's Waterfront Home

David's dream home was on the oceanfront. No high-rise condominium for him. "Why, they're no more than filing cabinets for old fogies. No thanks!" he said.

He would retire in a few years. The incoming tides would rejuvenate him, and he could swim almost every day, he explained. But he couldn't afford his dream. So he decided to settle for a house on the river. Same story, too costly.

Not being one to part easily with his dreams, David decided

that a small house with a brook or pond and rambling garden would be fine. Again, he stumbled over the bottom line. So he had an inner temper tantrum: he became depressed.

"After all these years, after all this work, prices have climbed so high I can't afford what I've worked for," he said. He became apathetic, aloof, and silent. He also began to suffer from headaches. His children offered many alternatives, including their own homes, but he refused, and sank further into his gloom.

David's eldest son, an architect, sympathized with his father's thwarted dreams. He talked to David about his own dreams, which were much the same as the older man's, and of the house he had in his head for himself and his family, and planned to build. His father listened and eventually was able to talk to his son, looking for an answer to his own dilemma. The son turned to the Japanese techniques of "expanding" and "borrowing" space.

He showed his father a "handyman's special" house he'd found in a stable, older neighborhood in the throes of gentrification, where many people his father's age lived. The house was the right size, had good basics, and could be affordably renovated and retrofitted. Plantings, including many mature trees, and fences already were in place.

"We're three miles inland. Where's my water?" the older man snapped.

"Just a minute," his son said, and he unrolled a plot plan he had drawn that showed a small koi pond and a lap pool close to the house, imparting a waterfront illusion. Dense ground covers and plantings at the fences fooled the eye into "seeing" acres of woods beyond the house. The design included large rocks, a "riverbed" of pebbles, and a path winding beside it.

When David's house was finished, visitors would say, "Oh, I see you have your own pool."

"No," he'd respond. "My own river!"

Chapter Eighteen

SCALE
Too Big or Too Small?

The only true measure of aging is the erosion of one's ideals.

—AUTHOR UNKNOWN

MANY ELDERS who want to use large, heavy furniture originally purchased for their former, larger homes are fooled into thinking that if furniture dimensionally fits into a small space, then it "fits." Yes, a 7-foot sofa will fit on a 9-foot wall, dimensionally. But visually, the sofa may look strange or tend to make you feel oversized, stifled, or crowded, and can interfere with your personal sense of space. The reason? *The scale is off.*

Further, the space into which the furniture is placed is related to action—what can be done in a given space—not only what a room looks like. For example, furniture that is too bulky or close together restricts passage, which can cause accidents and may hinder personal interaction, though the piece physically fits in the linear space.

Scale refers to the proper proportion of articles to humans and to other objects in a room, and to the space that surrounds them. Because the eye measures size by comparison, things become bigger or smaller according to where and with what they are placed. Furniture scaled too large for a room will cause the room to feel too small; furniture scaled too small for the room will cause *you* to feel too big. Always consider human scale.

Scale is especially important in small elder homes. Psychologists say that people often feel that small homes return them to their most comfortable

Scale your furniture to your room.

psychological space—a happy childhood, perhaps, or the early years of marriage. Folks also tend to gravitate toward furnishings that symbolize those happy times. Sentiment is fine—but, sometimes, sentimental treasures just don't work. Nancy had this experience . . .

Nancy's Favorite Things

An elderly lady, Nancy, had fine aesthetic appreciation—for everything except size. Tall, buxom, and very attractive, she still worked part-time as a model for an upscale store that catered to large women. She and her husband, Tim, who was also a large person, had purchased a small "old folks' home," as they called it, for their retirement years. In an expansive showroom that displayed many different periods of furniture, Nancy immediately was drawn to some small Victorian chairs with curvy configurations and delicate limbs.

Tim's red flag went up. "Nancy," he said, "Let's go to . . ." but he never got to finish his sentence.

"Aren't these chairs precious?" she cooed. "They would fit into our living room. You know, by that big window."

"Nancy, they'd be too small for that window," Tim answered, really meaning that the chairs were too small for her, but he could not bring himself to say it.

"Then let's put them someplace else."

"I really don't think they . . ."

Nancy suggested other places for them, all vetoed by her husband. Finally, in desperation, he said, "I really don't think you would find them sturdy."

"Sure they are," she countered and sat down heavily on one of them to prove her point. The chair crashed, her skirts flew, Tim cussed, and the manager came running. Fortunately, nothing was injured but her dignity, and Tim, embarrassed, paid for the chair.

Why the chair incident? The reason later revealed itself when Nancy spoke fondly of her mother and the happy times they had spent in her turn-of-the-century childhood home. Memories had engendered the need for Victorian things. Later she and Tim did purchase some chairs of that period, of larger scale and sturdier construction. They rescued an antique oak dining table from an aunt's basement and retrieved a few Victorian accessories to add some period flavor to the otherwise contemporary home. But

Tim would not accept the kind offer of a curvy, spindly chair, literally on its last legs!

No one ever knew for sure whether Nancy realized why she had gravitated to Victorian objects, but she seemed happy blending into her present life the good memories of her past. Family antiques had brought home to her a sense of rootedness and connection. And those with an appropriate scale fit into her home.

Being aware of scale helps you to choose the right furniture to bring from your big old house or to buy in a furniture showroom, and helps you avoid the wrong furniture, even if the tape measure says it will fit.

KEEPING TO SCALE

SIZE BY COMPARISON: Recognize that empty rooms appear smaller than those even minimally furnished. Place a large chest in a bare room; the chest seems small by comparison, so the room "grows." It is easier to "see" the size of a room with the chest in it because you are familiar with its size and can measure the surrounding space instinctively with your eye. This is why some lamp manufacturers will photograph their table lamps next to standard beverage bottles, so the viewer is able to measure the size of the lamp by the size of the familiar bottle. This usually has more meaning to the eye than numerical notations.

LARGE AND ORNATE PIECES: "Flavor" a small space with heavy things rather than furnishing it completely with them, to avoid making small spaces appear even smaller. Finding smaller-scaled furniture may take some searching in today's market of trendy overstuffed upholstery and ornate wood pieces.

SMALL PIECES: Also avoid furnishing with only small things. A mix of small and large things is best. Many small pieces may cause a room to appear cluttered, emphasize its smallness, and deprive it of importance. For example, if linear space permits, use a 6- to 8-foot sofa or combined sectional modules, instead of a 4-foot loveseat and small chairs. The sofa will anchor the room and tend to elongate the wall behind it.

INCHES MAY COUNT: Look for buffets 15 instead of 18 inches deep, sofas 32 instead of 35 inches deep. Some manufacturers make furniture compatible with small rooms, but not many. Most follow trends.

DON'T DISCARD
ALL YOUR OLD THINGS

GOOD DESIGN IS TIMELESS: Why change just for the sake of change? Many retirees, particularly those who have relocated to warmer climates, dispose of all their old, often traditional, furnishings in favor of new trendy items in the stores. Later on, most wish they hadn't. Be careful not to give in to change simply for the sake of change.

NEW THINGS ARE EXPENSIVE: In many cases good quality has diminished, and handcraftsmanship all but disappeared. Keeping an eye to scale, carefully evaluate your present furnishings. Refinishing, reupholstering, recycling are good options. Also consider sentimental value of your furnishings. Our homes are scrapbooks of our lives.

> **⌇ ELDER-AID:**
> Is that old carved sofa too heavy, too fancy, for your living room? Ask a good upholsterer about turning it into a headboard.

TOTAL REFURNISHING: On the other hand, if you can afford it, change is good for some people, giving them a new lease on life. Even then, do not eliminate *all* familiar large pieces. One large-scaled piece in a small room—an ornate sofa, perhaps, or a carved sideboard—will add individuality and character. Just be sure that you maintain *proper scale, negative space,* and *balance.* Eclectic interiors are fun, fashionable, and very warm. With this in mind, remember that furniture periods fall in and out of favor, so resist being swayed by photographs in trendy home magazines, pushy salespeople, and even your own peers.

MEASURE, MEASURE, MEASURE

Tape in hand, remember the following eye-foolers when shopping:

~ Large items of furniture always appear smaller in large stores and showrooms, even to a practiced eye. The space is big, so the furniture looks small, especially if it is displayed next to even larger pieces or groupings.
~ Large items of furniture will seem larger when surrounded by the clutter of antiques shops, as an example.
~ Small items will appear smaller in large and busy showrooms. Removed from this environment, they will gain in importance and, often, visual size.

PHOTOGRAPH BEFORE PURCHASING

~ If possible, request photographs with measurements; many vendors supply copies of catalog pages. Or, with permission, measure and take the photos yourself.

~ Photos and measurements in hand, mark off the space the furniture will require in the room it is to occupy. You can do this by temporarily marking cut-pile carpet with a pointed instrument (the vacuum cleaner will remove the marks), or with removable chalk. Then replicate the furniture with mock-ups or articles of like size (please refer to part 3 for more detail on mock-ups).

ACCESSORIES

The principles of small versus large furniture hold true for small versus large accessories. Although the warmth and interest generated by personal bric-a-brac are as important in small rooms as any other, many little things spread about make for *clutter,* the enemy of small spaces. Many elders have trouble with this because of nostalgic connections. For example, small pictures may be charming, but spread about an area they will emphasize smallness by fragmenting the wall space and causing the eye to hop from one thing to another. Instead, join them into an attractive grouping, possibly a pyramid arrangement to suggest height. Conversely, one large piece, optimally with deep perspective, will draw the eye to the space, add depth, and unify the furniture grouping below it.

Understanding scale is a major factor in designing a small home. Be aware that, in itself, nothing is too big or too small. The question is: Big or small as compared to what? A cabin is small when seen with a castle; a castle is an atom on the face of the Earth.

Scale is an ongoing evaluation of the size or character of an object as compared to the size or character of other objects in the room, and as compared to people. *Human scale* is the most vital consideration of any home. The scale of your surroundings and its furnishings can make you feel Lilliputian, or like the Jolly Green Giant, when all you may desire is to feel comfortably human in a human-scaled home, amid human-scaled things. In the end, paying close attention to scale is paying close attention to your own well-being. A small-scaled home is a gift to yourself, and to the Earth.

Chapter Nineteen

BALANCE, UNITY, AND HARMONY
Three Friendly Ghosts

The sense of comfort is the outcome of balance, while marked un-balance immediately urges a corrective.

—ALBERT H. MUNSELL

YOU CAN'T HOLD THEM in your hands, or touch them, but you can see them, and, most importantly, you can *sense* when balance, unity, and harmony are askew; you feel it when something is "off." Adhering to the premises (and promises) of *balance, unity,* and *harmony* will help bring these qualities into your home, and into your life.

Design is a matter of the relationships among all the parts of the whole—in this case, your house, its site, its furnishings, its mechanical systems, and its occupants. Considered together, they help to achieve beauty and proper function. Because there are no "rules" to applying these premises, you have unlimited possibilities to express your individuality. Balance, unity, and harmony do not imply monotony. To the contrary, interesting variety used in proportionate amounts makes for warm and interesting rooms.

BALANCE

Balance affects the way you see and experience space. Flowing smoothness encourages your own psychological equilibrium. Space flows more freely when the senses are not jarred by objects or colors too "heavy" or too "light" for the area. How do you achieve balance?

Balance the "weight" in your rooms.

EQUALIZE VISUAL "WEIGHT": Knowingly or unknowingly, balance usually is the aim of good composition. The distribution of groups should be approximately equal so that no part is overwhelmed by mass while another is relatively empty. For instance, if all the heavily upholstered pieces were on one side of the room and spindly chairs and small tables on the other, the room would visually "tilt."

EQUALIZE COLOR AND STRONG CONTRASTS: Bright colors or patterns, and sometimes shapes, carry great visual weight. Used all together in one room, or in one part of a room, their combined strength will create the same imbalance as furniture weight. Distribute strong tones and patterns throughout.

EQUALIZE RELATIONSHIPS: Pay attention to how furnishings work with each other. You don't need a Ph.D. in design to know that a skinny table looks strange with a bulky club chair, or that a heavy chair derides a dainty desk.

UNITY

Holding to a color scheme or feeling of furnishings (shapes, weight, and mood, not period) of furnishings is almost as important to small spaces as scale. Unity simulates the sense of expanded space, and creates a oneness, a congruence of color, patterns, shapes, and angles, sometimes all. Especially as we grow older, color rhythm becomes important; that is, that color carries the eye from place to place as a kind of "road map." Sudden breaks in visual continuity may cause feelings of confusion and agitation. To "follow the yellow brick road" is not just for kids.

If you're visually impaired, be careful. While it's true that repeating major background colors throughout, in the floor and woodwork, for example, tends to extend space visually, this may not be a good idea for you. Sudden breaks in color may cut up the space—but they also define areas. Sometimes you can't have it both ways. Which is more important to you?

You can create a feeling of unity in your home in a variety of ways.

EXTEND PATTERNS: Repeating colors or patterns from one area to another tends to join the areas together, expanding space, as opposed to cutting them apart with different color schemes. For example, repeat small amounts of a medium or bright color from the living room to the entry or dining room. You can physically cross a threshold, but the mind retains initial impressions and carries them from room to room.

EMPHASIZE RELATED FORMS: Unity, or rhythm, is strengthened when the shapes of the furnishings echo the architecture and each other. Picture the smoothness of a room with a rounded fireplace opening enhanced by rounded seating, round or oval tables, or dollops of a soft, swirly fabric. The effect is one of harmony, the other side of unity.

HARMONY

Also called consonance, harmony is the flow of design elements that gives you pleasant feelings of accord, as similar people get along well together.

AVOID SHARP INCONGRUOUS CONTRASTS: Overpowering pieces that diminish small ones, or a sudden burst of strong color or pattern, can "upset" the rest of the furnishings.

COMPLEMENT FURNISHINGS: Choose or place furnishings with an eye to their complementing, not matching, each other. Sameness robs each piece of interest, regardless of its individual beauty. Try not to furnish in only one period. Matching "suites" of furniture often can be boring and feel heavy, and may crowd small homes because they dominate the space.

CREATE FOCAL POINTS: If you own, say, a weighty (and expensive today) dining room set that's too large and heavy, you may still be able to use it in a small home. For example, think of using a china cabinet, breakfront, or buffet as a focal point in the living room, moving the host and hostess chairs elsewhere as a matching pair, and leaving the sideboard in the dining area. Remember that it's usually more interesting when all the wood tones in a room are not the same. Trees don't match.

While most folks have pretty good instincts about balance, unity, and harmony, it's comforting, nevertheless, to think of them as three friendly ghosts looking over your shoulder to guide the formulation of your house plans. Let them help you.

Chapter Twenty

THE CAST OF COLOR
Paint It Pretty

Color is a basic human need, like fire and water—a raw material indispensable to life.

—FERNAND LEGER

COLOR IS indispensable to life. Beyond its visual and aesthetic effects, humans respond to color to heal the body and calm (or agitate) the mind; to communicate; to connect with music, food, odors, and form; to influence learning, even to indulge in psychic and psychedelic phenomena. Experts have demonstrated that color affects all aspects of human beings: physical, emotional, mental, and spiritual. Primitive humans identified their world by color: the red color in the sun was the color of fire, the white of water, the black of Earth. Or, stated another way at other times, color came from the elements. Earth, fire, water, and air. And through the ages, color always has borne mythological, symbolic, and religious importance. Color affects all of Earth's inhabitants, even as color is drawn from the verdure of Earth itself and its minerals, and from the skies, the water, and yes, even smoke and fire. It's fascinating to note that nature has conditioned humankind to feel most comfortable with the dark values of the earth beneath our feet, medium values surrounding us, with light values overhead.

It's not happenstance that, as we age, most of us prefer homes that are light and airy, their interior colorations selected simply because we like

"Change" room dimensions with color.

them. Like magic, such homes raise our spirits, are easy to live with, and usually form flattering backgrounds. The magic—and it is magic—is imaginative use of color and light, which transforms spatial proportions, enhances or dims details, influences perception, performs myriad decorating and psychological tricks. It's not difficult to make magic with color and light in small homes, and at little, if any, additional cost.

Don't be afraid of color. It doesn't cost any more than the innocuous whites and beiges we've somehow surrounded ourselves with for so many years. Get to know what color can do for you. Forget the confining "rules" of yesteryear and enjoy today's bold new tones—if only in small doses—for their psychological impact and safety features, as a tool of self-expression, an exponent of the joy of life! Before you begin, however, here are some basics you might want to know about working with color.

- ~ *Dark colors absorb light,* and tend to make small quarters seem smaller.
- ~ *Light colors reflect light,* and tend to make small quarters seem larger.
- ~ *Warm colors advance,* dominate space, and seem to "fill" it.
- ~ *Cool colors recede,* and seem to expand space.

COLOR VALUE

Value refers to the intensity of the color, strong to weak. Walls will seem pushed back, ceilings raised or lowered, when you apply the above maxims.

FORESHORTENING: To visually foreshorten a long, narrow room, cover the far walls with a color that is darker, and preferably warmer, than that on the long walls. Placing large pieces of dark furniture at either end will produce almost the same effect.

NARROWING: To visually narrow a wide room, use a warm, darker color on the sidewalls, a cool, lighter tint or off-white on the shorter walls. However, to maintain a spacious look, avoid saturated dark colors. Also remember that too much dark color can be depressing, so try to use it as accents, not in large quantities.

AIRINESS: Use light, cool color values in small homes. By reflecting light, not absorbing it, small homes seem to "breathe" better, creating a feeling of airy spaciousness.

INTIMACY: Do not always eliminate dark colors. A small dark room painted in a deep, saturated tone creates a feeling of intimacy. But avoid dark colors if they make you feel as though the walls are closing in on you. Think of powder rooms, dens (where dark paneling is so popular), or a small library, where a very personal, womb-like ambiance is desired, and there is no hope of "stretching" the space effectively, regardless of what you do. *A caveat:* Contrast the furnishings with the walls to ensure clear definition.

CEILING HEIGHT: To "raise" a low ceiling, paint it the same color as the walls, if that color is a light value. To "lower" a high ceiling, paint it a darker value than the walls and bring the color down on the walls 6 to 10 inches.

COLOR INTENSIFIES: Remember that color intensifies. In other words, the more you use of it, the stronger it will seem. Color reflects on itself. With this in mind, choose a lighter value of the same color if it is to be used in large quantity, and avoid shiny surfaces.

COLOR CONTRAST

Another basic principle is that strong contrasts cause light elements to appear lighter and dark elements to appear darker. Match your sofa to the wall behind it and it tends to "disappear." No contrast. Upholster a fine little chair in a bright color or pattern, and its size and importance increase.

Good color contrast contributes to elder safety. Furnishings that contrast with each other do not "get lost" and cause accidents. But, yes, sharp contrast does take up more visual space. How much is too much? That depends on the room and on individual physical abilities and preferences. However, assuming that you have no unusual physical problems and that stretching space is important, here are some tips for using color effectively.

MONOCHROMATISM: Monochromatic (literally, "one color") schemes will visually increase the space. Little contrast translates into blending floor coverings with furnishings with draperies with walls, woodwork, and cabinetry—a gradual joining of various shades of a single color. To stretch space even further, touches of this one color should be carried throughout the residence, thus avoiding abrupt space breaks to the eye. For the same reason, dark woodwork is not a good idea. Will using only

ELDER-AID:
To avoid the possible boredom of a monochromatic color scheme, and to increase definition, paint doors and woodwork in a strong contrasting color; burgundy or dark blue in a beige room, for instance.

one color be boring? Unsafe? Possibly. Avoid boredom and the danger of things blending too closely with each other by shades and textures, as well as accent colors and achromatic elements.

TEXTURES AND SHADES: Consider all the shades, textures, and variations one color can offer. Warm beige, evolving from orange, for example, ranges from cream to peach to orange to terra-cotta to brown. This continuum could be the basis of a warm and very interesting environment. Take care to use the saturated (deep) tones in small quantities.

ACCENT COLORS: Use strong accent colors on small pieces, easily changed with the season or your mood. Choose the complement of your basic color, the one directly opposite it on the color wheel. In the above-cited warm beige scheme, the accent would be blue, the opposite of orange. This can be interestingly varied, too. If you've used lots of warm peach, accent it with blue-green; if your beige contains yellow, try blue-violet. Check a standard color wheel for opposites.

FOCAL POINTS AND COLOR RHYTHM: Use accent colors at focal points of a room rather than scattered about indiscriminately. Also use some matching accents in adjacent areas. This careful "color rhythm" can lead the eye to space beyond the room, thus helping to extend its visual boundaries.

ACHROMATISM: Use achromatic (literally, "no color") elements with any color scheme. These include wood, metals, glass and clear acrylic, stone and clay, and foliage.

THE MOODS OF COLOR

Mental health professionals have proven that color can influence the way you feel, physically and psychologically. To many people, color even carries with it special meanings. From the ancient Indian Vedic mystic texts to New Age metaphysicists, the seven colors in the rainbow spectrum have been correlated to the seven energy centers of the human body, the chakras. For example, the heart is green, the throat blue, the solar plexus yellow, and so on.

Yet, there are no academic, fixed rules about color selection. We all see color differently, and our frames of reference produce personal reactions. Color evokes memories, good and bad, which will affect emotional response and, therefore, choice. People who work in special color atmospheres normally will not choose those colors for their homes, such as scrub-suit hospital green or Howard Johnson orange. Also, where sunlight is abundant, such as in the tropics or semi-tropics, many people (usually brunettes) show a preference for warm, vivid hues. Where there is less sunlight, such as the more polar regions, most people (especially blondes) prefer cooler colors and softer tones.

Color also is rich in cultural significance. In parts of Islam, for example, a green toilet seat would be considered sacrilegious because it is believed that green was the color of the prophet Mohammed's turban, so the color is held in high regard. In China, products wrapped in pink sell better than, say, green, because pink signifies good luck. The meaning of color varies dramatically from culture to culture. Color is a serious study, taught in universities, utilized by industry and merchandising experts, bought and sold, and people's ignorance of color is exploited by for-hire "experts" and trend-setters. Color experts travel the world to conduct seminars for design professionals on the chemistry, application, fads, fashion, and technicalities of color.

The origin of all color seen in the world is light, in the form of sunlight traveling to us in waves. The eye develops the images formed on the retina and transmits them by way of the optic nerves to the brain center. Technically, there are only three colors in the entire world, the primary colors of red, yellow, and blue, from which all others stem. Other hues are secondary and tertiary colors, and mixtures or gradations, blendings with each other and with white or black. White is considered the absence of all color; black, the absorption of all colors.

THE MEANINGS OF COLOR

The following simplistic generalization is accepted by most color specialists, and, although extremely controversial, according to diagnostic tests color preferences also are accepted as clues to human personality.

RED: Red is a primary color. Most shades of red are stimulating to the brain, pulse, and appetite—the color of fire, blood, and danger. Raw red overstimulates (we "see red"), while "bubble gum pink," also called "pacifying pink," has a quieting effect. Pink also can be festive or a nursery color.

According to color psychology, red indicates people of vital force, sexuality, and action. Red may be chosen by people with physical or mental exhaustion, and is disliked by those who lack vitality. Vivid tones are preferred more by women than men.

ORANGE: Shades of orange are mixtures of yellow and red. Intense orange values increase tension, irritation, sexuality, and creativity. It also is said to convey joviality, gregariousness, and exuberance. Soft orange and peach suggest warmth and convey most of the positive qualities of orange without garishness, and are easy to live with. Psychologically, orange and red have similar effects on mood.

BROWN: Brown is a cozy, warm, earthy color. Brown is physical, often selected by those leaning toward security and conservatism, and often is the least-liked color, especially by children.

YELLOW: Yellow is a primary color. Calming, yellow creates a sense of well-being. Reminiscent of the sun, it suggests warmth, cheerfulness, and longevity. But take care—it also is the most difficult color to see, reflects poorly, and sometimes, depending on the shade, makes the skin look jaundiced. Orange-yellows generally are more flattering than green-yellows. Yellows are said to be liked by intelligent, innovative people of great expectations, particularly of happiness. They are disliked by those disappointed in life, isolated, or suspicious.

GREEN: A mixture of yellow and blue, green is tranquil, soothing, refreshing. Green suggests optimism and growth. It's also considered the color of creativity. Midpoint between warm (yellow) and cool (blue) colors, green is the easiest to see, and good for aging eyes. Blue-green is supposedly most popular among those who exhibit constancy and perseverance, seek security, and resist change. It is disliked by those who fear failure, loss of wealth or status.

BLUE: A primary color, blue is serene, refreshing, and calming, although gray-blue also can be cold and depressing (we "feel blue"). Blue is said to lower blood pressure and to create an atmosphere of trust. In mid-range intensity, blue is easy to care for and live with, and blends well with most other colors. Think of blue skies. Dark blue is seen as love of accomplishment, order, and peace. Rejection of blue may be a signal of personal rejection or strange behavior.

PURPLE OR VIOLET: Purples are mixtures of blue and red. This is a puzzling color. Depending on shade and texture, purple can mean anger (purple rage), be stimulating, depressing, or intimidating, or evoke feelings of spirituality and regality. Difficult for most people to live with in quantity, purple can be a good accent tone. In color psychology, purple indicates a dream made fact, enchantment. Avoidance may signify avoidance of close relationships.

GRAY: Gray shades can be mixed in various combinations, but generally this color is thought of as a blending of black and white. Gray is noncommittal. It reduces emotional response and creates a nondistracting environment. Used with small strong accents of warm yellow, turquoise, or russet, for example, gray makes for a restful, sophisticated interior. Considered "neither here nor there," gray usually is selected by persons who wish to be left alone, yet rejection indicates a desire to participate in life, to avoid isolation.

BLACK: Not classified as a color, black is considered the absorption of all colors. In large doses, black is threatening, representing gloom and death. When used sparingly, it promotes feelings of elegance, sophistication, and drama. It is said that black is selected by those who revolt against Fate.

WHITE: Also not classified as a color, white is considered to be the absence of all color. However, remember that white light contains all colors. Neither stimulating nor calming, white does tend to reflect the colors and influence that surround it. Pure white can seem sterile or unimaginative. In recent years, all-white interiors have been sought-after for their feelings of luxury and elegance, but they are not for easy-care, comfortable elder homes. Even all-white kitchens and bathrooms can cause glare that, in turn, often is the cause of accidents.

BEIGE AND NEUTRALS: Also called achromatic (literally "no color"), beiges do not seem to have characteristics or influence of their own and blend easily and absorb the characteristics of other hues.

MULTI-COLORS: All colors applied in full intensity are overpowering to most people, tending to minimize the occupants, and close in space, but in small dollops, rainbow tones add liveliness and personality.

COLOR TRENDS

What currently is "in" and makes you feel up and in step today very well may give you the old-hat doldrums tomorrow. If you are interested in what colors are destined to be "hot" in home furnishings, look to the ready-to-wear racks of women's apparel in better stores. Colors are that trendy! Unless you have the means and commitment to keep up with the fads, select what *you* like, what is appropriate and personally flattering, not what's in.

THE COMPLEXION OF COLOR

It is true that the "cool" colors—green, blue, and violet—evoke feelings of coolness, while "warm" colors—red, orange, and yellow—evoke feelings of heat both physically and emotionally. This should help you to create your own color scheme. Most people, for example, would not choose to live in an ice-blue room in Detroit in the winter time (which is most of the year) or in a hot pink one in Miami any time of the year. Most importantly, warm or cool, remember that the colors chosen for your home are backgrounds for living, and should articulate the often delicate balance of mood, function, and the people who live there.

COLOR CLUTTER

Unrelated, dissonant colors and patterns cause as much disturbance to the eye and psyche as too many objects, and similarly make homes appear smaller. Colors and patterns are visual objects. In tight quarters, it's a good idea to limit yourself to one major pattern, originating in the floor covering, upholstery, or drapery fabric, on the walls (art collections produce a great deal of pattern), or in collectibles. A good rule of thumb is to avoid vivid prints if your room is built around collections, especially of art.

COLOR SCHEMES AND ADAPTATION

Stores and magazine advertisements all compete for the consumer's dollar, often using color as magnetic eye-appeal. While rainbows never change, color fads and "rules" invariably do, offering variations and staggering combinations that are confusing and, often, unrealistic. The answer, of course, is to ignore the tastepushers' choice and look within for answers. Your favorite colors may already exist in your home, or in your closet or your backyard.

Borrow color schemes: Adapt a color scheme from an existing dominant pattern in the room, for example from a gay chintz, an Oriental rug, wallpaper, or a favorite painting. The palette has already been created by experts. Extract the most dominant color and vary it in several shades throughout the room (for a monochromatic scheme). The next most important color then can be used for accents. Minor patterns, such as narrow stripes, tone-on-tone fabrics, or mini patterns similar in color and feeling to the dominant pattern certainly can be used. Textures should be varied. Think of color and pattern in small rooms as ice cream—the smoother, the better. A taste treat!

TRUST PERSONAL PREFERENCES: Look to your own wardrobe for your colors of preference. Over the years, most of us do establish strong personal instincts and color attachments by which we often are known. Things "look like" us. It definitely is *not* an exercise in vanity to select colors that become you, especially when you're older and physical characteristics such as hair and skin color may have changed. Stand before a mirror and drape some garments about yourself to determine which colors complement your physical type. Then drape yourself in the decorative fabrics (or close replications) that you want to use in your home. They should be at least as becoming. If not in your own home, where? For a complete home makeover, you probably should *not* go to your closets for ideas because your clothes probably reflect old color habits. Allow your new interiors to dictate a new wardrobe. There was an incident of a young woman who bleached her hair ash blonde to "go" with her new pastel blue living room. She liked it so well, she's been a blonde ever since!

> **⌐ ELDER-AID:**
> If you work amid dull tones, you might want your home to be bright and sassy, or, if you're exposed to bright colors at work, you may enjoy a soft serene environment at home—regardless of your wardrobe.

USE A COLOR WHEEL: Look to a standard color wheel for guidance. Analogous (related) color schemes, composed of one color and one or several neighboring colors on the color wheel, such as shades of red, red-orange, red-violet in various intensities, or green, green-blue, and green-yellow. Analogous schemes lead to harmony and unity. Complementary (contrasting) color schemes are based on any two colors directly opposite each other on the color wheel, such as variations of red and green or yellow and violet. Complementary schemes offer a wider range of possibilities, as well as a balance of warm and cool hues. One scheme is not better than another; it's a matter of personal choice.

PRESERVE FAMILIAR FAVORITES: Don't change the color scheme you established a long time ago—providing that it is familiar, comfortable, and flattering to you. However, consider that some refreshing touches may be in order, such as adding splashes of new color in reupholstering, color accents, art, or the like.

COLOR SCHEME INSPIRATION:

~ Start a scrapbook of photographs of interiors that appeal to you. After a while, the photos will show you which colors (and styles) you gravitate toward, and, ultimately, will make you happy, and perchance fulfill a longtime dream.

~ Study firsthand the magnificent colorations of nature in your own backyard, a park, or a nature preserve, and bring those colors indoors for continuous enjoyment. Joining your home to the outdoors is a good way to "stretch" space in compact quarters.

~ See model homes, furniture stores, TV decorating shows, designer show houses, restaurants, and lobbies of public buildings, for exposure to what's available today, and to recognize both your preferences and dislikes. Take photos, if you can.

~ Visit museums and art galleries, for a source of stimulation and to zero in on colors of paintings that attract you, and to learn how the colors are used in combination with each other. You might want to consider a course in art appreciation or purchase a few books with good reproductions of famous art.

~ Seek help—if you can't view your home objectively—from someone close to you with a "good eye," or you might ask your children or friends who know you well; their opinions and observations could be valuable. Perhaps help from a color consultant or design professional might be in order.

Color is a study in its own right, so fascinating and far-reaching that tomes have been written and technical manuals compiled about it. You may want to investigate some books on color, written from psychological, physiological, medical, mythical, chemical, or practical points of view (please refer to the bibliography).

Après-Ski Lessons

For centuries, medical science has recognized the psychological as well as physiological effects of color on human beings. As a case in point, an experiment held some years ago proved the influence of color on body heat. Two groups of skiers, shivering from the cold, were ushered into two different rooms. In the room decorated in shades of red, orange, and beige, the skiers immediately began to remove their outer garments. As was expected, in the blue, green, and white room, the skiers huddled together and continued to shiver—even though both rooms were the same temperature!

Chapter Twenty-one

LIGHTING
Looking Is Not Seeing

If you can see, you can hear with your nose and smell with your ears.

—GREGORIAN CHANT

LIGHT AND COLOR are inseparable. Without light, there is no color. Put another way, color is how you light it. Light is a form of energy to which living creatures react immediately, often subconsciously. Light may be absorbed, reflected, or allowed to pass through, depending on the material to which it is applied. Light is forever a blessing. A Zen philosophy states that if you really see the things around you, you're not lonely anymore. Objects speak.

Sometimes light, even more than color, can alter the visual dimensions and mood of an area, or can highlight objects of importance, or camouflage defects. Light can enhance or impair the effect of any interior, can change, often destroy, the most meticulously executed color scheme. It molds and brings cohesion to spaces and directs the eye.

Light also has profound effects on our physical selves. Although not completely understood by science, it is believed to affect vital parts of the brain. The intensity of the light and color around us affects our moods, even those of color-blind people. A pleasant level of light can stimulate and arouse us, while darkness can provide visual shelter, privacy, and psychological feelings of security. Consider the theater, where the lighting director creates the mood of a performance. A set illuminated with bright light portrays cheerfulness; washed with cold, dull tones, gloom prevails.

Lighting is important to the environment. The fenestration (windows and other openings) in your home should be carefully evaluated prior to selecting or building your new home, if possible, keeping in mind that careful location will reduce fuel and electricity consumption, operating costs, and impact on the environment.

For maximum efficiency and comfort, your home should have both natural and artificial light sources, of both high and low intensities. Lights in a cheery welcoming foyer, for example, have a different effect than gentle up-lights that cast sensuous shadows on the ceiling. To avoid accidents, forget the theatrics. Here are some (but not all) of the lighting and light sources you will need, alone or in combination with each other.

Task lighting.

TYPES AND SOURCES OF LIGHTING

Walk into a lighting store, and you're sure to be dazzled by the vast display of lighting fixtures, methods, designs, color, and cost, for lighting your home. It's a dizzying, confusing, *electrifying* experience. Different features have different characteristics and serve a wide variety of purposes. Catalogs are filled with literally thousands of choices. The following are the kinds of lighting most used in residences.

TASK LIGHTING: This provides good visibility for activities such as reading or sewing and varies from simple portable lamps (best placed about 15 inches above the work surface) to recessed spotlights, to some hanging or wall-mounted lights, to extensive networks such as under-cabinet or baseboard lighting in a kitchen.

ACCENT LIGHTING: Similar to task lighting, accent lighting also is directed at particular areas, but is primarily decorative. Ceiling spotlights, for example, can be placed to beam down on specific objects such as sculpture, paintings, furniture, and areas of color. Accent lighting

Accent lighting.

Wallwashing.

Track lighting.

does not need to be near the object or area it illuminates, and often is more effective placed at a distance, on the ceiling or at floor level, sometimes behind plants or furniture.

WALLWASHING: Another kind of accent lighting, wallwashing can be done with track lights, recessed ceiling fixtures, or uplights placed on the floor. It is used primarily for its dramatic effect, to highlight textured walls, fireplaces, and such, and should be aimed at an angle to throw the texture into relief. Wallwashing is best used with stronger light elsewhere in the room, for effect and safety.

INDIRECT LIGHTING: This technique reflects light from other surfaces such as the ceiling, often from concealed lighting sources under valances or behind tall cabinets. General, or ambient, illumination fills a room with diffuse, indirect light, much like sunlight, and provides gentle overall visibility. It's a good idea for elders to augment indirect lighting with task lighting, and possibly with path illumination—that is, lights carefully placed to facilitate way-finding.

WARM/COOL LIGHTING: The above methods of lighting can be executed by "warm" incandescent lamps that emit heat, including the more recently popular tungsten-halogen varieties that economize electricity, but can be uncomfortably warm. "Cool" fluorescent (also called low-intensity discharge) lamps, that emit no heat, are best avoided for elder eyes. Both warm and cool lights are available in a wide choice of color shades, and it's wise to try out many bulbs in your own home.

Many designers and retailers like to play visual tricks with light. Jewelers, for example, use lighting made especially to enhance the brilliance of gems, and meat marketers display their wares under lights that intensify blood red. Designers have the most fun with light. It must be said, however, that it's important to install good, clear light where needed, such as at entrances, hallways, and on work surfaces. However, here are some of the more common visual tricks:

~ Blur wall definitions and "enlarge" a room with uplights behind large pieces of furniture.

~ "Push" walls outward to "enlarge" the space within the room by washing the walls from any direction.

~ "Alter" a room's proportions, much the same way you would with light and dark colors. "Raise" a ceiling by bathing it in light; bring it down by keeping it in shadows. Foreshorten a long narrow room by concentrating light on the long walls, with less bright light at either end.

~ Create "paths" of light to delineate areas without erecting walls, or to guide you from place to place (way-finding).

~ "Paint out" or change color with light. For example, obscure an unsightly ceiling in shadows by mounting lights below the ceiling surface, and directing the light downward. Experiment with colored lights to vary the results.

~ Bring the outdoors in with landscape lights to "remove" walls. Be very careful about this application; it's an effective eye-fooler and can cause accidents.

~ Install dimmer switches (reostats) to regulate brightness and control glare. Reostats create a candlelight effect over a dining table or in a spa, for example.

~ Change colors and textures by changing lights, ranging from natural daylight to cool white light to warm pink. Experiment; bulbs are not expensive! Here is Gerry's near-catastrophic experience:

Shedding Light on Magic Carpets

Gerry was very pleased with the two Chinese Art Deco carpets she had purchased at auction. They were luxurious. The silky fibers had been hand woven into interesting patterns, and the somewhat iridescent violet, gold, and green colors had originated from natural, not synthetic, dyes. She called them her "magic carpets" that would complete her Art Deco room, and felt that the carpets' colorations would blend nicely with the fabrics already there. The carpets were delivered in the afternoon, and she was glad to see her assumptions had been correct; they looked at home, as though they had always been there. Then the sun set, and lights were turned on. Disaster!

Artificial lighting changed the colors of the carpets, and, far from complementing the room, set them at war with each other. The green turned a sickly chartreuse, the purple became magenta, and the gold amazingly seemed laced with red. Gerry was dismayed. Now she hated the carpets—and they were so expensive! It had never occurred to her that this could happen, and she certainly had not checked the lighting in the auction house. Few people would! The rugs could not be returned, and she could not afford to reupholster. It was a sad time for her. What to do?

It seemed the most sensible approach would be to change the lighting. After days of trial and error—and more expense—the problem remained. Gerry decided to enlist the help of a lighting consultant, who was able to arrive at the right combination of light bulbs and lighting techniques, so that Gerry and her magic carpets could live in harmony, after all.

The profusion of information available about lighting methods, installations, styles, and sources is often confusing, even to design professionals. It may be worthwhile to work with a lighting expert, particularly when eye care requires special applications. Consultations can be arranged, sometimes without charge, from your local power company. Or check with a knowledgeable employee of a good lighting store. Your best consultant may be a lighting engineer who sells only her or his expertise, or a design professional who has had special lighting training.

Proper lighting will maximize the size of your small home. Without good lighting, all else is lost. Please refer to part 1 for more suggestions for special lighting for elders.

Chapter Twenty-two

TRANSPARENT AND REFLECTIVE MATERIALS

Things That "Aren't There"

True distance is not the concern of the eye; it is granted only to the spirit.

— ANTOINE DE ST. EXUPERY

Because they tease the eye to pass through or beyond them, transparent and reflective materials project feelings of negative space and add airiness to an area; they almost "disappear." For example, glass-top and acrylic tables command very little visual space. Small accessories such as baskets, boxes, and pedestals of glass, acrylic, mirror, and other reflective materials work the same way, and tend to eliminate spottiness in small rooms.

Be careful, though, because *transparent and reflective materials can cause accidents!* Because human eyes may find them difficult to distinguish in certain lights, be sure see-through furnishings are clearly identified with colorful accessories and/or adjoining furnishings, and not placed in the path of normal traffic. Use these materials judiciously, where the feeling of space is most needed. Too much of a good thing is boring, and looks contrived, even cold. Have you ever tried to snuggle up in an acrylic chair?

MIRRORS

Strategically placed, mirrors can "double" narrow spaces (such as Janice's dining area; see page 137), adding depth, light, and overall visual spaciousness and glamour. Mirrored walls are used extensively in model homes and lobbies.

RIGHT ANGLES: Place mirrors at right angles to a good view to bring more of it inside. Installed on the sides of a bay window, mirrors will expand the view and tend to obscure the side supports.

WALLS: Mirror the walls (possibly the ceiling?) of an unimpressive entrance way for a dramatic effect—however, be careful because you may experience some confusion and strange incidents.

CONVEX: Make a big first impression with a round convex mirror (one that bulges out) hung near the entranceway to give an expanded reflection of the surrounding room.

SMALL AND ODD SHAPES: Group small-framed and odd-shaped mirrors as wall treatments for areas such as powder rooms or small hallways. Breaking the wall space here, as opposed to that of large walls, avoids accidents and adds interest.

PLASTIC VS. GLASS: Consider plastic mirror instead of glass mirror. It is less expensive, less apt to bounce noise about, and is available in tile form. But keep in mind that it scratches more easily and tends to conduct static electricity.

Bring the outdoors in.

Too Many Mirrors

George wanted mirrors installed on the sliding doors of the closet in the entry hall of his new condo. It looked so glamorous in a model apartment he had recently seen. When the job was done, he didn't like it. "Now I have the opposite wall two times and can't find the closet."

He got the idea of mirroring all the walls in the long narrow entry hall, and would not be dissuaded by suggestions of patterned wallpaper that would tend to make the hall seem shorter, warmer, and quieter. No, George wanted the entry hall mirrored, and a mirrored doorway built at the end of the hall to match. He was warned it would look like a bowling alley. But he had it done anyway.

He invited his older sister, who was very nearsighted, to visit after the installation was complete. She rang the bell and opened the unlocked door. She entered, turned around, and left. "Oh, excuse me," she said to her own image. "I must be in the wrong apartment."

DISADVANTAGES OF MIRRORS

Mirrors have their value, but too much of a good thing can backfire.

GLITZ: Too much mirror changes glamour to glitz. It can make an area feel and look like an amusement park fun-house, like George's entryway (see "Too Many Mirrors," above).

COLD: Too many hard reflective surfaces cause a room to look chilled.

GLARE: Mirrors cause glare by reflecting and doubling the light. Mirrors lightly tinted in gray, bronze, or rose are softer.

NOISE: Too many mirrors produce a noisy "echo chamber" effect because a mirror is a non-sound-absorbing hard surface, causing sound to bounce. This may cause problems for hearing-impaired people. Therefore, buffer mirrors with sound-absorbing furnishings.

DANGEROUS ILLUSIONS: Mirror installations that can cause accidents include architectural illusions such as mirrors used to complete a curve or arch, mirrors on the walls of a narrow hallway to "add width," or mirrors placed at the end of a hallway or at the top of steps to create "depth," which can be lethal.

REFLECTIVE FURNITURE

While not transparent, chrome, stainless steel, or brushed aluminum materials do reflect the colors around them and tend to make the furnishings "shrink" to fit small spaces. This may be desirable in some cases but, again, it also may cause accidents because there is no contrast. Other achromatic materials such as light-colored wood and wrought iron also tend to claim little dominance of their own, depending on style and quantity used, and may be more suitable than mirrored or other shiny, metallic materials.

GLASS IN ARCHITECTURE

Glass—clear, tinted, or reflective—is a favorite material for modern and some post-modern architecture. Glass probably is the best trompe l'oeil (eye-fooler) of all. It adds to the visual size of interior areas by molding outdoors and indoors together into a single spatial experience, while permitting maximum light to penetrate. Look for glass in:
- ~ large window areas, skylights, and "bubbles" that splash natural light through the house, clerestory windows (those placed near tops of exterior walls as well as interior partitions), transoms, and gable windows;
- ~ glass doors on wall-mounted cabinets;
- ~ glass shelves; in front of windows in the kitchen, for example, these are handy for herbs, which can be aromatic and very attractive;
- ~ windows installed close to the floor in order not to interrupt the scenery—but be sure they are clearly marked to avoid accidents;
- ~ tall windows, which tend to increase room size by drawing attention upwards, are especially effective in combination with high or vaulted ceilings;
- ~ glass-block walls, partitions, and windows, which provide both light and privacy.

ACRYLIC IN ARCHITECTURE

Acrylic (a hard, lightweight, glassy synthetic resin), used extensively in industry and aerodynamics, has come into the house in attractive home furnishings, and in effective architectural elements. Some uses for acrylic in the home include:
- ~ dividing areas without creating visual barriers—but must be clearly identified to avoid accidents;

~ imparting a "floating" effect; see-through stair-cases, for example, seem weightless, suspended in air, and are very dramatic;

~ replacing glass between banisters, and for balcony railings instead of opaque materials, to create a spacious effect.

DISADVANTAGES OF GLASS AND ACRYLIC

LACK OF DEFINITION: This is the very reason glass helps to make small spaces seem larger. Yet glass can also create visual confusion. Many folks, not just elders, have been known to walk into glass doors, and reflections in glass (as well as mirrors) can be misleading. For safety's sake, use glass and acrylic judiciously, and be sure they are clearly marked or tinted. Further, if you are visually impaired, note that see-through elements can cause accidents for the very reason they seem to expand space: The eye passes beyond them. Problems with vision are problems enough!

GLARE: More of a problem with glass than acrylic, glare adversely affects aging eyes.

NOISE: Hard surfaces such as glass (acrylic is softer) are conducive to noise, and should be counterbalanced with lots of sound-absorbing materials such as carpeting, upholstery, and fabric-clad walls. Glass also is more likely to permit sound penetration. Hearing-impaired folks probably will have a hard time with the sound-bouncing quality of glass, and possibly acrylic, particularly where high ceilings also exist and cause confusing "echoes."

LOSS OR COMPROMISE OF PRIVACY: This is an important consideration to many people.

LOSS OF HEAT AND/OR COOLED AIR: Glass permits heat exchange from the interior to the exterior of a house. This loss is an important consideration. Think about energy-efficient windows, insulation, heat-conserving window treatments, and maintenance. These can be expensive initially, but they usually pay for themselves in a relatively short period of time.

> **ELDER-AID:**
> When all else fails, use paint or paper to create feelings of spaciousness. You can create *trompe l'oeil* (eye-fooler) windows, possibly with actual shutters or panes of glass, opening into imaginary landscapes and gardens; murals with deep perspective; even sky, stars, and clouds on the ceiling. Wallpaper stores offer a large variety.

Chapter Twenty-three

ONE-ROOM LIVING
Divide and Conquer—The Space

*Utopia is everyone's vision of the perfect life; your Utopia is not
necessarily mine.*

—AUTHOR UNKNOWN

IT'S A FACT: homes built today have fewer walls than those built
twenty years ago, resulting in less defined areas. These homes include
"great rooms," where the walls and corridors have been eliminated and
most daily activities take place (some great rooms have separate sleeping
quarters), or efficiency apartments, or "mother-in-law" cottages, or
lofts, or almost any living space where you literally live in one room. No
rules for comfort or pleasure can ever be set down; habitats vary, and so
do the people who occupy them. However, the following suggestions will
help to divide and conquer your one-room space without limiting flexibility, controlling privacy, noise, and light, while still retaining feelings of
openness.

THE GREAT ROOM—OR GREAT CONFUSION?

To satisfy the largely American obsession with spaciousness, which has
come to denote status as well as notions of comfort, many people are at-
tracted by what appears to be affordable spaciousness, homes that are
built on a "great room" concept. The idea is not new—generations of
Homo sapiens have lived and bred in one room, often along with their

livestock—but the term "great room" is a relatively new innovation. In all probability, it was an idea of builders or architects who were challenged to provide space, which was dwindling, while holding down prices, which were rising. And the new name "great room" was born. The idea worked, but as is the way of most new things, the name soon was applied to any one-room space, from one-room cabins to spacious lofts.

And confusion often followed.

Unlike many other cultures, most Americans are accustomed to departmentalized living—a room for this, a room for that—and find it difficult to adapt to spaces with no walls, where activities easily spill into each other. The problem worsens when children and grandkids come to visit.

The following are some suggestions for adopting undefined space in most types of undivided dwellings. Please keep in mind that not all suggestions will work for everyone or every one-room home; sometimes so-called rules must be broken, or at least bent a little! As always, adapt what applies to you.

DIVIDE THE SPACE ACCORDING TO FUNCTION: Dining and entertaining facilities, for example, should be fairly close to the kitchen area, with lounging, TV, and music places not far away. On the other hand, private areas such as study, work, and sleeping spaces are best located away from living or communal areas.

DIVIDE THE AREA IN UNOBTRUSIVE WAYS: Do not attempt to form "rooms" with ceiling-to-floor draperies, blinds, and the like, lest the illusion of open, flowing space be spoiled and the space "shrinks." (A sleeping area might be an exception.)

USE COLOR AND LIGHT TO DELINEATE THE SPACE:
~ Try "color coding," an effective means of separating the areas and guiding the eye by color (a technique frequently used for guiding people to specific areas in public buildings). It is important that the transitions be gradual and interrelated. As an example, picture the living area in shades of blue accented in green; the private area in light green and accented in deep blue.
~ If you're planning a monochromatic scheme, which is the best choice for visually expanding space, areas can be set off from each other by various shades of one color. Joanna (see page 187) used a pale, soft green in the living areas as a bow to the outdoors,

darkening the green as the purposes of the areas changed. She also used different accent colors, such as gold, russet, and bright blue, in different areas. In this way, the spatial flow was not disrupted.

~ Good lighting is essential to point up the color differentiations, and to avoid accidents. Remember, without light, there is no color!

DIVIDE SPACE BY FURNITURE ARRANGEMENT: For example, a sofa with its back to the dining area automatically separates two parts of the great room. Back the sofa with a serving table or buffet for further definition. A desk or easel would indicate a workspace. A planter, étagère, or baker's rack might set off an entryway. Upholstered pieces placed at right angles to a wall make for a cozy conversation place. Place the seating face-to-face for hearing- and sight-impaired folks.

DIVIDE SPACE WITH PLANTS AND ART: Medium to large plants, which are relatively inexpensive, soften areas as they separate them. Try to match or closely blend the containers, and add a piece of outdoor sculpture for a garden effect, space permitting. Sometimes, plants of varying heights are all you need to divide the space. Free-standing large sculpture, stained glass panels (for light penetration), and handsome folding screens only partially extended into the room are other beautiful ways to separate areas.

DIVIDE SPACE WITH CHANGE: Varying flooring color or material is a simple but effective means of visual division in large areas, and also lends direction. Consider inserting feature stripes or pattern in resilient flooring, or combining tile and carpet, or hardwood and ceramic tile, as examples. Changes in color, texture, and style all signal change of function. To prevent tripping, be sure all flooring materials meet within ⅛ inch of each other, and avoid area rugs.

ELDER-AID:
To eliminate the "color clutter" of books, or to add a strong color accent in one-room living, take the "French library" approach. Jacket books in a single color, and mark them clearly.

USE BUILT-IN CABINETRY AND SEATING AS DIVIDERS: Although this can be quite expensive, it generally lessens the amount of furniture you need to buy and effectively utilizes space, particularly odd corners, structural columns, spaces around windows, and the like. Ready-made entertainment units and wall systems (low, 30 to 36 inches, if free-standing) also can be used. Both organize clutter, the enemy of small and great rooms alike.

Joanna's Chicken House

Joanna, a retired social worker and an artist, said she would be happy to give up her big house if she could find another home in the right location, of the right size, and at the right price—and the walls didn't close in on her. She had looked for months and finally located an idyllic place where everything seemed just right except that there were no interior walls. It was an old former chicken house on a subdivided farm, an idea that appealed to her. But there were problems.

"There's one large, gorgeous room that has to be the kitchen, living room, dining room, bedroom, guest room, and studio, too," she explained. "It's open and airy, and the beautiful grounds outside seem to come right in through the windows. And I can have a garden."

So?

"So it scares me," she said. "I don't know what to do with a one-room chicken house!"

Nevertheless, Joanna purchased it because she loved the openness and the view, saying she would find a way to "divide and conquer" the space. Eventually, she did turn it into a perfect home for herself without installing walls or disrupting the open flow, which was the lure of the place.

In addition to the interior design, Joanna's house presented a challenge she wasn't sure she could handle: She wanted an ecological home, sustainable for her own lifetime and beyond. She had purchased the property because it felt so right for her plans, and she could envision its potential, even though it meant rethinking all she had ever known about heating and cooling a house, energy conservation, and efficiency—which wasn't much.

Joanna read every helpful book she could find, spoke to dozens of people, and finally hired a building contractor whose specialty was housing that incorporated features for sustainable living, including passive solar heating and cooling and generating energy. And she later was able to "lend" the surplus energy to the local power company, and retrieve it when needed in the cold months. And, imagine, no utility bills.

"It was a real challenge," she later said, "but challenges are what make life interesting!"

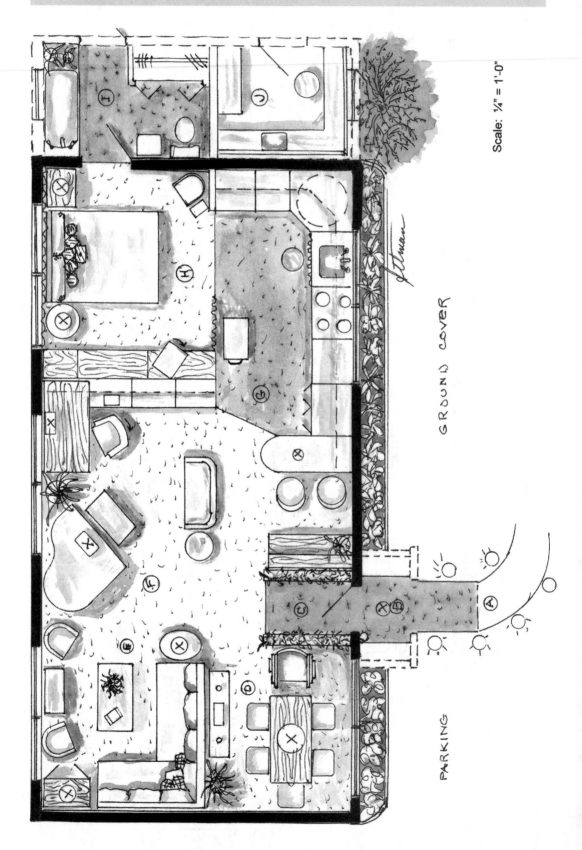

Scale: ¼" = 1'-0"

GROUND COVER

PARKING

Joanna's chicken house.

A   walkway: sensor lights, ramp
B   overhang (building add-on): sensor ceiling light, ledge, bench, grab bar, outdoor carpet
C   entryway: outdoor carpet continued, see-through trellis dividers
D   dining area: wheelchair accessible; glass-topped sofa table
E   living area: sofabed, matching sofa, cabinet, two comfortable chairs, TV, tea table (lightweight metal and acrylic)
F   music area/home office: piano and bench; loveseat and table; desk with typing-height open extension; swivel chair; files
G   country kitchen: antique hutch, low breakfast bar and chairs, cart on wheels, kitchen-grade carpet. Appliances include: side-by-side refrigerator/freezer, cabinet over; ovens; cooktop; sink (open under with curtain); corner cabinets with turntables; washer and dryer, cabinets over
H   sleeping area: queen-sized bed; round table, end table with shelves; open low chest; two dressers backing office equipment; swivel TV on dresser; mirror on back of bathroom door; drapery for privacy, if needed; small chair
I   bathroom (building add-on, outdoor accessible): standard plumbing fixtures, closet
J   potting shed: open shelves, sink, pegboard on walls, stool

X = lighting
= = depicts add-ons

LOFTS

Now that we are living longer, healthier lives, lofts are beginning to appeal to elders who like the big-city convenience and excitement they generate, not just to younger folks as they did in past years. Lofts are perhaps the greatest great rooms of them all, offering more space than most other flats, rental, co-op, or condo. They can also be designed to allow for the safety, comfort, and accessibility elders may require—so long as the utilities and elevators are working.

Urban pioneers have recycled old, sometimes derelict and abandoned, commercial buildings into spacious dwellings that have found much favor among those willing to convert the large former mills, factories, warehouses, even silos, into desirable places to live. In the beginning, the pioneers were artists seeking cheap dwelling and working space (many as big as 4,000 to 8,000 square feet with quality light through 8- to 10-foot windows), followed by developers who turned them into urban chic. Examples are the Soho district of Manhattan, Pike's Market in Seattle, and Ghiardelli Square in San Francisco, to name but a few.

Unlike the one-room residences mentioned above, the problem with lofts usually is *too much space* for intimate residential use. A large space can be handled in myriad different ways, with no restrictions on style. It can be whimsical or elegant, a cozy home or a workshop, or all and sundry combinations thereof. It can be whatever you want it to be.

Nevertheless, most of the suggestions listed above for dividing space—defining by furniture placement, color, flooring, built-in cabinetry—also work well in large areas. Lofts do present some major differences in design considerations, however.

COLOR: No need to skimp on range or intensity of color so long as it is relatively unified from area to area. Large window areas may require dark or saturated wall color, at least in part, to absorb the glare.

FURNITURE ARRANGEMENTS: USE whatever defines the areas and is comfortable. Taste, as always, is up to you, in loft and cabin alike. Lofts offer unlimited opportunity and freedom to find stunning new design solutions not often found within the four walls of suburbia. Many loft residents opt for "floating" furniture; that is, placing cozy groupings in the middle of empty spaces, almost like sculpture. It's fun to see old friends in new places.

FLOORING: Work with the flooring that's there, if possible. Large ex-

A Haven in Heaven

Thomas and William had been lifelong partners. Now at retirement age, they chose to live in a loft. But not in the city.

Their dwelling was comprised of the two top floors of a reclaimed grain silo in Michigan, outside a large industrial city. An elevator took them to the sleeping, exercise, and bathing areas on the next-to-top floor, and a beautiful recycled stairway then led them to the spacious living areas above. The bedrooms faced a rising sun on the river and, away from the din and dust of the city itself, they enjoyed vivid sunsets that transformed the skyscrapers to castles in the sky. An additional adventure was actually watching their chandeliers move and feeling the building sway to winter winds. This is not for everyone, perhaps, but it is a delightful haven in heaven, as they call it, for themselves and frequent guests.

panses of flooring are expensive to change. Some old buildings already have beautiful wood flooring hiding under the veneer of time, waiting to be refinished; others are concrete, to be painted, stenciled, carpeted, or tiled to define areas. Remember to hold to safety considerations previously outlined.

BUILT-INS: While always attractive (and expensive, unless you can do it yourself), built-in furnishings usually are not necessary in large spaces. Movable furniture probably is a better choice, to rearrange at will and take with you should you move to more conventional housing. Commercial storage units often are used in lofts to complement the industrial setting, and are relatively inexpensive. Two-sided 4- to 8-foot shelving units create partial non-confining walls.

WALLS: With plenty of space, walls or partial walls or high dividers can be utilized where necessary, to set off the kitchen, bathroom, sleeping, and work/study areas, for example. Take advantage of the museumlike setting to display collections of major art and artifacts.

ARCHITECTURE: Unique architectural elements of old industrial buildings are treasures, and should be retained and used to embellish your own loft. They may include previously mentioned hardwood floors, plus columns, iron dividers and nameplates, fans, dramatic stairways (watch out for those!), window trim—even beams and old brick. One common practice is to "lower" the ceiling and paint out the pipes with black, while carefully positioning "invisible" down-lighting on furniture groupings or art. This method of lighting also divides the space.

The above are only some of the ways to divide great room space, provide for separate activities, yet maintain openness and hold down costs. Once you begin to consider great rooms and lofts as real possibilities for a unique home, you are sure to come up with many ideas of your own. Unconventional space often generates unconventional—and exciting—innovation.

Chapter Twenty-four

LET YOUR SENSES LEAD YOU

There is nothing in the intellect that is not first in the senses.

—THOMAS AQUINAS

No ONE CAN DESIGN a home, any home, by intellect alone. Certain things please you, others do not. It's not necessary to know the reasons; that they are not to your liking is quite enough. Or that you find them pleasing, comforting, exciting, beautiful. Ultimately, taste is irrational. Gut feelings come from the senses. First we sense, then we think. Life is a multisensory experience.

The gifts of the senses are mesmerizing, memorable . . . the changing colors of autumn, the bouquet of newly mown grass . . . a glorious work of art . . . the touch of love. Forget for a few blessed moments the admonitions of logic and allow your senses to maximize the magic of ordinary moments. Let them lead you.

First we see. Perhaps the best understood of the senses, sight leads us to behold and evaluate our world—not by monetary worth, but by sensuous reaction. How does what we see affect us? It is the eye that brings us into relation with the space, color, and light of our environment. Sight is perception, the magic wand that brings ideas to life. The eye is the lens of the soul.

Sight tells us what is beautiful (or ugly), spearheads our views of life. While no one can define beauty in a simple sentence or two, it is, in essence, what flows from the senses and imagination and gives us pleasure. Everyone *looks,* but it takes a lifetime to *see.* Let your home pleasure your eyes, your imagination, and your soul.

And we touch. The luxurious feeling of velvet in our hands, plush carpets underfoot, silky fabrics, rough towels, smooth sheets are pleasantly familiar to us all. "Touch is the most personally experienced of all sensations," writes Dr. Edward T. Hall, a renowned anthropologist. A lover's hands, a baby's cheek, a sweaty brow.

Texture, the way things feel and the way our minds interpret them—roughness, smoothness, softness, rigidity, raised pattern—is appreciated almost entirely by touch. Texture also affects color by causing light to bounce or be absorbed in certain ways. We "see" by touch; we "touch" by sight. The two cannot be separated any more than shadows can exist without light.

It's fun and revealing to cover your eyes and make a "touch test" of your furnishings, particularly if you plan to reupholster. Sometimes our things are so familiar that we forget that the feel of them may not be pleasant. And touch-test new fabrics, too, before you buy them.

Touch also tells us about temperature and motion—hot tubs and cool pools, warm fires, hot towels, the breeze on our cheeks. Think of the touch-oriented goodies with which you can indulge yourself: electric blankets, shower massagers, whirlpool attachments, inflatable pillows for your bath, upholstered seats for your bottom.

And we hear. The pleasures of the ear are many: music, laughter, the rumble of the sea, a pot on the stove, sometimes silence, blessed silence. Yet sound is a two-faced friend, welcomed as good sound by some, scorned as noise by others. Fill your home with the sounds of your own pleasures, such as beautiful music that can be savored again and again, or the whir of a favorite tool, or the purring of a cat. Keep in mind that women generally are more sensitive to sound than men, particularly high-pitched sounds, and may even be sensitive to sounds beyond the conscious hearing range.

And we have the sense of smell. The odors of places and persons evoke deeper memories than either sight or sound. They invade your thoughts, sometimes most unexpectedly, whenever these odors are duplicated, and have a profound effect on your moods and performance.

Take a "touch test."

Experts cite fruit scents that can induce women to buy certain things, or cloves to calm you, and peppermint to elevate your mood, even to relieve headaches, for example.

So fill your elder home with the smells you like the best, not necessarily perfume or potpourri, possibly things from nature: leather, spices, pine, eucalyptus. Or the odors of the things we like to do—clay, paint and turpentine, wood, food on the stove, flowers from the garden. Make it *smell like home.*

And we have the sense of taste. A good meal—or a good drink—is as good for the soul as it is for the stomach. The old saw about reaching a man's (or woman's) heart through the stomach is true. And contentedness brings the other senses to life.

Finally, there is the sixth sense—your personal sense of beauty. Call it instinct, insight, the recognition of elusive excellence, it is that particular awareness that creates harmony between yourself and your home. It is a very special gift. To surround yourself and your special persons with your favorite things is an act of truth and love, more valuable than all the well-meaning decorating guides ever printed.

Following is part 3, "Planning Your Home—Your Way." It will show you how to plan your home on paper, to "see" it before you've sewn a stitch, or nailed a nail, or parted with a penny.

PART III

PLANNING YOUR HOME— YOUR WAY

Chapter Twenty-five

THOUGHTS ARE THINGS

The need to be creative is the need to transcend the passive role of being created, to express individuality.

—ERICH FROMM

Now for the fun—the actual down-to-earth, pencil-to-paper, out-of-theory-into-life designing of your home. *Your* home.

This will be a valuable experience, enabling you to "see" your home, and to "experience" its ambience before it is even begun. Imagine that! Plans you can hold in your own hands are sure to supplant with positive expectations any negative thoughts you may have, and they will eliminate lurking fears of living captive in someone else's idea of how your home should look or feel. Only your own imprints can make a house feel like *yours*. Designers and developers long have known that, even in furnished dwellings, space must be left for people to add some of their own things, their imprint in the sealing wax of design.

We all have thoughts about how we want to live. *Thoughts are things.* But thoughts need to be anchored. Plans for your home will shift from vague ideas to reality as you set them down on paper. When fragmented thoughts and unanswered questions are transmuted from fleeting mental flashes to tangible form, the task is defined, and can go forward. Each idea, each detail, will come to life as you work—and sometimes will take on a life of their own. It's amazing how a single random thought can beget a whole new way of life. Mitchell was an example . . .

Glory in Being Special

The son of vintners, Mitchell was born in Napa Valley, California. In college, he earned an advanced degree in agriculture, intending to apply his knowledge to the land as his forebears had done. But a bright future with a large company, and more money than he had ever known, lured him away from the land to the laboratory. Several promotions and much money later, he was, by most contemporary standards, considered very successful. At age fifty-five, he was glad to take an early retirement from the corporate rat race . . . but to what? he'd ask. However, Mitchell's wife, Joan, a former CEO, had no reservations about joining friends who now lived in a luxury retirement community.

She was examining various floor plans offered by the consortium that owned the mega-complex. For a very high purchase price for an apartment that would consume a sizable part of their savings, plus a monthly maintenance fee, they were promised life care in the meticulously landscaped golf course, Olympic-pool plush, spa-director-planned, recreation-gourmet cuisine community. The units were unfurnished, allowing for residents' personal interior preferences. This day, Joan was struggling with which possessions to take with them when they moved. Mitchell was taking a golf lesson at which he was doing poorly, and muttering about the stupidity of a "bunch of sheep chasing after little balls in minuscule holes." He returned home sweaty and swearing, calling up more sphincters and orifices than most people knew they had. Joan surmised that he had had a bad fairway day.

"Hello, dear. I think I've got it figured out," she said cheerfully. "If we take Unit B-3, we'd have room for *our* sofa and entertainment unit and *our* king-sized bed. It only costs a little more than Unit B-2."

"Joan, the more I think about retiring to *this*"—he swept his hands toward his golf clubs—"the more I want to keep working!" His face lit up with a single thought: "Let's go back to my mountains and grow food the way food should be grown: to feed people, not 'engineered' to feed the bottom line. I've had my fill of that. It's been years since I've tasted a tomato that tastes like a tomato!"

"Don't be silly," she said. He stormed away. But that single thought grew in his mind.

For many years, Mitchell had had flashes of the purple mountains, the scarlet skies, and the blessed rich earth smell of his youth. But he'd convinced himself that that was a lifetime ago, and it was dead, and his life was in the here and now. Still, he wasn't always so sure.

Golf that he couldn't and didn't want to play? A regimented community after years of corporate regimentation? A social director paid to be sociable? Living in an expensive chicken coop looking out over other expensive chicken coops?

Mitchell didn't think so.

Joan was not easily convinced. The country club way of life was just fine, thank-you-very-much, she said. So he escaped happily to his mountains, she to her friends on the golf course. Did they live happily ever after they separated? Joan refused to discuss it.

Mitchell established a small organic vegetable farm that soon took over most of his land. Then he purchased adjoining acreage, "to keep another Silicon Valley from encroaching," he said. But his motivation ran deeper, back to his younger days of working the land with his folks. His present productivity and plans for the future brought him happiness, but still, he missed Joan. His letters to her were glowing and very poetic, and before long, she rejoined him.

Applying his scientific knowledge and her business acumen to organic farming, Mitchell and Joan created a solid business. The demand for organically grown foods was growing, and, in the years to come, their name and logo were to become a nationally recognized symbol for healthful eating.

Signing herself "The Farmer's Wife," Joan kept in touch with her friends. "We're doing important work here," she told them, "feeding people without chemicals, pesticides, or genetic engineering. We feel very special."

Like so very many elders these days, Mitchell and Joan adopted the right idea about elder living: *To glory in being special.* We elders are the new "me generation," taking a front-row seat alongside energetic, talented people of all generations, commanding equal respect and consideration. We are taking advantage of our lives, realizing that these years can be the very best of all to explore, create, enjoy. This may also be the time to create your smaller, timeless house to serve and pleasure you and your family, for lifetimes of safety, comfort, accessibility, and independence: a home you will never outgrow.

No one can plan this home better than you. While it is true that some of us may be more "artistic" or inherently better at it than others, your design capabilities may surprise you. It matters little that your life experience may not have included drawing house plans, or drawing anything at all. Even those who can't "draw a straight line" find it possible to plan and produce delightful homes in which to relax and feel good about their accomplishments, about themselves. You can be one of them.

Designing your smaller independent home is an exciting and exceedingly rewarding thing to do, a great gift from you to yourself. You don't need a Ph.D. in design, nor expensive computer-aided design equipment, just some simple tools or user-friendly computer software, and most importantly, the desire to do it. Frequently, it's possible to "eyeball" space and to know instinctively how to place the furniture and how it will look. But in terms of planning for the future, as you will see, it's much to your advantage to work with reasonably accurate floor plans (or blueprints, if you have them), to spot at a glance where trouble spots lurk, and then go forward to create your safe and comfortable home—your way. Just do it!

But first, here are four maxims to help you achieve the best results:

BEGIN WITH A DREAM: No matter how unrealistic it may seem at first (do you want butterflies on the ceiling? or a place to breed iguanas?), your dreams will lead you to possibilities. Then follow up with floor plans for direction, replications for substance, and color for life.

DISCOVER THE FUN: Know that planning your home can be a happy time. Begin with a smile on your face and fun on your mind. Especially cultivate the ability to find humor in your own quirks, foibles, and the inevitable mistake or two. You have lots of company.

STAY COOL: Don't be overwhelmed by the previously offered information, instruction, admonitions, and, perchance, confusion! These have been one-size-fits-all preventions for woes that frequently befall elder homes. Not everything will be for you. No two people live the same, nor age the same. *Determine for yourself* what changes fit your particular circumstances of health, lifestyle, budget, and space.

BE YOURSELF: Well-meaning as friends may be, they are not you, and have their own agendas. Nobody but you knows what you feel, how you think, what you can do, and sometimes even you are not sure until you try. Beware the must-haves and should-haves handed down by "experts" and purveyors of fads and fashions. Their job is to feather their own nests, not yours. Follow your own plans, and go with whatever works and works for you and gives you pleasure.

Chapter Twenty-six

VISUAL AIDS
See It Before It Is

To feel beauty is a better thing than to understand how we come to feel it.

— GEORGE SANTAYANA

It is possible to "occupy" your future living space, to get the feel, the spirit of it, in advance. Visual aids make this easy. They are valuable planning tools, the reason design professionals spend so much time, and charge accordingly, for their presentations. The importance of visual aids is emphasized by designers' use of CAD (computer-aided design) systems that can cost up to millions of dollars. CAD "walks" viewers electronically and instantly through the interior from various angles and distances, makes changes in design, lighting, and color at the tap of a few keys—and can do it from almost anywhere in the world. Picture this: you are in your office in New York and want to see how the plans are progressing for your retirement home in Palm Springs, California. Presto! You are there electronically, and can see your home and confer with your designer across the continent.

Costly electronic visual aids are used extensively by large design firms and corporations to project their ideas to clients and CEOs. You can get a similar feel for an environment you have not yet seen by pulling together some of your own visual aids: floor plans, freehand sketches, swatch boards, paste-ups, mock-ups, even scaled models. Not electronic, but fun. If you prefer to design by computer, user-friendly software also is available. But try the old-fashioned way first.

It is neither necessary nor important to create professional-quality renderings. All you need are simple, neat plans that will help you to visualize and experience your home before the fact. Remember, though, that accuracy counts; the more accurate your final plans, the more fixed in your mind they will become, and they will help you to stay on course. Changing plans generally is the most common reason for mistakes and added expense.

Be adventurous—it's only paper! Try any arrangement that you can imagine, no matter how inappropriate it may seem. The best ideas sometimes happen this way. If that plan is not workable, simply throw it away. Then try something else. Solutions don't leap off the plan the moment you commit measurements to paper. You'll be in good company. Trial and error is also the way many professionals achieve their design solutions.

Before the Fact

Rochelle and John were newlyweds. They had rented a one-bedroom apartment and moved in with some makeshift furniture, a mattress on the floor, and boxes of wedding gifts piled in a corner. There was an uncommon amount of clothing, possibly a kind of compensation to Rochelle for being deaf and, unfortunately, also beset with deteriorating vision. By her own admission, she was a clothes collector who rarely parted with anything she could wear. Looking her best was extremely important to her.

John, also hearing impaired, was a technician at a TV station, whose own clothing consisted of little more than basic essentials. He was a writer, an avid reader, a fixer and collector of this and that. Storage in so small a place was a big problem. Space also had to be found for two TTYs (special telephone communication systems for the hearing impaired).

Matters were further complicated by Rochelle's preference for elegant, formal furnishings in a place more suitable to simpler, smaller things. That the designer didn't know sign language made communication difficult. Floor plans became their means of working together.

Solutions to storage problems and furniture placement depicted on paper, along with actual large samples of fabrics, tile, and carpeting, allowed them both to "see" their apartment long before they chose the furniture, and enabled changes to be made based on personal needs and physical limitations.

For example, special lighting was imperative because of Rochelle's poor vision. Sharp corners on furniture needed to be eliminated wherever possible to prevent injury to her. Rochelle's extensive wardrobe needed to be double-hung and arranged according to type and color to help her start her day. And, yes, it was possible, despite communication barriers, for the designer to show her how and where it was better to forego some, but not all, of her preferences for elegant furniture.

Although this was an extreme situation, it nevertheless demonstrates the importance of floor plans as tools of design—and communication among parties—for conceptualization, visualization, guidance.

FLOOR PLANS

Think of floor plans as road maps to design destinations. Rich in visual detail, they are representations of color schemes, traffic patterns, furniture groupings, and modifications to prevent accidents, that you can "live in," "walk through," look at, touch, and change at will. Use floor plans to:

~ designate boundaries and guidelines;

~ help prevent accidents by pointing up, in advance, the obstacle courses and booby traps of your home;

~ designate the items needed to age-proof an area, enabling you to prioritize your needs, organize time, and budget money;

~ keep you on track, even though time may elapse between shopping trips;

~ prevent costly mistakes such as buying pieces too large, too small, or not elder-friendly, or arranging furniture inappropriately, or choosing fabrics or colors ill-suited to your needs;

~ act as a powerful psychological incentive to actualizing your home more quickly;

~ encourage patience by serving as visible promises of things to come;

~ determine the feasibility of modifying or re-allocating your present space, before calling the builders;

~ help all participants (including a designer if you hire one) to make intelligent decisions on issues of safety and comfort, individual and communal space use, aesthetics, and financial considerations.

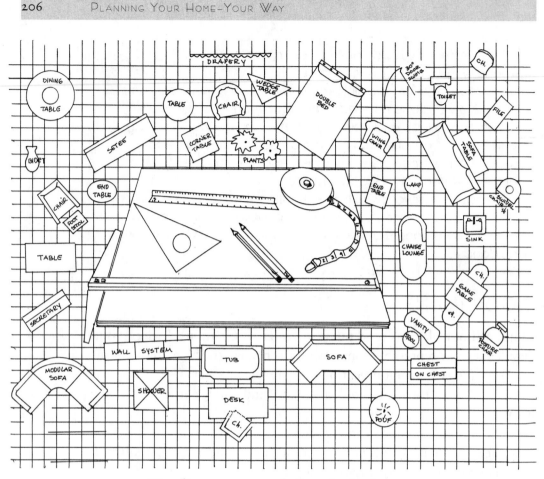

Visualize your rooms before they're begun.

HOW TO DRAW FLOOR PLANS

Space is difficult to "see." The eye measures space mostly by comparison. When a mature tree seems tiny, we recognize the vastness of the countryside; when even one piece of familiar furniture is placed in an empty room, we are able to approximate the size of the room by visually measuring it against the size of the familiar furniture. But when that one piece is not there or, worse, the room is crowded with other people's things, your eye becomes confused and you tend to estimate space inaccurately, if at all.

Merely knowing that a room measures, say, 12 feet by 15 feet, and has "good wall space" and an eastern exposure certainly is not enough to plan its furnishings. A reasonably accurate representational drawing, such as a floor plan of the room, is in order.

Because it would be impractical to make life-sized plans or patterns of rooms and furniture, scaled plans were devised to represent in miniature the actual space. "Scale" here refers to measurements that are represented according to the proportions of an established scale, such as our feet and inches.

SCALE: Quarter-inch scale, generally used for residential planning, means that $\frac{1}{4}$ inch on a standard American ruler equals 1 foot of actual space, and is written $\frac{1}{4}$" = 1'-0". In other words, an inch on a standard ruler would equal 4 feet of actual space.

MODIFICATIONS: Scale can be changed whenever appropriate, and is so noted on blueprints. Large buildings and their interiors usually are drawn to $\frac{1}{8}$-inch scale (half the size of $\frac{1}{4}$-inch scale), while plans for furniture and custom cabinetry usually are drawn to $\frac{1}{2}$-inch scale (twice the size of $\frac{1}{4}$-inch scale) or larger. The $\frac{1}{2}$-inch scale works well for planning details and elevations (please see below) and is easier to read. It's best to find your own way.

PERSPECTIVE: Floor plans represent your home seen as though you had cut the building in half horizontally and then looked down on the room and its furnishings as though you were a fly on the ceiling. The view clearly depicts the arrangement of rooms, location of hallways, doors, windows, stairs, and other features, and can show you potential trouble spots such as where floors may be slippery or uneven, where windows will cause glare, and narrow doorways.

TOOLS YOU WILL NEED

Tools for drawing house plans need not be complicated or expensive. Investigate art supply stores, blueprint shops, building supply stores, or stationers. You can also order tools from companies that sell home-planning kits, usually advertised in home furnishing and interior design magazines. You surely will find many kinds of more complicated (and expensive!) equipment, inks, and paper products, but the following are adequate:

~ A tape measure at least 8 feet long for convenience. Or you may prefer a room measurer that rolls on the floor, or, getting fancy, an electronic instrument that measures with a light beam. Check them out at your hardware store. Many people record the measurements on tape, to be applied later, but this leads to confusion more often than not.

~ Sharp number 2 pencils, or softer sketching pencils, for noting measurements; harder drafting pencils, good to use with carbon or transfer paper.

~ Erasers, preferably the "kneaded" kind that do not leave residue.

~ Colored pencils, pastels, or pastel pencils, markers, water color, or whatever medium you can handle best for coloring plans, the simpler the better.

~ Bristol board (a heavyweight, smooth paper "board"), or cardboard, or construction paper for mounting floor plans, photos, swatches of fabric, floor covering, paint samples, and the like.

~ Pad of graph paper of ¼-inch squares. (Be careful, those with other sized squares are available.) A scale rule may be used as an alternative to graph paper. To use a scale rule, measure off space by the quarter-inch (or half-inch) on the rule, instead of counting off squares on the graph paper. Be careful to select the correct scale; they range from ³⁄₃₂ to 1½-inch, all clearly marked. This technique takes a little more time until you become accustomed to using it, but is far more versatile and exact.

~ Quarter-inch scale templates of basic furniture forms; and templates of basic architectural elements such as door swings, stairs, and plumbing fixtures. Cardboard cut-outs made to scale may be used instead of templates to represent furniture. Templates are easier to use and usually are more accurate.

~ A pad of tracing (visualization) paper.

"ROUGH" DIAGRAMS

In a "rough" diagram, accurate scale is not necessary, only the shape of the room. Be sure to sketch it large enough to contain notations.

MEASURE INDIVIDUAL WALL SPACES AND OPENINGS: Sketch in walls, doors, windows, and arches, on the rough plan just as they appear in the room. Note these measurements on the plan. Include door and window trim as part of the wall measurements.

MEASURE FEATURES: Note all jogs, irregularities, and fixed features, and write in corresponding measurements. For example, to add a fireplace, as shown in figure B (page 210), measure the hearth and mantle and place them on your plan. Do the same for built-in cabinets, shelves, dividers, radiators, air conditioners, columns, exposed pipes, or anything else that is a fixed part of the room. Note their names.

INDICATE OPENINGS: Note direction of door swings, casement windows, and other moving features (figure C, page 211).

THE "GOOD" PLAN

This plan will be the "armature" of your design, much like the understructure of a sculpture, to guide you and to keep measurements, architectural elements, and exposure before you at all times. Don't plan or buy anything without it! And take your time drawing it. It's okay to mess up at first; just try it again. It's only paper. However, once the plan is finished, make several copies to work with.

DRAW ROOM SHAPES: Count off squares on the graph paper (or use the scale rule). Using your rough plan as a guide, accurately draw in the basic room shape on your "good" plan. Each square represents 12 inches or 1 foot on the ruler. For areas less than 12 inches, approximate part of a square that equals the number of inches; for instance, 6 inches equals half a square (figure A, page 210).

ADD WALL THICKNESSES: Designate exterior walls by about 6 inches (half-squares); interior partitions, by about 4 inches or less (figure B, page 210).

INDICATE OPENINGS: Locate windows and doors on the walls according to the measurements on your rough plan. Are hallways the minimum 42 inches wide to accommodate possible walking aids? Are doors a minimum 32 inches wide? Can you chart a workable emergency evacuation route? (Please see part 1.)

MEASURE: Take overall measurements, length and width, of this room at its farthest points. Place measurements to the sides of the room plan.

CHECK MEASUREMENTS: Add up the individual measurements on your long walls (wall space plus windows plus doors). The total should equal your overall length measurement. Do the same for the width.

DRAW ONE ROOM AT A TIME: Add adjoining areas later on a larger sheet of paper, as you get the hang of it, or work with drawings of individual rooms.

FINISHING THE DRAWINGS: Erase unneeded lines at doors, windows, and other openings. Add arrows

> **ᕫ ELDER-AID:**
> Another way to experiment with room arrangements is to move scaled ($^1/4$" = 1'-0") furniture cutouts about to find the best arrangements. Make them from lightweight cardboard or poster board, or use ready-made room planning kits.

CREATING PLANS.

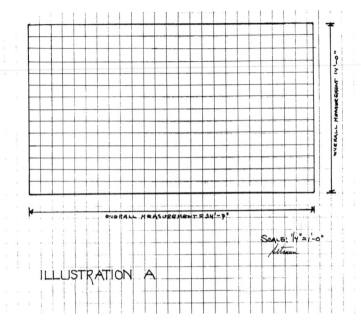

First, draw the overall measurement of your space, to scale.

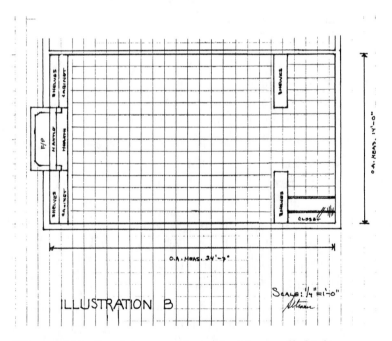

Next, add in fixed features, irregularities, wall thicknesses, and interior partitions.

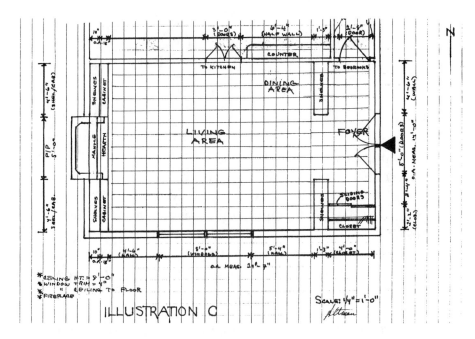

ILLUSTRATION C

Name the spaces, noting the direction of door swings and other moving features.

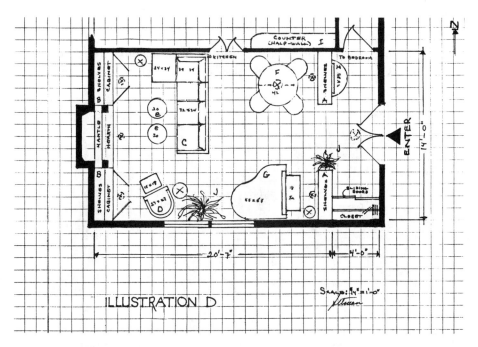

ILLUSTRATION D

Finally, add finer details, including furniture and color selections, to your master plan.

to indicate room entrances. Label the spaces. Now check your plan against figure C (page 215). Did you forget anything?

ANNOTATIONS

~ Record window heights and placement on the walls (an elevation is handy here; see below).
~ Record ceiling height (draw to scale on elevations).
~ Record architectural details such as moldings, columns, and flooring (elevations, photographs, or freehand sketches are helpful).
~ Record room exposures, to be considered when planning lighting, window coverings for insulation and to eliminate glare, choosing colors and fabrics, and furniture placements. Will you rise with the sun, dine at sunset? Or will you hide from the sun, street noise, or a bad view?
~ Record size of access doors, elevators, stairways, and landings for possible wheelchair use, and also for delivery of large furnishings.

ELEVATIONS

Elevations usually are included in architectural schematics for exterior views, millwork, and the like, and also are rendered in color for profes-

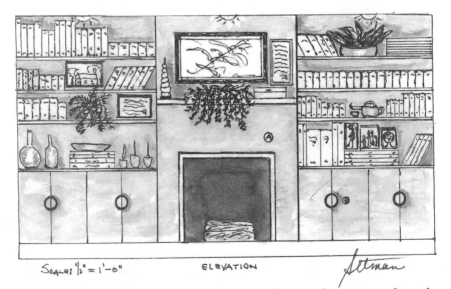

Scale: ½" = 1'-0"   ELEVATION

An elevation of Flo and Henry's fireplace wall. (See the master plan of their retrofit, page 116.)

sional design presentations. Generally, they are not necessary for average home planning. However, they can be helpful. Elevations:

~ are front views, showing what you would see standing across the room;
~ have no perspective (things appearing smaller as the distance increases between viewer and object, or becoming larger as distance *decreases* between viewer and object);
~ are *drawn to scale,* showing length, height, divisions such as windows, doors, bookcases, and the like.

Elevations can be helpful in determining details of your rooms such as wall arrangements, window treatments, or built-ins, and in planning kitchens and bathrooms for accessibility of cabinets, appliances, plumbing fixtures, and whatever needs a closer look. (Please refer to the following elevations that depict two window covering choices for a living room.)

OVERLAYS

Overlays help to eliminate the confusion that can occur with the convergence of too much information on one drawing.

~ Use separate sheets of tracing (or visualization) paper that fit over your drawing to note electric and TV outlets, wall and ceiling lights, telephone jacks, etc. Also note whether the locations need to be changed; electrical outlets should be about 18 inches from the floor, for example; light switches, about 48 inches from the floor.
~ Use separate sheets of tracing paper to record necessary structural changes, such as adding ramps or changing types of doors, and mechanical changes such as relocating or changing sinks or appliances.
~ Use separate sheets of tracing paper to try out furniture arrangements and color schemes. Draw them in with ¼" = 1'-0" scale templates, a new sheet for different arrangements and colorations. In this way, you can compare them side by side. Experiment—and watch your room come to life!
~ Plan traffic patterns that are *obstruction-free,* and that provide convenience and comfort.

FINISHING THE PLANS

~ Draw your final furniture and color selections, renovations, and so forth, on your master floor plan (figure D, page 211).

~ Color the drawing according to the colors and fabrics you have selected. Snips of fabric to be used in the room also can be attached to furniture drawn in on the plan instead of coloring it. This is a quick-fix method and certainly worth trying, but it does not show color in its proper proportion to the room. For example, red accents will look like too much red in a $\frac{1}{4}$-inch scale drawing, and pattern is lost.

SWATCH BOARDS AND PASTE-UPS

Your personal decorating guides, swatch boards and paste-ups provide graphic, overall pictures of your rooms by displaying their components at a glance: dimensions, furniture arrangements and preferences, colors, and textures. There are several ways to create these. Some folks prefer to keep swatch boards of fabrics and colors by themselves. Another way is to make a "decorating book" by affixing samples to fold-out pages of a loose-leaf notebook, along with notations, prices, and purchasing information.

Swatch boards are fun and easy to make. Paste actual samples of selected materials—upholstery and drapery fabrics, wall and floor coverings, paint chips and sheets of Bristol board or cardboard. Affix floor plans of rooms in which the materials are to be used. Then add notations such as A-B-C or 1-2-3 to furnishings on your plan, with corresponding notations to the materials. Use arrows, if they do not cause confusion. Swatch boards and paste-ups are useful in the following ways:

~ To match and blend color and pattern, and generally coordinate all design materials. Always resist purchasing one material without first checking it against the others. Large samples are best.

Do not select large patterns from small swatches without first seeing them in samples of a "full repeat" (the entire pattern) to check them in combination with other furnishings in the room. Live with the fabrics for a few days, if possible; large and bright patterns can become

> **✍ ELDER-AID:**
> You can purchase $5 sample pots of brand-name paints for testing, instead of costly quart sizes. The sample covers an 8-by-8-foot test area, enough to tell what a room will look like. Participating dealers are listed at www.finepaints.com or phone 800-332-1550.

wearying after a while. If large samples are not available, ask to order a memo sample from the factory or distributor. Be willing to pay for it—it's much less expensive than making a costly mistake.

View fabrics, especially patterns, from a distance of ten feet or so for overall effect. If you are nearsighted, remove your glasses, or squint if your eyes are okay. You may find that the color to which you matched your walls has practically disappeared!

The same is true for paint and wallpaper. It's better to buy small quantities of paint or a single roll of wallpaper to apply to your walls than to have to repaint or repaper a whole room. Paint dries darker and varies somewhat according to the light, such as in corners of rooms; wallpaper varies according to dye lot (be sure to check dye lot numbers).

~ For measurement references of specific areas. For example, doorway widths are critical for movement-impaired folks, or for selecting large furnishings such as sofas or entertainment units.

~ To help you to stay on track as you shop, and avoid temptations. The stores are full of beautiful home furnishings, and it's easy to be thrown off course. If you do decide on an item not on your plan, or a more expensive one, swatch boards will show you where to re-allot space and money.

~ To become personal spec (specification) sheets similar to those used by professional designers and purchasing agents. Just add price, size, and ordering information to individual items, preferably on a separate sheet of paper attached to the spec sheet, or in your decorating booklet.

~ To mount catalog or magazine clippings, photos, or drawings of the type of furniture you want to purchase next to their representational wood chips or fabrics. Pictures do not have to be of specific furnishings, but accurate enough to convey the general feeling. You may prefer to paste these to separate boards or in your booklet.

OTHER HELPFUL AIDS

PERSPECTIVE DRAWINGS: If you can draw them, quickie perspective sketches, no matter how basic, can give substance to your own thoughts or convey ideas to others. Accuracy is not essential, just the ideas. Note: Detailed, glamorous perspective drawings usually displayed at large design and architectural projects are done by professional artists and are very expensive. Usually, they are not necessary for home planning. But if you want to try it yourself, it's fun.

MOCK-UPS: These are three-dimensional representations of actual furniture to use when visualizing rooms from small-scale drawings is difficult. Try to replicate the width, height, and bulk of the furniture you want to use with almost anything that will stand in for the furnishings reasonably well, including cardboard boxes, heavy wrapping paper, layers of newspaper, or other pieces of furniture of approximately the same proportions. But don't expect any visual pleasure. Use them only to judge space. "Draw" the furniture in the carpet with a pointer or similar object. This is an easy way to see how much space furnishings require. The "drawings" are easily vacuumed away. Or use chalk on hard surfaces, also easily wiped away, or marking crayons on floors that are to be covered.

SCALED MODELS: Unless you enjoy building dollhouses, these are unnecessary, time consuming, and costly. Models are used primarily by architects for portraying building developments and large corporate and commercial installations, and as teaching devices in some design schools. Their value is questionable. But if you do enjoy dollhouses, or replica-building, indulge yourself. Some hobbyists have made scale models of their homes to use as birdhouses.

DESIGN PROFESSIONALS

The ranks of design professionals include architects, space planners, interior designers, decorators, and some furniture salespeople and artisans who have been trained or are well-experienced in home design. For simplification, I will refer to them all as "Desi."

Because it has taken a long while for interior design to become recognized as a bona fide profession, most states still do not require the licensing of its practitioners. And so there exist the "pros," the accredited or licensed design professionals, and a diverse array of "cons," who pass themselves off as pros. Here's how to tell the difference:

~ Check professional qualifications, licensing, and references before hiring any designer. Elders need to be very sure that Desi or someone on staff has passed the ADA (Americans with Disabilities Act) examination. Professional (not trade or associate) membership in the American Society of Interior Designers (ASID) usually indicates bona fide professionalism, but, unfortunately, not always, any more than M.D. after a person's name guarantees the degree of medical proficiency.

~ Inspect Desi's work, preferably actual commissions. This "live" approach probably is your best assurance of professional design capabilities. Photographs can be staged and misleading. Designers pay a great deal of money to professional photographers who know the tricks and have the equipment to take glamorous shots to whet your appetite. Desi's own Polaroid or normal snapshots probably are more accurate, although less glamorous. Try not to let period furnishings or color sway your judgment.

~ Ask for references and check them. If Desi is to handle large sums of your money, it might also be a good idea to check credit ratings, and check with the local Better Business Bureau and the Department of Consumer Affairs for complaints. Also meet in person with a former client, if possible.

~ Interview several designers, just as you would interview several applicants for any job. Pay particular attention to how much time Desi spends asking about your wants, needs, and problems, and how much time is devoted to how Desi wants your home to look. Clock it.

It is important that you like your designer personally and that communication is easy between you. Desi will become another member of your household for a while. A good job depends on your full participation and cooperation. You are a member of the design team.

Also consider your *price, service,* and *quality* requirements. Remember that every retailer, including Desi, can offer only these three commodities, meaning that if you buy price, you may not get service and quality; if you buy quality, it's worth more; if you buy service, don't expect low prices. Beware of anyone who promises all three. Also be aware that design professionals' stock-in-trade includes the Three T's: Time, Training, and Talent. Expect to pay for them.

FINAL DESIGN TIPS

First, *learning to see* is probably the most helpful skill to develop in this frenetic, speed-crazy, dot-com world. Everyone looks, but who really *sees* beyond today's window dressings and subterfuge to substance, truth, and beauty? Seeing is a magic wand to inspire thought and generate new ideas.

Your creativity will be stimulated by visits to new places—museums' decorative arts wings, showcase houses, model homes, furniture store displays, or friends' homes. Such visits will help new ideas to take root, and possibly solve old problems in new ways. Carry a notepad or small recorder to anchor those trigger flashes of insight, flights of fancy, even genius. Interior design publications are other good sources of ideas. Many of today's pros (and cons) have learned their trade from these magazines, trade manuals, and catalogs, and from the multitude of books that cover every aspect of design.

Try to notice the basic architectural assets and flaws of an area and how they are handled—the use of color, lighting, and contrast; how harmony and balance were achieved; furniture styles and materials that were used and their functions; and any other design wizardry that catches your eye. Most importantly, note where and how elder safety and energy-saving considerations have been incorporated—or ignored.

Beautiful and clever as some model rooms are, they may not be adaptable to your home, having been designed to sell real estate or home furnishings or decorating services. Your home is a place for people.

It's helpful to take notes or, with owners' permission, photographs of particularly well-designed areas. Also, for future reference, keep a scrapbook of rooms and furnishings that appeal to you and, possibly, a journal of how-tos. And take your time. Like good wine, taste and selectivity take time to mature.

Help can come from Aunt Tillie, or your best friend, or someone whose home you admire, or your artist friend, or your antiques dealer, or anyone whose taste you trust, and who is willing to take you on as a client, or simply is willing to help.

No one ever has been able to prove that professionally trained designers will do the best job for every individual. Knowledge can be licensed, artistry can't. Many a decorator has built a reputation on artistry alone, and has turned out good, even memorable, work. A person whose artistic ability was inborn, not acquired, and improved on by time and experience, may be all you need, degrees notwithstanding.

The story still circulates about Lee Radziwill, Jacqueline Kennedy Onasis' sister, who at one time had turned her hand to

Ready to go!

interior decorating for a living. When questioned about her credentials, she stated, "Oh, I have a way with the visual!"

It requires a great deal more than good taste or a way with the visual to design a home for safety and independence. If your home is to accommodate your special needs or limitations, first consult an expert in this field—then address the visual. They can be worked as one.

Designing your own home is not foolproof, but is the best of all possible gifts you can present to yourself. It may be the most creative/boring, easy/challenging, gratifying/frustrating, love/hate experience you will ever have. Smart elders, indeed, smart people of any age, plan their homes by maintaining their determination to *live independently* as they age. If you approach this project with optimism and confidence, so it shall be.

END NOTE

THE FIRST MISSION of this book has been to help you prevent accidents, ensure comfort, and maintain an independent, sustainable lifestyle in your own home as you age. Its second mission has been to explain basic interior design elements to help you derive the most possible living pleasure in smaller living space. Thirdly, pencil to paper, it teaches how to plan that space. Awareness of safety measures and design elements sharpens your perception of techniques used by professional designers and elder housing experts, swathing a path for you to follow—but on your own terms, no one else's.

There has been yet another underlying mission of this book: to suggest that we ponder the possibilities of the future, as we live longer and better lives. The coming years may improve us, or they may not, but surely they will afford us the opportunity to help, not harm, the world we live in. Perhaps we can guide new generations to be more caring than the last, rather than richer, to improve the only technologies that matter—the means of making our world a healthier, more peaceful, more beautiful, and infinitely happier place for all its beings.

Still, beyond all help—beyond price, design, and all illusions—home is a matter of the heart. Create it your way, with love and enthusiasm, optimism and confidence in all your tomorrows!

BIBLIOGRAPHY

Accessible Space Team, *Accessible Design Review Guide: An ADAAG Guide for Designing and Specifying Spaces, Buildings, and Sites.* New York: McGraw-Hill, 1996.

A Consumer's Guide to Home Adaptation. Boston: Adaptive Environments Center, 1993.

Birren, Faver, *Color and Human Response.* New York: John Wiley & Sons, 1978.

Chiras, Daniel D., *The Natural House.* White River Jct., Vt.: Chelsea Green, 2000.

The Doable, Renewable Home, D-12470. Washington, D.C.: American Association of Retired Persons (AARP), 1994.

Don't Move! Improve!, D-16048. Washington, D.C.: American Association of Retired Persons (AARP), 1993.

Edwards, Betty, *Drawing on the Right Side of the Brain.* New York: G.P. Putnum's Sons, 1989.

Elements of an Energy-Efficient House, DOE/CO 10200. Washington, D.C.: U.S. Department of Energy, 2000.

Exercise: A Guide from the National Institute on Aging. Gaithersburg, Md.: NIA Information Center, 2001.

Goldsmith, Selwyn, *Designing for the Disabled,* Second Edition. New York: McGraw-Hill, 1967.

Gussow, Joan Dye, *This Organic Life.* White River Jct., Vt.: Chelsea Green, 2001.

How to Protect Your Home, D-395. Washington, D.C.: American Association of Retired Persons (AARP), n.d.

Lansprey, Susan, and Joan Hyde, eds., *Staying Put: Adapting the Places Instead of the People.* Amityville, N.Y.: Baywood Publishing Company, 1997.

Leibrock, Cynthia, and Susan Behar, *Beautiful Barrier Free: A Visual*

Guide to Accessibility. New York: Van Nostrand Reinhold, 1993.

The Perfect Fit, D-14823. Washington, D.C.: American Association of Retired Persons (AARP), 1992.

Mace, Ron, *Universal Design: Housing for the Lifespan of all People.* Washington, D.C.: U.S. Department of Housing and Urban Development, Office of Policy Development and Research, 1988.

Residential Remodeling and Universal Design: Making Homes More Comfortable and Accessible. Washington, D.C.: U.S. Department of Housing and Urban Development, Office of Policy Development and Research, 1996.

Rickman, L.A., *A Comprehensive Approach for Retrofitting Homes for a Lifetime.* Upper Marlboro, Md.: NAHB Research Center, 1991.

Roschko, B.A., *Housing Interiors for the Disabled and Elderly.* New York: Van Nostrand Reinhold, 1991.

Safety for Older Consumers. U.S. Consumer Product Safety Commission, Washington, D.C., 1986.

INDEX

Put $50 out there and just see what comes back from

the Invisible Universe

THE INVISIBLE UNIVERSE is a virtual and virtuous "place" for people who want to be on the leading edge of sustainable living. For a $50 membership fee (annual), you receive the following benefits:

1. A free book. (Our selection will change from time to time, but at the moment new Denizens receive *Slow Food: Collected Thoughts on Taste, Tradition, and the Honest Pleasures of Food*, a $24.95 value.)

2. A free trial subscription to (your choice) *Natural Home Magazine*, *Mother Earth News*, *Permaculture Magazine*, or *Resurgence Magazine*. A value of up to $25.

3. A one-year membership in Co-op America, entitled to their full benefits, including a copy of their indispensible reference *The Green Pages*. A value of $30.

4. Free admission to Convocations, festivals that celebrate sustainability. These carry a dollar value of $25, but how do you really attach dollars to learning and fun?

5. The Hub enewsletter and *The Junction*, Chelsea Green's print newsletter.

6. Access to the unpublished Invisible Universe Web site where Denizens are encouraged to mount the soapbox, show off, or just noodle around.

7. A free gift anytime you visit the Solar Living Center or Terra Verde. Just identify yourself as a Denizen of the Invisible Universe and show your invisible membership card.

8. Free shipping on all Chelsea Green books—for Denizens only!

. . . and much more

Midwest Renewable Energy Association

Co-op America
building an economy for people and the planet

This is the club for people who don't join clubs, an organization for people who prefer exclusivity with a common touch. To learn more or to join the Invisible Universe:

CALL us toll-free at 1.800.639.4099
VISIT our website www.chelseagreen.com

the
invisible
universe

BOOKS FOR SUSTAINABLE LIVING

CHELSEA GREEN PUBLISHING

C HELSEA GREEN publishes information that helps us lead pleasurable lives on a planet where human activities are in harmony and balance with Nature. Our celebration of the sustainable arts has led us to publish trend-setting books about organic gardening, solar electricity and renewable energy, innovative building techniques, regenerative forestry, local and bioregional democracy, and whole foods. The company's published works, while intensely practical, are also entertaining and inspirational, demonstrating that an ecological approach to life is consistent with producing beautiful, eloquent, and useful books, videos, and audio cassettes.

Shelter

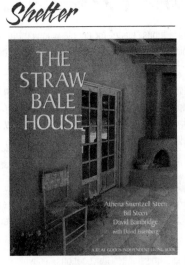

The Straw Bale House
Athena Swentzell Steen, Bill Steen,
and David Bainbridge
ISBN 0-930031-71-7 • $30.00

Food

Four-Season Harvest: Organic Vegetables from
Your Home Garden All Year Long
Revised and expanded edition
Eliot Coleman
ISBN 1-890132-27-6 • $24.95

Planet

Believing Cassandra: An Optimist
Looks at a Pessimist's World
Alan AtKisson
ISBN 1-890132-16-0 • $16.95

People

slow food

IDEAS + INFORMATION = INSP